SINDHIS
IN GLOBAL CONTEXT
PAST, PRESENT, FUTURE,
AND ORIGINS
(2600 BCE TO…)

SINDHIS
IN GLOBAL CONTEXT
PAST, PRESENT, FUTURE,
AND ORIGINS
(2600 BCE TO...)

DR. MAQBOOL A. HALEPOTA

Copyright © 2024 Dr. Maqbool A. Halepota, All rights reserved.
Author's photo taken by Jon Simpson

No part of this publication may be reproduced, stored in a retrieval system or transmitted in any form or by any means, electronic, mechanical, photocopying, recording or otherwise, without prior permission of Halo Publishing International.

The views and opinions expressed in this book are those of the author and do not necessarily reflect the official policy or position of Halo Publishing International. Any content provided by our authors are of their opinion and are not intended to malign any religion, ethnic group, club, organization, company, individual or anyone or anything.

For permission requests, write to the publisher, addressed "Attention: Permissions Coordinator," at the address below.

Halo Publishing International
7550 WIH-10 #800, PMB 2069,
San Antonio, TX 78229

First Edition, July 2024
ISBN: 978-1-63765-584-9
Library of Congress Control Number: 2024904095

The information contained within this book is strictly for informational purposes. Unless otherwise indicated, all the names, characters, businesses, places, events and incidents in this book are either the product of the author's imagination or used in a fictitious manner. Any resemblance to actual persons, living or dead, or actual events is purely coincidental.

Halo Publishing International is a self-publishing company that publishes adult fiction and non-fiction, children's literature, self-help, spiritual, and faith-based books. We continually strive to help authors reach their publishing goals and provide many different services that help them do so. We do not publish books that are deemed to be politically, religiously, or socially disrespectful, or books that are sexually provocative, including erotica. Halo reserves the right to refuse publication of any manuscript if it is deemed not to be in line with our principles. Do you have a book idea you would like us to consider publishing? Please visit www.halopublishing.com for more information.

This book is dedicated to my beloved motherland of Sindh. The land that has been the victim of invaders and aggressors since time immemorial. But in the end, it has always conquered all its conquerors with nothing but pure love!

چائُتِ پائي چِتَ مِ، سَنهو کَتيو جَنِ:
تِنِ جو صَرافنِ، دُکو داخِلِ نہ کيو.

With rancor in their souls, those who crafted, thin and fine
Theirs, the appraisers did not accept even an ounce!
~Shah Latif

مُحَبَتَ پائي مَنَ ۾، رَنديا روڙيا جَنِ؛
تِنِ جو صَرافَنِ، اَڪَ توريو ئي اَگھائيو۔

With love in their souls, those who crafted, thick and rough
Theirs, the appraisers accepted unmeasured!
~Shah Latif

موٽِي مانڊاڻ ڪِي، واري ڪيائِين وارَ:
وِجُون وَسَڻ آئِيُون، چَوڏِسِ ء چوڏارِ.
ڪي اٽي ويٺيُون اِستَنبولَ ڍي، ڪي مَٽيُون مَغرَبَ پارَ:
ڪي چمڪَنِ چِينَ تي، ڪي لهَنِ سَمَرقَندِينَ سارَ:
ڪي رَمِي ويٺيُون رومَ تي، ڪي ڪابُلَ، ڪي قَندارَ:
ڪي دَهلِيءَ، ڪي دکَنِ، ڪي گَڙنَ مَٿي گِرنارَ:
ڪَنهِين جُنبِي جيسَلميرَ تان، ڌَنا بيڪانير بَڪارَ:
ڪَنهِين ڀُڄُ ڀِچائِيو، ڪَنهِين ڍَٽَ مَٿي ڍارَ:
ڪَنهِين اَچِي اَمَرَ ڪوٽَ تان، وَسايا وَلهارَ:
سانئِيمَ! سَدائِين ڪَرِين، مَٿي سِنڌُ سُڪارَ:
دوسَ! مِٺا دِلدارَ، عالَمَ سَڀ آبادَ ڪَرِين.

Hovering clouds only return to rain tumultuously
Thundering and lightning all over
Some rained over Istanbul, some congregate to the west
Some light up China, some turn to Samarkand
Some travelled to Rome, others to Kabul and Kandahar
Some roamed over Delhi, some Deccan, some thundered over Girnar
Some soaked Jaisalmer, some bloomed Bikaner
Some blessed Bhuj, some flooded Dhatt
Some crossed over Amarkot to refresh the meadows
My Lord, forever keep Sindh flourishing
Oh, the sweet beloved, oh my friend, make the whole world prosperous
~Shah Latif

The Nation's Task

*For centuries the nation's millions slept
At last they wake, they see, they cry —
"Freedom must be saved, or Orient's ancient nations die."
From cities and hamlets and hoary hermitages,
From fiery Mussulmans and mild men of the Aryan Race,
Comes freedom's cry with new devotion to India's cause.
It is the cry of comrades who forget feuds of yesterday
And stand together for faith and fatherland.
This cry is the message of India's long exile.
This cry is the speech of her sorrows, her night of pain.
Not ours only, the cry hath come from the Great God-Heart.
I hear it in birds and flowers and trees.
In the Sindhu immortal and the surge of the sea.
I read it in the star that gazes with golden eye,
And sing it at the master's feet —
"Freedom must be saved, or Orient's nations must die."
Freedom's flag they bore and lifted high —
Socrates and Jesus and St. Joan of Arc,
And Muhammad the praised, and Mazzini, Mansur,
And many more...God's Rebels...in east and west.
With bleeding hearts they bore it on the world's rough road,
Silent in the midst of the lies,*

Calm in the midst of tumult, strong under every strain,
And worshipping the Beautiful in bitter struggle and pain.
'Tis the banner of the immortals!
It calls us through the dins and the dark of today.
It calls us to prove our manhood in the strength of the Pure and the meek!
It calls us to a new consecration,
To make life an oblation,
To seek not greatness but the service of the nation,
To adore Allah the Merciful midst struggle and strife,
So may the people enter into freedom and life.
~Professor Sadhu T. L. Vaswani

Contents

Foreword	21
Introduction	25
Where Is Sindh?	31
The Origins of Sindhis	53
Sindhis in Prehistory: Life and Times in Ancient Sindh	63
Myth and Realities	
Pre-Mohenjo-Daro—Mehrgarh	71
Mohenjo-Daro (2500 BCE): Cradle of Indus Valley Civilization	81
The Story of Excavation and Man of Mohenjo-Daro	89
Vedic Era	107
Aryan Age	110
Sindhis Under Persians (519-400 BCE)	117
Sindhis Under Greeks	119
Sindhis Under Maurya Dynasty	123

Bactrians (Bahktarians) and Other Foreign Invasions in Sindh	124
Rai and Chach Dynasties	126

The Arab Era — 133
    Dahir—Hero or Villain? — 149

Sindh: The Melting Pot of Faiths — 155
    Sindh, Beloved Country of the God — 155
    Religion of the Indus — 156
    Rigveda and Sindhu — 160

Reclaiming Sindh: History of Haakims, Native Sindhi Rulers — 183
    The Habbari Dynasty — 184
    Soomra Dynasty in Sindh — 185
    The Sammas — 189
    Arghuns and Tarkhans — 195
    Kalhoras — 198
    Talpurs — 202

The British Raj — 205
Hur Movement for Freedom of Sindh — 219
The Hero King and His Valiant Hurs — 219
Partition, Flight, and Plight of Sindhi Hindus — 245
Disenfranchisement of Sindhis in Sindh — 269
    The Lahore Resolution — 269
    One Unit—The Darkest Years in Sindh's History — 277
    Water and Lands of Sindh Under One Unit — 280
    Exploitation of Mineral Resources — 282

Mass Influx of Immigrant Populations into Sindh	284
Apartheid Against Sindhis	287
Sindhi Nationalist Movement	293
Sindhi Nationalist Movement Pre-Partition	294
Sindhi Nationalist Movement Post-Partition	297
March 4th—The D-Day of the Sindhi Nationalist Movement	304
Sindhi Nationalist Movement Post-One Unit	310
Sindhudesh Movement	317
The Rise and Fall of Bhuttos	325
Sindh Under Martial Law	357
Catastrophes of Martial Law	361
Yahya Khan—The Martial Law of Paradoxes	367
Zia and His Martial Law—Model Dictator of Asia and Mother of All Martial Laws	371
Pervez Musharraf—Pinochet of Pakistan	381
Emergence of Sindhi Diaspora	389
Melluhas in Mesopotamia— Indus Villages in Mesopotamia	390
Sindhis Come to Rome	394
Sindhworkis, Merchants of Sindh	395
Sindhi Diaspora Organizations	402
Future of Sindhis	409
Excellence in Education, Sciences, Arts, and Literature	417

Selected Bibliography 423
Acknowledgments 437
About Dr. Maqbool A. Halepota,
MD, FACP, CPE 441

Foreword

I am the founder of the Congressional Sindh Caucus (CSC) in the House of Representatives of the United States of America and have been its chairman since 2010. But my connections to Sindh are much older and deeper.

My connection to Sindh is rooted in my family history. Through his work, my grandfather was stationed in the province of Sindh. He experienced the rich culture, language, and unique way of life in Sindh. The people of Sindh have been under attack by major governmental bodies and security forces in Pakistan for far too long. Political activists defending Sindhi rights are subject to arrests, disappearances, tortures, and even killings. The native Sindhi language and culture is woefully underrepresented in Pakistan's government. The people of Sindh have much to be proud of, and through my work with the Sindh Caucus, I have pushed the US to reach out to Sindhis in their own language and to address human-rights challenges in the region. I encourage Sindhi Americans to be involved in the political process and encourage their representatives to be active on Sindhi issues in Congress.

In my roles as founder and chair of CSC, I have focused on human rights and the rule of law in Pakistan, particularly Sindh. Over the last decade, we have dedicated our efforts toward protecting the geographic, demographic, cultural, linguistic, and ecological heritage of Sindh and its people, particularly their dedication to religious tolerance. Unfortunately, the human-rights picture in Pakistan and Sindh is not good.

As chair of the Congressional Sindh Caucus, I have repeatedly drawn attention to these human-rights abuses in Sindh, especially the issue of forced disappearances. Although we have been able to save the lives of many young men, still these individuals oftentimes later turn up dead, and no justice is ever served.

In the past few years, the United Nations Human Rights Committee, Amnesty International, Human Rights Watch, and the State Department's own Report on Human Rights have all noted serious concerns about extrajudicial, targeted killings and disappearances in Pakistan, particularly in Sindh.

We are also extremely concerned about the destruction of the rich cultural, linguistic, and social fabric of Sindh, especially the continued construction of numerous dams on River Indus, the only lifeline for a rapidly exploding population in the region. The destruction of one of the largest river systems in the world, including its delta, if unchecked, will result in an ecological calamity of colossal level, which the planet cannot afford. This will not only have disastrous effects on the region, but also on the world as a whole.

Atrocities of this type cannot go unanswered. It is our obligation to speak out and demand accountability. That is why this book is so important. *Sindhis in Global Context: Past, Present, Future, and Origins* provides the general public and policymakers an opportunity to learn about the fraught history and contemporary issues facing the province of Sindh and its people. I hope this book will inspire others to work to hold accountable those people and nations responsible for such abuses.

No one knows more about the issues faced by the people of Sindh than Dr. Maqbool Alam Halepota. He has been the most ardent advocate for Sindhis and Sindh in the US for more than two decades now. This book details thousands of years of the Indus Valley and its peoples. It is a testament to the hardships Sindhis have faced throughout the centuries, and the bright future ahead if the Sindhi diaspora all over the world conquers their religious prejudices, forgets and forgives the mistakes of the past, and rebuilds their bonds with the land of their forefathers.

Dr. Halepota's message is simple: Sindhis must come together to invest in and develop modern-day Sindh for the betterment of Sindhi society. A powerful lesson for a people with a rich culture and history that should be made known to the international community.

I, like Dr. Halepota, am a strong advocate for the Sindhi people and for bringing to light the issues they face. This book describes in great detail the current situation and makes a strong case for Sindh to acquire the level of autonomy promised to it in the 1940 Pakistan/Lahore Resolution. This resolution was the very basis for the creation of Pakistan and the reason for Sindh to join the Federation of Pakistan.

Dr. Halepota and I have fought for the human rights of the Sindhi people. I believe that the people of Sindh should have the level of autonomy they aspire to, consistent with a united and successful Pakistan. This was the original dream of the founders of Pakistan.

Brad Sherman

Congressman Brad Sherman,
Member of the US House of Representatives

Introduction

"**A**re you from India?" asked the elderly lady sitting next to me. It was March 1992, and I had just arrived in the Unites States of America. I was on a subway train from Brooklyn to Manhattan.

I had grown up in Pakistan. It had been hammered into our minds all our lives that we were Pakistanis. We were totally different than the Indians, who were our worst enemies and the greatest threat to our very existence.

So my response was a vehement no. "I am from Pakistan," I further explained, shocked at the idea that someone could mistake me for my worst enemy.

"Is that next to Israel?" she asked, trying to carry on the conversation.

But I was done with this dialogue. Not only did she not know the difference between Indians and Pakistanis, but she didn't even know where Pakistan was located on the world map. So I decided to move to a different section of the train and was able to get away from that poor elderly lady who had obviously sensed that I was new to the country and was just trying to make me feel welcome.

Since my arrival in the United States more than thirty years ago, I have never been able to escape the question "Are you from India?" I have been asked that question thousands of times, to the point that I have now stopped clarifying the response, just to avoid the follow-up query as to where in the world Pakistan is located. But being repeatedly asked if I was from India also led me to ask myself the following questions:

Who truly am I?

Is everything that I was told while growing up in Pakistan about India and Indians really true?

Are Pakistanis and Indians really that different from one other?

And as I dug deeper into these questions, I realized that I actually am from India. As a matter of fact, I am more Indian than most people who were born in India!

You see, the South Asian subcontinent derives its name, the Indian subcontinent, from the River Indus, also called the Sindhu. And I was born in Sindh, which gives the River Indus its name of Sindhu, distorted in the English language to Indus.

The more I dwelt into my own identity, the more cognizant I became of the absolute necessity to make the world aware of one the oldest and greatest civilizations known to human history—the Indus Valley civilization, or the Civilization of the Valley of Sindh—and its inhabitants, the Sindhis. The original Indians.

The necessity of this work became even more urgent and important when we started advocacy on behalf of the oppressed people of Sindh a decade and a half later. I was amazed by the lack of knowledge about Sindh, even among the most educated and worldly aware decision-makers in Washington, DC. Though, unlike the elderly lady on the train in Brooklyn, these Washingtonians were aware of where Pakistan was. But, unfortunately, that pretty much was the extent of their knowledge about the region. Most of them thought of Pakistan as a totally homogenous country in which every citizen looked the same, spoke the same language, and pretty much followed the same ideology. Even some of the top decision-makers had no idea of the racial, national, linguistic, religious, social, historic, and topographical diversity that existed in Pakistan.

The typical image of a Pakistani in Washington, DC, and in the United States in general, was that of an angry male, with a long beard, burning a US flag, as shown in every caricature of a Pakistani in the US media. They had no idea that Pakistan also consisted of Sindh, the cradle of Sufism, love, and peaceful coexistence for more than 5,000 years.

Thus, this book is a humble attempt at introducing Sindh and Sindhis to anyone who may be interested in learning more about us. It is especially for those who were born and bred in Sindh but are not aware that they are Sindhis, or do not want to own their own motherland. For those who may have roots in Sindh but have never been there themselves. And for those whose forefathers may have been forced to leave their ancestral land.

This book will take the reader on a journey through Sindh's glorious past and make them aware of Sindh's current painful, sorrowful existence as it gasps in its struggle to survive. It will give them some idea of how Sindh's lifeline, the mighty River Indus, is being completely choked to death by construction of countless dams. Hopefully, it will also encourage sons and daughters of the soil, those living in Sindh and abroad, to do everything possible to save our motherland, which has been plundered by too many for too long. This must be stopped before it is too late.

This should serve as an SOS call: Save Our Sindh!

Where Is Sindh?

Oh, dear Queen, my empire has Sindh, Sauvīra, Saurashtra, Kashi, and Kaushal, and these provinces produce an infinite variety of luxuries; name them, and they shall be yours.

~Mahābhārata

Sindh was a country that existed long before the word *Hind* became familiar to the human ear, a 5,000-year-old civilization that was born on the banks of the ancient, mighty River Indus, contemporary to the Mesopotamian and Egyptian civilizations. It stretched from present-day Karachi, Pakistan, in the south, to Kandahar, Afghanistan, in the north.

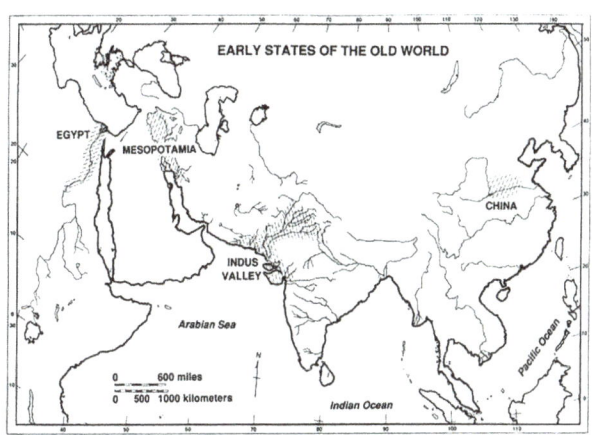

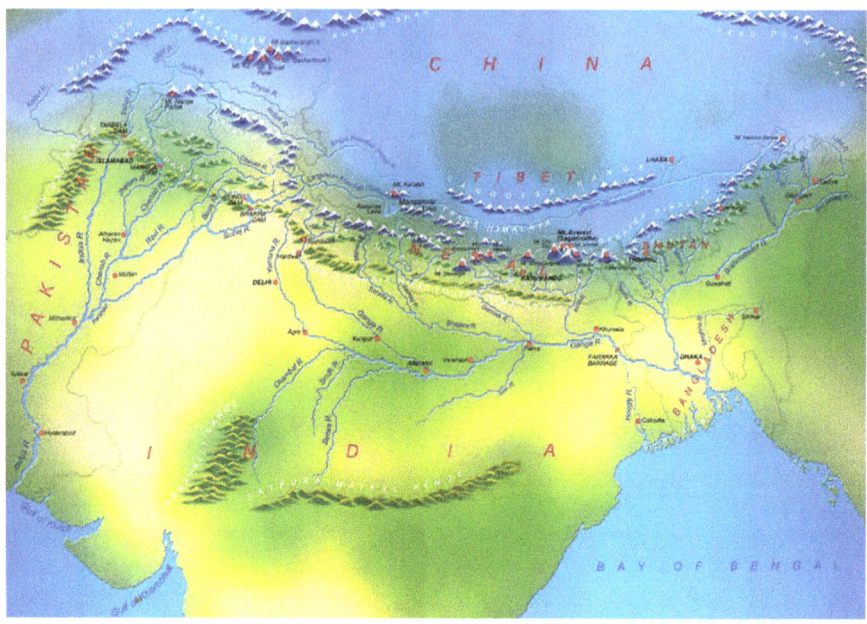

Its port cities and metropolises had trade links with the rest of the world, including Lanka, Egypt, Babylon, Mesopotamia, Central Asia, and China. The Rigveda mentions Sindh as "Sapta Sindhu," the Country of Seven Rivers. The Mahābhārata mentions Sindhu as an independent country and counted it in the "Halls of World Guardians":

> *Sarūpa, Virūpa, Mahāśiras, Daśagrīva, Vālin, Meghavāsa, Dusavara, Kaiṭabha, Viṭaṭūta, Saṃhrāda, Indratāpana.*
>
> *All hosts of Daityas and Dānavas, with their bright earrings, all garlanded, diamonded and divinely garbed, all receivers of boons and champions, all beyond death, all always held in the noose of the law and observant of their vows, attend on the great-spirited God Varna in his hall.*

It also refers to Sindhu as one of the sacred rivers:

> *The four oceans and the rivers Ganges, Bhagirathi, the Kalindi, Vidisha, Venna, Narmada, Vegavāhinī, Vipasa, Śatadru, Chandrabhaga, Saraswati, Indravati, Vitasta, Sindhu, Devananda, Godāvarī, Krishnavenna, Kaveri, best of rivers, these other rivers and fords and lakes, wells and springs in bodily form, Yudhishthira, and ponds and tanks in bodily form, O Bharata, the Quarters, earth and all the mountains and all water creatures wait upon the great-spirited God.*

The Rigvedic literature mentions Sindh as follows:

> *The Sindhu too is flowing with a current of fresh blood. (3:223)*

> *The seven large rivers including the Sindhu, though flowing eastwards, then flowed in opposite directions. The directions seemed to be reversed and nothing could be distinguished. Fires blazed up everywhere and the earth trembled repeatedly. (5:84)*

> *The spot where the Sindhu mingles with the sea, is that Tīrtha of Varuna. (3:82)*

> *There is a celebrated Tīrtha of the name of Sindhuttama. (3:82)*

The journey of Sindh is as old as the sojourn of Sapta Sindhu, or the River Indus itself. In the prehistoric period, Sindh and

Sindhu were documented in traditional history as Itihasa, Upanishads, and Purana (Pothi and Puranas). The two great books of history of the period happen to be Ramayana and Rigveda. Thus, these periods are named the Ramayana and Rigvedic ages.

The Mahabharata narrates the great war fought over the abduction—by the King of Sindh, Raja Jayadratha—of Draupadi, one of the hundred common wives of the Pandava brothers, from their house in the forest. The Pandava brothers went to retrieve Draupadi, defeated Raja Jayadratha, and captured him. In the war, Abhimanyu, the son of Pandava brother Arjuna, and his personal wife, Subhadra, were killed by Raja Jayadratha.

The Mahabharata praised the horses and heroes of Sindh:

> *Horses belonging to Sindhu breed were used extensively in the Kurukshetra War. (7:24)*

> *Steeds consisting of the best of the breeds as also of those born in the country of the rivers, and of those belonging to Airavat and Mahand Sindhu, and of those of Vanayu also that were white in hue, and lastly those of hilly countries were the different types of horse employed in this war. (6:91)*

The Rigveda describes Sindh as follows:

> *The Sindhu is rich in horses, rich in chariots, rich in clothes, rich in golden ornaments. Well made,*

rich in food, rich in wool, ever fresh, abounding in Silama plants, and the auspicious river wears honey, growing flowers. (Rigveda X75)

In the Rigvedic period, Aryans lived in the Sindhu valley. According to Rigveda records, steeds from Sindhu:

...were lean-fleshed, yet strong and capable of a long journey, endured with energy, strength of high breed and docility. Free from inauspicious marks, with wide nostrils and swollen cheeks, free from faults, fast as the winds. (3:71)

The second book that documents Sindh is Mahabharata, which chronicles the great war that dates to 3102 BCE. This proves that Sindhu civilization is older than the Rigvedic and Mahabharata.

This was also confirmed by Abū Rayḥān Muḥammad ibn Aḥmad Al-Bīrūnī, one of the greatest Islamic scholars of all times. He came to India in 1030 ADE and documented that "today marks the 5,000-year anniversary of the Mahabharata War," which means that Sindhu civilization goes as far back as 4000 BCE.

According to Mahabharata, during the Kurukshetra War, the Kauravas lost, and most of them were killed, including Raja Jayadratha. The Pandavas won the war, and Yudhishthira, the eldest Pandava brother, ascended the throne. The Ashuddhi era was ushered in. The present Punjab and other surrounding provinces came under their kingdom. But still Sindh remained under non-Aryan rule.

Raja Jayadratha, with help from the Aryans, built the city of Shivasthan. This name, over the centuries, morphed into Sevistan and now Sehwan, thus making it the oldest city of Sindh. Mahabharata narrates that Lord Rama took his *banvaas* (refuge) in Hinglaj, present-day Balochistan, not far from Karachi. According to Ramayana, on his way to Hinglaj, he meditated near present-day Keamari, on an oyster rock called Ramakharroka (Glimpse Window of Ram). Hinglaj remains a place of pilgrimage for Sindhis of all faiths and beliefs to this day.

Shah Abdul Latif Bhittai, the greatest poet of the Sindhi language, describes in detail his pilgrimage to Hinglaj in Sur Ramkali. A whole chapter in his collection of poetry (*Shah Jo Risalo*) is dedicated to Yogis. Based on the narratives in Ramayana, it was a common belief that Lord Ram had rested in a garden in present-day Karachi, which was named Ram Bagh. After the Partition of India, the name was changed to Aram Bagh.

Ramayana also mentions Serendib and Bhavandib (Java and Sumatra) and the Red Sea. It documents the coronation festivities of King Yudhisthira, in which a delegation from Rome came with gifts. It also describes that Lord Ram awarded Sindh to his brother Bharata in return for his loyalties. King Bharata extended his kingdom to Gandhāra, the city named after his wife, Gandhari.

After the Mahabharata War (fought in the battlefield of Kurukshetra, north of present-day Delhi, in 3102 BCE), the entire India experienced a great deal of disaster and damages that were followed by great migrations. Many from Sindhu

Valley migrated and set up their trade bases at Abyssinia. Many from Madhya Pradesh migrated toward West Asia and America. The Native Americans originated from the ancestry of those migrating from India and Sindhu Valley.[1]

Rigveda demarcates the Sindhu Valley on the banks of Sapta Sindhu, including present-day Punjab, up to Kandahar. Rigveda termed the people living on the Sindhu as Aryans. The sacred scripture of Zoroastrianism, *Avesta*, has used Hapat Hindu, pronouncing the letter *s* as the letter *h*, which means Sapta Sindhu, the Country of Seven Rivers. Thus, Iranians changed the word *Sindhu* into the word *Hindu*. Persians replaced the letter *s* of the Sanskrit word *Sindhu*, for the river, with the letter *h*, and the Greeks with the letter *i*, so that Sindhu became *Hindu* to the Persians and *India* to the Europeans.[2] According to a local myth, the prophet Noah had two sons, Hindh and Sindh, whose descendants settled in current Hind (India) and Sindh (Indus Valley).

Religion had no influence on the public lives of the people of the Sindhu Valley civilization. There is plenty of historical evidence that the earliest Sindhu civilization, consisting of metropolises like Mohenjo-Daro and Harappa, had a classless and secular society.[3]

---

[1] Chaman Lal, *Hindu America* (Hassell Street Press, 2021).

[2] Suhail Zaheer Lari, *A History of Sindh* (Oxford University Press, 1995).

[3] Naval Viyogi, *The Founders of Indus Valley Civilisation and Their Later History: v. 1 (The history of the indigenous people of India)* (Samyak Prakashan, 2015).

Rigveda offered the dates of Supta Sindhu civilization at 1500 BCE, but archaeological evidence suggests even earlier. According to Rigveda (II-40-6), Aryans lived in the Indus Valley. In the Yajurveda period, they left Sindh and settled in Madhya Desh (Midland). They opened *vidyalas* and *pathakshalas* (reading houses) in Madhya Desh, thus creating ancient scriptures in the form of Upanishads, Vedas, and Puranas.

The ancient scriptures record Sindhu. The Puranas praise the wages and richness of Sindhu:

> *And this, enemy-tamer, is the great Fort-of-the-Sindhu, where Lopamudra met Agastya and chose him for her husband.*

Sindhu is held by Hindus in high esteem and is considered a holy river, a purifier of all evils. Many worship the river Sindhu.

It originates from Lake Manasarovar in Tibet and flows to Keti Bandar, Sindh, where it merges into the Sindhi, or Arabian Sea.

Sindh was the place where the foundation of Hinduism was laid because of hymns of Rigveda written on the banks of the river Sindhu. The Vedas include the names of Sindhu up to thirty times, using it to refer to goddess (Rigveda 1-114) and river (Rigveda 10-75).[4] In the words of Sir John Marshall, "The Indus civilization was built on cults of Siva and Mother Goddess."

Sindh is currently the southern province of Pakistan, with Karachi as its economic and political nerve center. Sindh consists of Larr (Lower Sindh), Wicholo (Central Sindh), Uttar (Upper Sindh), and Kachho, Kohistan, and Thar (arid and mountainous land), most beautifully described by the great poet Shaikh Ayaz, as:

لاڙ وچولو اتر "
ڪڇ ڪراچي بندر
هيڏو سارو جر ٿر
ڪيڏو ڪوهستان
سنڌودیش مهان

Larr, The middle, and North Kach, Karachi Port
The vast deserts of Thar and Kohistan, The land of Sindhu is sacred.

---

[4] K. R. Malkani, *The Sindh Story* (Sindhi Academy, 1984).

Sindh is naturally endowed with coastlines, the river delta, and, most of all, the sweet and fresh waters of the Indus River, along with enormous deposits of natural resources including oil, gas, and coal. Seventh-century Sindh was divided into four governing principalities: Upper Sindh, Middle Sindh, Lower Sindh, and Kutch.

Sindhu civilization has been a melting pot of religions: Jainism, Buddhism, Hinduism, Islam, and Sufism. Sindh has been either part of the travel itinerary or the destination of many historical figures, including Lord Rama, Buddha, Jesus, Rishis, and Manis. That is the reason Sindh became a sanctuary of religious pluralism, although Sindhis have always had their own religion in the form of a unique brand of Sufism.

The center stage of Sindhu civilization, culture, and commerce was Mohenjo-Daro, governed by people of Dravidian origins. Mohenjo-Daro, situated on the Indus River, was the first metropolis that had urban town planning, a sewage system, city life, arts, and sports. It is believed that they were highly intellectual people who invented board games like chess. Even with their intellectual and social evolution, they were a peaceful group of people, as no weapons of war were discovered in the excavation at this archaeological site. However, tools used to cultivate and harvest wheat and cotton crops were unearthed.

According to the observation of Sir John Marshall on the discovery of the mounds from Mohenjo-Daro:

> *Before the rise of Maurya Empire a well-developed and flourished civilization had existed in India for at least a thousand years; yet, of the structural*

monuments erected in those ages not one example has survived save the Cyclopean walls of Rajagriha.

The Indus Civilization is example of archaic sociocultural complexity, but without a state.[5]

Modern-day archaeologists, including Gregory L. Possehl, term the first-ever Bronze Age of Mohenjo-Daro as the Indus Age. The people during the Indus Age lived in a casteless society, free from socioeconomic classes; each citizen was an equal and independent member without the concept of a sovereign power or entity. This was very different when compared with its contemporary civilizations of Mesopotamia and Egypt. A potter of Mohenjo-Daro lived in a multistory house consisting of many rooms. His house had a well, a bathroom, a beautiful veranda, and a vast compound. In contrast, potters in Mesopotamia lived in single-room houses. In Egypt, the army of slaves lived in barracks.[6]

This urban civilization was spread over a vast geographic region from the mountains of Baluchistan to Afghanistan, to the coastal regions of Makran, Sindh, and Gujarat.[7]

---

[5] Gregory L. Possehl, *The Indus Civilization: A Contemporary Perspective* (AltaMira Press, 2002).

[6] S. R. Rao, *Lothal and the Indus Civilization* (Asia Publishing House, 1973).

[7] Jonathan Mark Kenoyer et al., *The Indus Civilization; Art of the First Cities the Third Millennium BCE from the Mediterranean to the Indus* (Yale University Press, 2003).

In the words of Naval Viyogi:

> *The cities of Sumeria, Akkad, and Babylon were also pucca like those of the Indus Valley, but they were not planned at all. They had only developed. The outer walls were ugly. The streets were similar to those of Rome, London, Paris, and Indian cities which had zigzag of paths. The excavated minor streets of Mohenjo-Daro are much more impressive in appearance than the wider ones, as the buildings on them are so much better preserved.*[8]

The bastion of the Indus civilization was Mohenjo-Daro. In the world civilization, it was the first city to have a developed urban society, elegant buildings, structures raised with kiln bricks, personal and public baths, colleges, and community halls. The architectural sites of Mohenjo-Daro offer compelling evidence of urban town planning and the avant-garde society of the Indus Valley Civilization.

---

[8] Viyogi, *The Founders of the Indus Valley Civilisation and Their Later History: v. 1 (The history of the indigenous people of India)*.

British archaeologist Sir Mortimer Wheeler said:

> *In 1921 at Harappa, a small town in Punjab, and in 1922 at Mohenjo-Daro in Sindh, evidence was recovered of an evolved urban culture nearly two thousand years older than any previously recognized in the Indo-Pakistan subcontinent... From the discoveries of the sites first explored, the culture was named as the Indus Valley Civilization. This name it retains, although subsequent research has revealed evidence of the civilization on the one hand westward to the Makran Coast and Saurashtra, and on the other hand eastwards into the Valley of Yamuna (Jamuna). Thus amplified, the civilization is apparently larger than its contemporaries in Iraq and Egypt.*

Mohenjo-Daro was the metropolis of the Indus Valley Civilization dating back to 3000 BCE; it stood as an entirely urban center and economic hub, using water as a means of transport over the floodplains of the River Sindhu and its tributaries. It remained in oblivion to the people of Sindh and the rest of the world until the dawn of the twentieth century.

In 1901, Lord Curzon, then Viceroy of British India, ordered an archaeological survey of India, and Sir John Marshall was deputed as its director general. Thus, organized excavations of Harappa and Mohenjo-Daro were initiated in the 1920s under Sir John Marshall. Excavation work of the archaeological sites of Harappa and Mohenjo-Daro continued until 1926 and brought to light this pre-Aryan civilization. Rakhal Das Banerji, an archaeologist from Madras, was the first who found some artifacts at the mounds of Mohenjo-Daro; this discovery led to the excavation and discovery of 1,200 sites representing the Indus Valley Civilization. The initial excavation sites were Ghaibi Dero, Dhamrah, and Dokri, thus paving way for the discovery of the Indus Civilization by historian Nayanjot Lahiri, called Banerji the Maverick, at Mohenjo-Daro.

These excavations revealed to the world that the Indus Valley Civilization stretched up the entire northwest region of India and included present-day Pakistan, Haryana, Rajasthan, and some significant parts of Gujarat and Uttar Pradesh. Mohenjo-Daro stood tall as the metropolis of the Indus Valley Civilization. It was first traced over 1,000 sites marked for excavation under Sir John Marshall, and it later became known to the world as the Indus Valley Civilization. The Indus Valley Civilization was four times bigger than Egypt and twice as large as Mesopotamia.

Discovery of the Indus Valley Civilization was a major archaeological find and a breakthrough in the tracing of human history. It disproved the previously held belief that the history of Sindh began with Aryans or Arabs. Recent discoveries of sites in Mehrgarh and Baluchistan have now extended the period of the Indus Valley Civilization to 8000 BCE.

Sindh, since the beginning of time, has been a green pasture for the armies of conquerors, wandering wild tribes, robbers, travelers, adventurers, refugees running away from persecution, and impoverished nomads in search of livelihoods for themselves and their livestock. Sufis, saints, dervishes, and lovers came to Sindh in search of peace, love, and spirituality; it was as if Sindh were a gigantic magnet attracting multitudes of human races. Kalidasa praised Sindh in his epic poem on rain, "Meghadūta."

> *The torrent passed, behold the Sindhu glide,*
> *As though the hair-band bound the slender tide;*
> *Bleached with the withered foliage, that the breeze*
> *has showered rude from overhanging trees:*
> *To thee she looks for succor, to restore*
> *Her lagging waters, and her leafy shore.*

Rabindranath (Thakur) Tagore mentioned Sindh in his well-known poem, "Jana Gana Mana," which is now one of the national anthems of India.

> *Thou art the ruler of the minds of all people,*
> *dispenser of India's destiny.*
> *Thy name rouses the hearts of the Punjab, Sindh,*
> *Gujarat and Maratha,*
> *of the Dravida, Orissa and Bengal.*

Chinese pilgrim traveler Xuanzang, known as Hsüan-tsang, who visited Sindh during the seventh century (641 AD), called Sindh Shin-tu or Sindhu, the Land of the Indus. He traveled extensively throughout India, including Gujarat and Malwa in Rajasthan, from where he entered Sindh. He wrote:

> *After going through the wild desert and dangerous gorges, crossing the great river Sin-Tu, we came to the kingdom of Sin-Tu (Sindh), which is one of the few described of having the Shudra king. (II-272)*

Ibn Battuta, describing the then-incumbent king of Sindh, revealed that Sindh was ruled by an indigenous king of Dravidian descent, whom Aryans considered Shudra, the outcast. Shudras are related by some historians to the founders of the Indus Civilization.[9]

Hsüan-tsang documented, based on his memory, that "Sin-Tu included the delta and the island of Cutch."

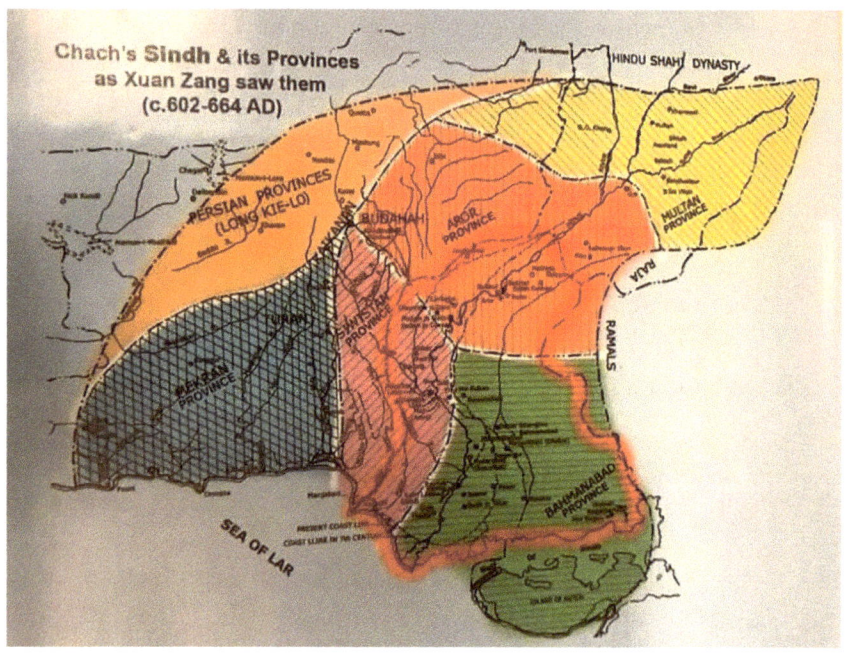

Zhen Zhang, an ambassador of Han who visited Sindh in the second century BCE (38-125 BCE), recalled Sindh by its Chinese name, Shen-tu (Sindh). Monk Faxian and the pilgrim

---

[9] Viyogi, *The Founders of Indus Valley Civilisation and Their Later History: v. 1 (The history of the indigenous people of India)*.

Hsüan-tsang left two reports detailing trade routes from Sindh to other countries and information about Sindh's ports, cities, and towns. The fifteenth-century Arab traveler Ibn Battuta chronicled his visit to Sindh in the following way:

> *When we reached this river called Panj Aab and which are the territories of the Sultan of India and Sindh, the officials of the intelligence service came to us and sent a report about us to the governor of the city of Multan. From Sindh to the city of Delhi, the Sultan's capital, it is fifty days' march, but when the intelligence officials wrote to the Sultan from Sindh the letter reached him in five days from the postal service.*[10]

Ibn Battuta spent some time in Sindh and has written about Lal Shahbaz Qalandar, whom he referred to as Usman Marwandi, and the City of Sehwan. Later, known as Qalandar Lal Shahbaz (decd 1274 CE), he became one of the most influential Sufis in Sindh.

Records of navigation routes by Greek sailors in 70-80 BCE show cities and ports on the river Sindhu. They mention that the Assyrians used a fabric called Sadin, an Indian cloth, with references to Sindhu or Sintu. This was reportedly traded between the coasts of Eden, Babylon, and ports of the River Indus. Thus, the traders of Sindh went to far-flung corners of the world from the cities and ports of Sindh. Their destinations included Serendib, Lanka, Africa, Russia, Persia, and Rome.

---

[10] Ibn Battuta, *Travels in Asia and Africa*, 1325-1354, trans. H. A. R. Gibb (Martino Fine Books, 2023).

Buddha, along with his swami Upagupta, visited Sindh during an expedition to spread the message of nonviolence or *ahnsawad*. Swami Upagupta was a guru to King Ashoka of the Maurya dynasty. After the death of Buddha, his blowing horn was sent to the countries where Buddha had set foot. King Ashoka also sent his blowing horn, or *shankh* in Sindh, over which stupas were built.

Hsüan-tsang describes numerous monasteries in Sindh and 1,000 monks of the Sammitīya school. These were the times when monasteries of Taxila were in ruins, but Sindh had an abundance of Buddhist places of learning and pilgrimage. The king of Sindh himself was a Buddhist, and "Upagupta often visited the place" (W II.252.3).

Buddhism had direct influence over Sufis and Sadhus of India and Sindh. In the eighth century, Bayazid Bastami visited his mentor, Abu Ali, a Sindhi Sufi master. This was when Sufism was flourishing all over the Islamic region.

Eighteenth-century poet and Sufi Shah Abdul Latif Bhittai is called the poet of Sindh's past, present, and future because of the mystic messages in his poetry. Shah Abdul Latif Bhittai was greatly influenced by the great Persian poet and Sufi Jalal ad-Din Rumi. Rumi's partner, mentor, and guide, Shams Tabrizi, was enormously influenced by the Sufi Bayazid Bastami. The master of Bayazid Bastami, in turn, was a Sindhi Sufi named Abu 'Ali al-Sindi.

Sindh was also visited by the great Sufi Mansour al-Hallaj around 896-97 CE. From Buddhist monasteries to Sufi shrines, to palaces of kings and battlefields, Sindhis excelled in all fields. Mohenjo-Daro, Jhoolay Lal, Shah Abdul Latif Bhittai, and the Sindhu River are icons of Sindh. Muhammad Qasim Farishta, in his acclaimed book *Tarikh-i Firishta*, called Sindh Neelaabor, Blue Water. On the other hand, nineteenth-century British explorer and adventurer Richard F. Burton described Sindh as the Unhappy Valley.

Historian Suhail Zaheer Lari described it perfectly when he wrote:

> *Sindh was also repeatedly occupied by empire builders from the north and west who wanted to gain access to the trade that tied the Indian Ocean to the Mediterranean, as well as by those who were running from the persecution of empire builders and looking for a place of refuge.*

Be it the Medes, the first historically documented foreigners who took refuge in Sindh, or the Achaemenes, Bactrians, Greeks, Sassanid, Samarians, Arabs, Mongols, Tarkhans, Arghuns, Pathans, Mughals, Portuguese, British, or the post-Pakistan influx of population, Sindh has always opened her arms and hinterlands for those who assimilate through a natural and historical process. But Sindh has always rejected those who have tried to usurp its resources.

Sindh is currently striving to regain its past glory. It has become merely a province chained by many treaties, ethnocentric hegemony, and betrayals by the current masters. It has not yet been determined how the Indus Valley Civilization was destroyed. Was it the wrath of Mother Nature or a man-made catastrophe?

Hugh Lambrick was of the view that it was the result of a natural disaster in the form of a flood.

> *We do not have the means at present of ascertaining whether the lowest and permanently drowned habitation levels under Mohenjo-Daro belong to the Indus Civilization, or to an antecedent culture. But it is a fair assumption that it was the Indus people who had built their first permanent settlement in such an exposed position. It may reasonably be inferred that the Indus people were never involved in a war with a formidable enemy until, perhaps, the very end of the many centuries of their rule.*[11]

To the contrary, E. Mackay and Mortimer Wheeler—who were directly involved in excavation of sites, preservation of artifacts, and examination of corpses at Mohenjo-Daro—believe that the end of the Indus Civilization was the result of a massacre by invaders. From Rao Jiwaji, the founder of the Rao dynasty and the ruler of Sindh from 489 to 652 CE, to Raja Dahir onwards, the history of Sindh is full of horses and heroes who, in Shah Abdul Latif Bhittai's words, "had few days to live."

---

[11] H. T. Lambrick, *Sind, Before the Muslim Conquest* (*History of Sind series, v. 2*) (Karachi: Oxford University Press, 1973).

To date, from Dara to Alexander, the Sindhis' nonviolent movements and their Sufi souls have always in the end defeated their oppressors. Pluralism has been the essence of the Sindhi people and society since time immemorial.

گھوڙن ۽ گھوٽن، جئَڻ تورا ڏينھڙا: ڪڏھن مَنجھہ ڪوٽن، ڪڏھن واھي رڻ جا.

> *Horses and Heroes live, but a few days,*
> *Either lavishing in palaces, or wandering in the*
> *sands of deserts.*
>
> ~Shah Lateef

From the end of the Indus Civilization to the beginning of the history of Sindh, there is a gap of one millennium, about which no recorded history is available. We are not aware of what happened to the Sindhu civilization during that millennium, but the salient features and culture of Sindhu civilization survived. This was only because of the resilience of the people of Sindh, who continue to face and fight back the intruders.

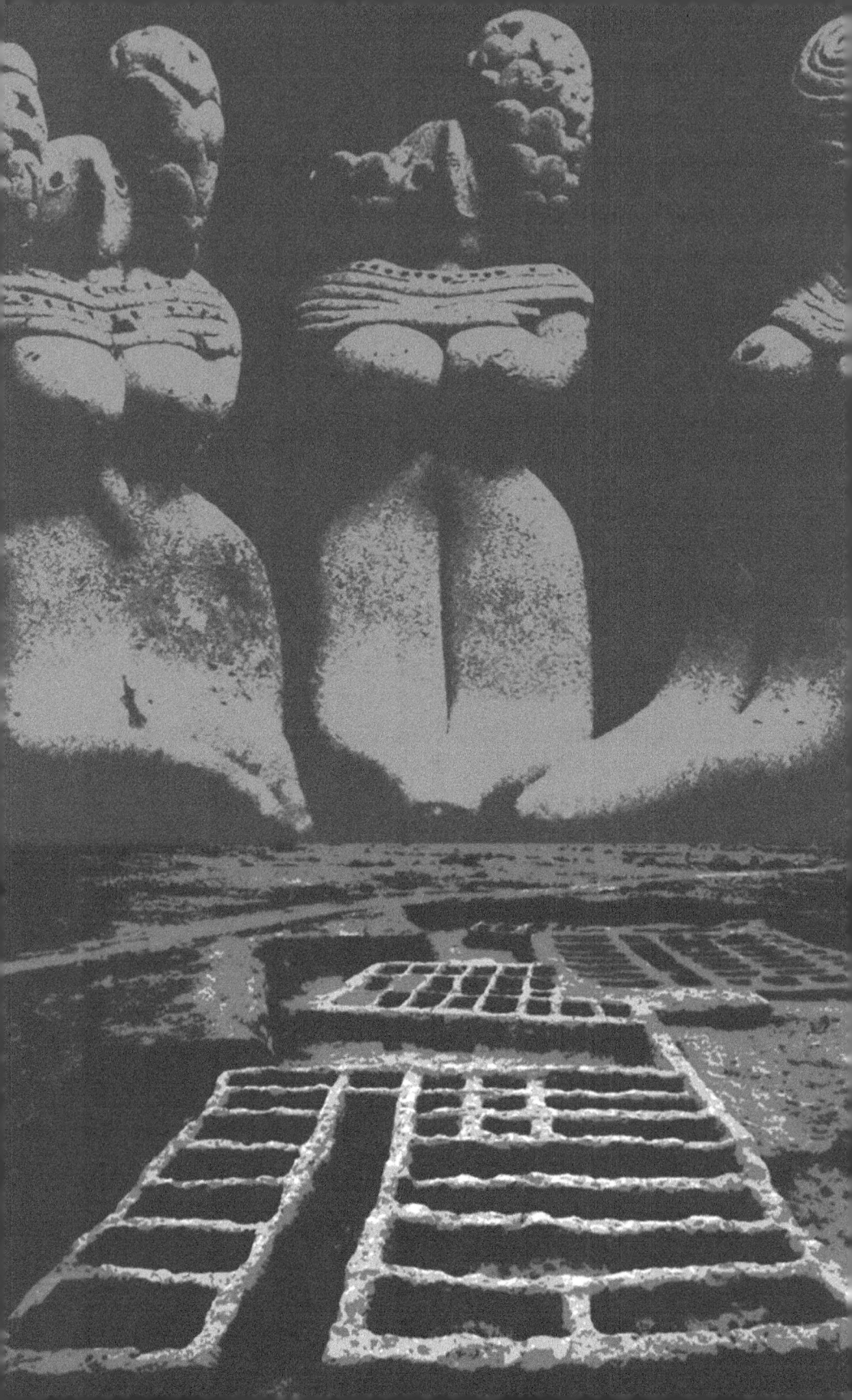

The Origins of Sindhis

About 150,000 years ago, there lived a woman on the continent of Africa. All living human beings are the direct descendants of this woman now called by geneticists and evolution historians as Mitochondrial Eve. Some 60,000 years ago, her children opted for migration to the north in search of their everyday food and scattered all over the planet. As the Ice Age depleted oceans, these migrating human populations started their land journey to Australia, the Americas, and Southeast Asia.

The first human migration occurred roughly 146,000 years ago from Africa. The journeys of these groups of people trace back the ancestry of the earliest migratory human population out of Africa along the Pacific. These tribes of hunters and herdsmen, who came from the Eurasian Steppe, established the earliest civilization of Sindh.

Mehrgarh appears to be the earliest discovered archaeological site of the Indus Valley Civilization. It precedes other sites, such as Mohenjo-Daro, by approximately 3,000 years, thus proving that the Indus Valley Civilization may be as much as 8,000 years old.

Fossils found in the Caspian and Mediterranean regions have similarities to the sites discovered in the Indus Valley Civilization.

The twentieth century saw miraculous breakthroughs with the introduction of DNA testing and further advances in molecular biology and forensic sciences. The twentieth and twenty-first centuries saw an array of new methodologies of research in molecular biology and forensic sciences, shedding new light on the origins of human populations and the history of evolution. Not only did this make the work of modern historians easier, but it also has virtually converted history into a science.

"In some sense, we don't want to talk to historians. There is a great virtue in being objective: you put the data in and get the history out. We think this is a way of reconstructing history by just using DNA," wrote Daniel Falush, Max Planck Institute of Evolutionary Anthropology, Leipzig, Germany, on the launching of "A Genetic Atlas of Human Admixture History," a global study on human genomes, including those of Sindhis, published in the journal, *American Association for the Advancement of Science*, 2014.

In 2009, anthropology historian, B. S. Ahloowalia coined a new term for the journey of humans—the Journey of Gene Flow. Since the 1980s, new research techniques and scientific studies in the disciplines of genetic sciences (genomics) through DNA profiling, analytical sciences on microsatellite markers, Short Tandem Repeat (STR), Y chromosome, and mitochondrial DNA have led to new discoveries in human phylogenetic trees, history of human populations, evolution, origins of human history, and their migration lineage.

Contrary to the other twenty-two sets of pairs of chromosomes in males, the Y chromosomes do not change to shuffle or recombine among both parents until they transform into the male progeny. So, the mutations among nonrecombinant male Y chromosomes happen to be stable and specific among populations in different geographical locations. The Y chromosome testing has been proved to be a reliable tool in the hands of anthropologists, bio- anthropologists, and geneticists to demonstrably prove the male parentage ancestry of mankind. Likewise, mitochondrial chromosome is passed by mother to children of both sexes. In such tests, microsatellites have been enormously effective in tandem to repeated series of two- to-six nucleotides.[12]

That is how the latest research traces the origins of modern humans back to Africa.[13] The method of Y-chromosome DNA testing and mitochondrial DNA analysis can safely assess the ancestry of modern humans back to millions of years. That is how the science of human genetics decoded that all modern human beings are the offspring of Mitochondrial Eve.

---

[12] Michael R. Green and Joseph Sambrook, *Molecular Cloning: A Laboratory Manual (Fourth Edition) Vol. 1, 2 & 3* (Cold Spring Harbor Laboratory Press, 2012).

[13] L. L. Cavalli-sforza, Paolo Menozzi, and Alberto Piazza, *The History and Geography of Human Genes* (Princeton University Press, 1996).

The latest inquiries into ethnic biology, biological anthropology, archaeology,[14] and zoo archaeology offer evidence that modern Sindhi humans had settled on the Indus plains even before the beginning of the Indus Civilization period.

This was further confirmed when modern-day archaeologists extended their research on the sites of Mehrgarh, Rohri, Amri, and Kot Diji, only to discover that the human population in the Indus plains preceded the Neolithic era, thus extending the life of this civilization from 3000 to 8000 BCE.

In the words of the great Sufi poet Bulleh Shah:

" اسان آدم کنون اڳي هيا سي, آدم ساڏا جايا "

I was here before Adam; Adam was of my progeny.

No organized religion is as old as the Sindhu Civilization. Hinduism is less than 3,500 years old, Buddhism is 2,500 years old, Islam is less than 1,500 years old, Christianity is about 2,000 years old, and Sikhism is about 500 years old. Judaism is the oldest religion; it originated in Canaan around 1500-1000 BCE.[15]

---

[14] Steven A. Weber, ed., William R. Belcher, ed., et al., Indus Ethnobiology: New Perspectives from the Field (Lexington Books, 2003).

[15] B. S. Ahloowalia, *Invasion of the Genes: Genetic Heritage of India* (New York: Eloquent Books, 2009).

Environmental, economic, and ecological changes have always been the primary reasons human beings migrated from one region of the planet to another. Tracing back roots of Sindhis by Y-chromosome markers, geneticists have identified the route of the earliest human population.

> *Invaders including the Aryans and Macedonians have all contributed to the ethnic variety of Pakistan's population, the Baluchis, Brahuis, Makranis, and Sindhis constitute the major Southern population. In present-day Pakistan. The major northern groups include the Balti, Burusho, Hazaras, Kalash Kafirs, Kashmiris and Punjabis.*[16]

These tests have provided insights into genetic variations and have been helpful in detecting the origins of modern man back to Homo sapiens in Africa. West Eurasia was the first habitat of Homo sapiens after Africa. From there, modern humans migrated to other parts of the world, as far as Mehrgarh and Indus Valley. Studies done internationally have found DNA variations among populations of the Indus Valley, including Sindhis.

A research paper titled, "Y-Chromosomal DNA Variation in Pakistan," presented at the Fourteenth International Congress of International Union of Anthropological and Ethnological Sciences in Williamsburg, Virginia, established that the original

---

[16] S. Q. Mehdi et al., "Where West Meets East: The Complex mtDNA Landscape of the Southwest and the Central Asian Corridor." *The American Journal of Human Genetics* Vol. 74, Issue 5 (April 2004).

populations of humans migrated to the present-day Sindh approximately 60,000 years ago.

> *These two regional groups might have originated as a result of two distinct waves of migrations, one from the North Africa and the other from the Sub-Saharan Region.*[17]

Thus, migrations and invasions of pasturelands contributed to the mix of origins of the people of the Indus Valley, including Sindhis. This genetic admixture of populations occurred before the advent of languages. "These results lend support to the hypothesis that peopling of Pakistan has been influenced by separate migrations from West Asia, the Levant, and Sub-Saharan Africa."[18]

These studies in disciplines of genomics clearly prove the different genetic origins of ethnic groups living in northern versus southern regions of present-day Pakistan. The ethnic groups living in the north are mostly of Indo-European and Sino-Tibetan origin; whereas those living in the south are of North African and Sub-Saharan origin.

---

[17] S. Q. Mehdi et al., "Clinical and Evolutionary Genetics of Pakistani Populations," ICGEB 10th Anniversary Symposium. Trieste, Italy (1997).

[18] S. Q. Mehdi et al., "The Origins of Pakistani Populations: Evidence from Y Chromosome Markers," *Genomic Diversity Application in Human Population Genetics*. Eds. S. S. Papiha, R. Deka, and R. Chakraborty. (Boston: Springer, 1999) p. 83-90.

The above evidence further confirms that these groups resulted in the ethnic variation of present-day Pakistan. Because of their strong endogamous, cultural, ethnic, and linguistic differences, they still remain alien to one another's culture and languages.

The studies recommended that carrying on more research will help in further understanding origins of the highly diverse ethnic groups living in northern versus southern parts of the Indus Valley. Hence, the historic struggle for Sindh's natural and historic rights.

In 1999, a multinational study on the presence of global distribution of haplogroup 3 and haplogroup 7 chromosomes was conducted by a conglomerate of scientists and geneticists, including molecular biologists and anthropologists from the UK, Germany, India, Pakistan, and Russia. This study produced the following findings:

> *In thirteen of the twenty-two populations, haplogroup 3 chromosomes make up one-fifth of the population or more. Thus, they account for a major proportion of Asian and European Y chromosomes. Within Asia, there is considerable local variation in frequency from population to population, without a simple overall geographical pattern.*

> *This is particularly noticeable in the Pakistani population, where the sample sizes are large enough to provide reliable frequency estimates. Among the Parsi, the frequency was eight percent (7/90), while, as noted above, it was fifty-two percent (38/73) in Sindhi.*

Within Europe, there is a greater gradient in frequency from northeast (high) to southwest (low).[19]

In 2004, a genomic study was carried out on twenty-seven groups consisting of different tribes, castes, and clans on their present genetic landscapes and geographic settings in Central Asia, the Iranian Plateau, and the Indus Valley. Their 910 mitochondrial DNA were taken, examined, and analyzed. This study concluded that "mt DNAs from Southwest Asia and Central Asian corridors show that the highest variations are found in populations located at the Indus Valley and Central Asia, highlighting this region as the place where Western Eurasian lineage meets both East Eurasian and South Asian groups."[20]

The amalgamation of different genetic components in this area may have resulted from the successive and continuous waves of migrations from diverse geographic sources at different time periods.

Sindh, the region Greeks called Sindhoomana, was referred to by its indigenous ancient children as Sind-hudesha. The Arab conquest of Sindh in 711 AD opened the floodgates for the

---

[19] T. Zerjal et al., "The Use of Y-Chromosomal DNA Variation to Investigate Population History: Recent Male Spread in Asia and Europe." *Genetic Diversity Application in Human Population Genetics* Eds. S. S. Papiha, R. Deka, and R. Chakraborty. (Boston: Springer, 1999).

[20] S. Q. Mehdi et al., "Where West Meets East: The Complex mtDNA Landscape of the Southwest and the Central Asian Corridor."

invasion of genes. This was followed by the incursion and settlement of Persians, Arghuns, Tarkhans, Pathans, and Afghans. Hindus, Bheels, and Mohanos were the original indigenous races of the Sindhu Valley.

The genetic scientists involved in detections of DNA variations among populations in the region do not rule out the contributions of invading races to the admixture of the population of Sindhis. This also conforms with the findings of historians.

As historian Sarah F. Ansari puts it, "The Sindhis from the southeastern province of Pakistan (Sindh) are of a mixed ethnic background."[21] However, Ansari and British explorer and historian Richard F. Burton both agree that ancient Hindus and races like Mohanos, Bheels, Chana, and Abras are the survivors of these invasions of gene flows in the Indus Valley.

Sindhis, be they from Sindh in present-day Pakistan, India, the Americas, Europe, or East Asia, contribute their unique genetic makeup to the human genetic world atlas.

---

[21] Sarah F. Ansari, *Sufi Saints and State Power: The Pirs of Sind, 1843-1947* (Cambridge South Asian Studies, Series Number 50) (Cambridge University Press, 1992).

Sindhis in Prehistory: Life and Times in Ancient Sindh

Myth and Realities

According to the *Oxford English Dictionary*, the definition of prehistory is "the period of time before the written record."

Ample records have been discovered of great civilizations—including the three great civilizations of Egypt, Mesopotamia, and the Indus Valley—prior to modern recorded history. These civilizations, contemporary to each other some 5,000 years ago in the Bronze Age, had developed a maritime trade relationship. The story of Sindh began with the first flow of the River Indus.

Long before modern technological advances of archaeology equipped with radiocarbon dating techniques and modern history, Sindh was documented in traditional Puranas (old scriptures) and Itihasa (traditional history). The epic Mahabharata also spoke of King Manu, the survivor of great floods. He was the founder of two races: Suraj Bansi and Chandar Bansi (Children of the Sun and Children of Moon).

According to Mahabharata and Puranas, these Children of the Sun and Moon founded the Kingdom of Āryāvarta (the land of the Aryans), which expanded over most of the northern parts of the Indian subcontinent. The descendants of Sooraj Bansis fought the Kurukshetra War to the north of modern Delhi in 3102 BCE. As documented by Dr. Hamida Khuhro, "The Sindhi King Jayadratha fought alongside the Aryans. Surrounded by 500 brave mountaineers, with his banner depicting a wild boar, he was killed in battle by Arjuna."

King Jayadratha's kingdom extended over Sauvīra, Sivi, Sindh, and many other parts of the regions of the subcontinent. The Mahabharata describes this great war and its period as the Age of Kali (the Age of Misfortune). According to research done by historian Bherumal Meharchand Advani, the Sindhu Civilization precedes the Age of Kali. An urbanized Indus civilization was found to have been documented by the Mesopotamians 5,300 years ago. The Mesopotamians had drawn graphics of trading ships floating over River Indus, bound for ancient Egypt and Mesopotamia. They called it Meluḫḫa, meaning a far and distant place in the east. This was described as the place where peacocks danced and gold was found.

The Mighty Indus: Sindhu Sauvir 1, or Golden River

As per an ancient myth:

> *In a village in the Himalayan Valley of Tibet, Sadhus (ascetic holy men), after their meditation over millions of years, captured the longest snake. The snake slipped from the hands of the holy men, and it sneaked through the Himalayas to the mountains, springs, glaciers, plains, deserts of Sindh, and finally it dived into the Sindhi Sea. A mighty river sprouted wherever the snake passed. Hence the Indus River was born.*

The records of the history of Sindh begin with the settlement of the first humans along the mighty River Indus, which starts in the vicinity of Lake Manasarovar in Tibet. It runs its course through the Ladakh District of Jamun and Kashmir and then enters present-day Pakistan through Gilgit-Baltistan. Flowing from north to south, the River Indus merges with the Arabian Sea not far from the metropolitan city of Karachi.

کو جو قَهَرُ کلاچ ۾ ڳهڙي سو نِئي،
خَبَرَ کونه ڏِئي، رَچَ کجاڑي رَندِيا؟

There is such wrath in Kulach, it devours each that dares to enter. No one knows how many has the vortex swallowed.

~Shah Latif

Kulach was the old name of Karachi when it was still a small fishing village The length of the river stretches up to 3,180 kilometers; it is the longest river of the Indian subcontinent. It has always been not only a lifeline to Sindh and its people (modern as well as ancient), but also a food basket for the region. "The Indus River and its tributaries produce annual flows of water that are, for example, twice that of the Nile in Egypt, and ten times the Colorado in the Southwestern United States."[22]

Scottish archaeologist Jane R. McIntosh, who carried out research on Indus Valley and Harappan civilizations along the Saraswati, Hakro, and Indus River systems, stated in her findings:

---

[22] Roger Revelle, "A Review of Problems in Achieving Efficient Use of Surface and Ground Irrigation Waters in Agricultural Development." (World Bank Report, 1963).

The most dramatic change took place in the region south of Indus River, where there is evidence that a great river system flowed in the Harappan period. Through ground survey methods of remote sensing such as satellite photography, many stretches of dry riverbed have been traced in Thar Desert and the Indo-Gangetic divide, often as much as ten kilometers wide, showing that they once had substantial rivers. The Ghaggar still flows in India while the Hakro that flowed in five major cavities of the Indus Civilization became a relic of history, leaving its ruins and some channels in present Cholistan.

The annual floods into River Indus and its sister rivers have always been a great source of silt and rich mineral deposits from the Himalayan highlands and Tibetan Plateau. These natural variations in the ebb and flow of the rivers have been the source of ever-renewing fertility of the Indus Valley region, which, in turn, has been the major reason for migration to the area.

دَهشَتَ دَمَ دَرياهَ مِ، جِتِ جايونَ جانارَنِ؛
نَكو سَندو سِيرَ جو، مَپُ نه مَلاحَنِ؛
دَرندا دَرياهَ مِ، واڪا ڪِيو وَرَنِ؛
سَجا بيڑا بارِ مِ، هَليا هيتَ وَجَنِ؛
پُرزو پِئدا نه ٿئي، تَختو مَنجهان تَنِ؛
ڪو جو قَهرُ ڪَنَنِ، ويا ڪِينَ وَرَنِ؛
اُتي اُٿتارُنِ، ساهَڙَ! سِيرَ لَنگهاءِ تُونِ.

There is terror in the river, It is home to many beasts
Sailors have no idea of the current, or a measure of it
Predators in the river turn at your roaring
Ships get drowned in the depths
No trace of their plank and pieces to be seen again
Such is the wrath of the vortexes, that no one can return
Oh savior, there, save those who can swim

~Shah Latif

In the words of a classical Sindhi poet of the sixteenth century:

هاک وهندو هاکڙو ييجندي ٻنڊ اروڙ
بيهه مڇي ۽ لوڙهه سمي ويندي سوکڙي

The flow of the River Hakra would be praised all over, Aror River will breech its banks
Lotus roots, and fish of all kinds will go to the Samoon King as presents

Sindhis also call it Darya Shah, or the King River. Peasant leader Hyder Bux Jatoi, who also coined the term "Jeay Sindh," perfectly portrayed the emotions of Sindhis about their beloved Indus River, in the following poem:

حيدر بخش جتوئي "حيدر"
درياهہ شاھہ

تون داخل ٿئين سنڌ ۾ تو اَخير،
جا آ عشق تنهنجي ۾ اصلا اَسير،
سحر وقت، سنڊي، اچي ٿي حقير،
ڪري تنهنجي پوڄا، مڃي توکي پير،
اي "سنڌو" سدائي، تون ڪر "سنڌ" سائي،
تون همنام سان رھہ، وفا سان هميشہ،
جو سنڌو سوا سنڌ ٻي ڪجھہ بہ ناهہ،
ڀلي آئين جي آئين درياهہ شاهہ!

You enter Sindh at the end
Which is afflicted with eternal love for you
Though for you it comes last
Sindh worships you and considers you its sage
O' Sindhu may you forever keep Sindh green
May you remain faithful to your namesake
Because without Sindhu, Sindh cannot survive
Welcome, welcome O' the King of Rivers

In the words of Alice Albinia, "From the deserts of Sindh to the mountains of Tibet, the Indus is worshiped by peasants and honored by poets, more than priests and politicians."

Sindhi Hindus recognize the River Indus as a place of rebirth or reemergence of Odero Lal, the reincarnation of God Krishna. Sindhi Muslims see the same saint as Shaikh Tahir and Khwaja Khizr.

British journalist Alice Albinia, who had undertaken an expedition of the River Indus from its delta in the ocean to its beginnings in Tibet, wrote:

> *Along the way, the river has more names than its people have had dictators.*[23]

---

[23] Alice Albinia, *Empires of the Indus: The Story of a River* (New York: W. W. Norton & Company, Inc., 2010).

> *Rivers have great influence on physical shaping of the country, its geography and history. Great upheavals occur on account of change of river's course. River Sindhu has also passed through such vicissitudes, has changed its course, and so on. Therefore, its present position cannot be taken for granted in dealing with its ancient history.*[24]

Many myths are attached to River Indus, including one that states if you throw any metal into the river, it will turn into gold, thus the name Sonmarg, meaning Place of Gold.

Pre-Mohenjo-Daro—Mehrgarh

Prehistory of Sindh dates back to the origin of River Indus. The actual age of River Indus remains undetermined. But archaeologists and zoologists believe that the Indus flowed 3,000,000 years before the appearance of Homo sapiens on the continent of Africa some 100,000 to 120,000 years ago.[25]

Some 60,000 years ago, Sindh was submerged and remained under the sea for 12,000 years. That delayed the Neolithic Period in the Indus Valley, thus Sindhu or Indus Civilization

---

[24] Gangaram Samrat, *Sindhu-Sauvir: History Begins at Sindh* (G. Samrat, 1984).

[25] Saiyid Ali Naqvi, *Indus Water and Social Change: The Evolution and Transition of Agrarian Society in Pakistan* (Oxford University Press, 2013).

attained the age of maturity later than its contemporary civilizations, like Mesopotamia, Egypt, and Babylon.

After 12,000 years, the sea began subsiding, which ushered in the Mesolithic Age. During the Mesolithic Age, the survival of humans depended on hunting in the forest and fishing from the river. According to historiographer M. H. Panhwar, forest hunting must have been moved from Deccan, Bengal, and Punjab to Sindh.[26]

> Nine thousand years back, the seacoast must have been north of Hyderabad, and possibly near Hala. The Indus fish and forests must have attracted large numbers of Mesolithic fishermen and hunters by this time. Sindh was capable of supporting higher

---

[26] M. H. Panhwar, *Chronological Dictionary of Sindh* (Jamshoro Sind-Pakistan: Institute of Sindhology University of Sind, 1983).

> *densities of population than any other part of the subcontinent under conditions existing then. It was probably during this time that crude raft boats and fishing hooks were evolved. Skin float and nets of fishing would probably have come late.*

> *Mohanos (fishing people) of Sindh are said to be ancestors of those who later built Harappa and Mohenjo Daro, popularly known as Indus Civilization.*

This was confirmed by Alice Albinia:

> *The unmechanized wooden boats they navigated along the Indus, propelled by the sails, rudders and poles, are identical in outline to boats sketched on five-thousand-year-old seals of Mohenjo Daro Civilization.*[27]

> *Mohanas are the direct connection to the prehistoric Indus River cult, if anybody has the answer to the mystery of its origins.*

Sir John Marshall was the first scholar to coin the name Indus Civilization. This civilization preceded the beginning of urban civilization or the city-states of Mohenjo Daro. Archaeological expeditions from 1970 to 1980 found ample evidence of the earliest human settlements from the Neolithic Age in Rohri, Amri, and Kot Diji. These are similar to Mehrgarh (7000 BCE to 3500 BCE, which was settled around some 7,000 years BCE).

---

[27] Albinia, *Empires of the Indus: The Story of a River.*

Mehrgarh is situated in the foothills of the Bolān Pass, at the edge of riverine areas of the River Indus. It is South Asia's oldest discovered settlement of the Stone Age, where prehistorical pastoralism existed. After the last Ice Age ended 10,000 years ago, the age of farming began. The new breakthrough in forensic and genetic sciences located the first farming humans and their settlements. The latest evidence discovered by zoo archaeologists at the Paleolithic sites of Mehrgarh, Kot Diji, Amri, and Rohri confirms the earliest human settlements in the area, which precede Harappa and Mohenjo Daro civilizations. Owing to the latest excavation by a French team in Mehrgarh, the history of Neolithic settlements is believed to be as old as 8,000 years BCE—rather than 3,000 years BCE, as was originally believed.

> *Further excavation and archaeological studies suggest human settlements in Mehrgarh were in the fourth millennium, while the human settlements in Amri were of the second half of that millennium. This site predates the agrarian Harappan culture that flourished in the fertile Indus Valley around 2400 BCE.*[28]

In comparison to the bordering areas of the Iranian Plateau and Central Asia, the geographic territories of Sindh were much more fertile ground for early settlement of hunting tribes and their animals because of its plentiful water and vegetation. The earliest inhabitants built their settlements along the riverine areas of Indus, similar to Mehrgarh.

---

[28] Richard H. Meadow, Ajita K. Patel, et al., *Indus Ethnobiology: New Perspectives from the Field* (Lexington Books, 2003).

These settlers navigated the seasonal variations in the ebbs and flows of the mighty River Indus and flourished along its banks. This encouraged the migration of more humans to the area. Having settled in the flood plains of the Indus, these people acquired techniques of sowing grains like barley and wheat. They also learned to domesticate and breed animals, including goats and sheep. Archaeologists and archaeology historians have termed the first human settlements in pre-historic Sindh as the pre-urbanization period, preceding the Indus Civilization.[29]

---

[29] Rita P. Wright, *The Ancient Indus: Urbanism, Economy and Society—Case Studies in Early Societies* (New York: Cambridge University Press, 2009).

These prehistoric settlements were dependent on changes in the course of the Indus and its sister rivers, Ghaggar and Hakra, which were controlled by climate changes, including monsoon rains and melting of glaciers in the north. Archaeologists and archaeology historians used to believe that civilization in South Asia started with the Harappa or Indus Valley Civilization in the Bronze Age. This theory was dispelled by Bridget and Raymond Allchin when they discovered sites of the Paleolithic, or Primitive Stone, Age in the 1970s.

The groundbreaking work of the Allchins was followed by a series of expeditions to unearth different layers from the Mesolithic and Neolithic periods in Sindh, which confirmed migrations and human settlements preceding the Indus Valley Civilization. Mehrgarh, Rohri, Amri, Kot Diji, Nal, Lasbela, and Shadi Shaheed were uncovered in the 1980s and 1990s. This further unlocked secrets of what archaeologist Jan R. McIntosh called, "Sindh, the Land of the Unsolved Mysteries." The discovery of populations and cultures of the Paleolithic, Mesolithic, and Neolithic periods were precursors to the Bronze Age Civilization called the Indus Valley Civilization.

Thus, prehistory of Sindh began in the Paleolithic Age, flourished in the Mesolithic or Middle Stone Age, and then transitioned to the Neolithic or New Stone Age. This stretched the origins of the Indus civilization to 9000-8001 BCE instead of 5000 BCE, as previously believed.

Sindhi historiographer M. H. Panhwar, through radiocarbon dating, chronicled Sindh's pre-Neolithic period as follows:

- *Early Paleolithic Period or Early Stone Age—100,000-40,000 BCE*

- *Middle Paleolithic Period or Middle Stone Age—40,000-10,000 BCE*

- *Late Paleolithic Period or Late Stone Age—10,000-3,000 BCE*

In this period, populations of hunters migrated into agricultural communities and settled on the plains of the Indus Valley and on both banks of the river. During early Indus periods, there was a tremendous increase in population because of annual floods, greenery, and a sufficient supply of fresh water. The rapid influx of outer populations added to current settlements and created new settlements.[30]

Earlier archaeologists who excavated and discovered Harappa and Mohenjo-Daro were not successful in bringing the prehistoric Indus Civilization into light, such as Amri, Ranikot, Johi, Kirthar Range, Rohri, Kot Diji, Kili Gul Muhammad at Kech, and Mehrgarh. These sites testify that these earliest human settlements paved the way for the much more mature civilization of Harappa and Mohenjo-Daro. Later archaeological researchers—such as Rita P. Wright, who participated in the excavations of Mehrgarh—discovered settlements of developed village life in the pre-urbanization period.

---

[30] Raymond and Bridget Allchin, *The Rise of Civilization in India and Pakistan* (Cambridge University Press, 1982).

Artifacts discovered at these sites also confirmed that domestication of plants and animals, along with the use of tools made of stone, had become prevalent among the first inhabitants in and around ancient Sindh. Bones of goats and sheep and grains of barley and wheat confirm that nomadic life had evolved into permanent settlements of varying magnitudes. With Mehrgarh being the center of the migratory populations from across Hindu Kush and the Iranian Plateaus, this later paved the way for the much more mature civilization of Sindhu, also called Indus Civilization.

Richard H. Meadow and Ajita K. Patel were pioneers in the fields of zooarchaeology and Indus ethnobiology. Zooarchaeology is the study and interpretation of animal remains recovered from archaeological sites. Ethnobiology examines the relationship between living organisms and human culture, whether prehistoric, historic, or contemporary.

> *We do not believe that it is now necessary to position the Harappan Civilization as having been the ultimate source of Chalcolithic culture(s) of Peninsular India. Instead, it was farming and herding practices developed in the prehistoric Indus, peripheral to the Indus Valley proper, that are more likely to have established the foundations for settlements to the east and south.*[31]

New research over the last five decades of the twentieth century validates organized civilizations in prehistoric Sindh, with

---

[31] Meadow, Patel et al., *Indus Ethnobiology: New Perspectives from the Field.*

settlements at Rohri, Amri, Kot Diji, Nal, Lasbela, and Allahdino (in Karachi) from the Stone and Middle Stone Age, long before the Neolithic period dawned over the Indus with the building of urban centers like Mohenjo-Daro.

Rita. P. Wright, shedding light on Mehrgarh, states, "The evidence from Mehrgarh has even greater significance to our overall understanding of the developments leading to the Indus Civilization."[32]

---

[32] Wright, *The Ancient Indus: Urbanism, Economy and Society—Case Studies in Early Societies.*

Mohenjo-Daro (2500 BCE): Cradle of Indus Valley Civilization

We are engaged in opening up an entirely new chapter of civilization The garden of Eden, which one did not require to be driven out.
~John Marshall

I stood on the mound of Mohenjo-Daro. As all around me lay the house and streets of the ancient city. What was the secret of this strength? Where did it come from?

~Jawaharlal Nehru

The Indus civilization, including its metropolis Mohenjo-Daro, remained buried beneath the deserts and plains of South Asia, along the mighty River Indus, for two millennia, until the second decade of the twentieth century, when native Indian Rakhal Das (R. D.) Banerji unearthed its first site. Banerji was an archaeologist from Calcutta; he was originally deputed to Sindh to oversee archaeological sites including Rohri, Sukkur, Khudabad, and Larkana.

On a chilly winter day of 1921, he got off Quetta Mail. He had traveled from Bombay to Larkana and from there to Dokri, headquarters of what was then the Labdarya taluk. He then rode on a tonga, or horse-drawn carriage, to reach his destination.

This man would put Sindh on the world map as one of the oldest civilizations on the planet. He was the first archaeologist to uncover the metropolis Mohenjo-Daro. Located along the western bank of the mighty Indus, this archaeological metropolis was a contemporary to the civilizations of Mesopotamia and Samaria.

It was during this tour of duty that Banerji discovered three seals, including that of the bull from Mohenjo-Daro. These seals were similar to ones found in Harappa.

From his camp in Mohenjo-Daro, he wrote to his boss, Sir John Marshall, the director general of Survey of India (1923):

> *At this time, I should bring to your notice that three different seals bearing the bull statant with a standard in front have been discovered. They are exactly similar to Cunningham's Harappa seals.*
>
> *I send impression of these three seals to you. Two of these belong to the same period. Unfortunately, the larger one is broken but in both of them the object in front of the bull is quite clear. It is really a standard. Both bulls bear a saddle on their backs and the inscriptions differ. The third seal is slightly later in date, according to my opinion, as the execution of the bull is not as good as in the case of the first two.*[33]

It was in 1918-19 when R. D. Banerji, then superintendent of the Western Circle, extensively travelled Sindh's archaeological sites, including shrines, tombs, and mosques. He visited numerous *stupas* of Buddha and Hindu holy places. In 1919, he discovered the above seals, beneath a stupa at the current site of Mohenjo-Daro, located within the Labdarya taluk of the Larkana District.

The *Gazetteer* of the Sindh government described this area of the Larkana District as "one of the finest alluvial areas in the

---

[33] Nayanjot Lahiri, *Finding Forgotten Cities: How the Indus Civilization was Discovered* (Permanent Black, 2022).

whole of Sindh, with a soil so productive that the district was called the Garden of Sindh."

It was so strange that the sites had never been mentioned in the archaeological world of India until Banerji set his eyes on the ruins. Unlike him, his predecessor, Henry Cousens, had surveyed Sindh fifteen years prior and called it the "Lowlands of Larkana," but he did not discover the ruins. Cousens described this area as "loaded with an abundance of soft, impalpable dust, which insinuates itself into every nook and corner."

Banerji's observations and experiences were quite different, as he was astonished to see the site: a Buddhist stupa standing tall at the mound, littered with burnt bricks, eighty to ninety feet higher than its surroundings. He was perplexed to note why the area was never mentioned previously, even though it was quite familiar and known to locals as Mohenjo-Daro.

A controversy over the actual name still goes on. There are two schools of thought: those who believe that the actual name of the site is Moen-Jo-Da-ro, or Mound of the Dead, and others who believe the name is Mohan-Jo-Daro, or Mohan's Mound, as Mohan is a common name among the local Hindu population. Since the separation of Pakistan from India, the former version has been pushed very aggressively for reasons not completely historically correct.

In 1924, Sir John Marshall published, in the *Illustrated London News*, an article with photographs of the site and artifacts from Mohenjo-Daro. This took Europe by storm, which had previously thought of Sindh and India as the land of the half-naked fakirs, sadhus, and ascetic people only.

The richest grain-lands of Sindh in the days before modern irrigation were the broad plains of Larkana, between the Indus and the Kohistan, or Kirthar, hills. It is in this district and one such small patch of barren land that Mohenjo-Daro, the Mound of the Dead, is situated. It stands on what is known locally as The Island, a long, narrow strip of land between the main river bend and the western-northern loop, its precise position being 27 19N. by 68 8' E., some seven miles by road from Dokri on the Northwestern Railway, and twenty-five miles from the town of Larkana. The mounds that hide the remains of the ancient city, or rather the series of superimposed one upon the other, are conspicuous from afar in the riverine flat. The actual area covered by the mound is now more than about two hundred forty acres.[34]

In the *Illustrated London News*, writing about the initial discoveries from Mohenjo-Daro and Harappa, Sir John Marshall said, "The Punjab and Sindh were enjoying an advanced and singular civilization of their own."

The artifacts recovered from the mounds of the Civilization of the Indus Valley, with its urban center of Mohenjo-Daro, vouched for themselves that civilizations can also be built without weapons, as no weapons were found among the artifacts.

---

[34] John Marshall, *Mohenjo-Daro and the Indus Civilization*, Volume One (Gyan Publishing House, 2020).

Banerji was the pioneer of the excavation of sites of Mohenjo-Daro and in other parts of Indus Valley Civilization. These sites had been buried beneath sand dunes, plains, and mountains in western, undivided India, including all of Rajasthan, the south and north of Sindh, Balochistan, and even beyond.

The Sindhu or Indus Valley Civilization stood tall among its contemporary civilizations of Mesopotamia and Egypt due to its unique qualities as a fully developed city-state river empire with a people's government system. Explorer and anthropologist Alice Albinia said, "Unlike Egypt with its pyramids, or Mesopotamia with its temples, their biggest structures were not symbols of monarchical tyranny or priestly power, but civic buildings such as public baths and grain stores." She also deduced from the discovery of the statue of a dancing girl at Mohenjo-Daro that this "society revered empowered women."

The architecture of Mohenjo-Daro was the first kind of urban town planning ever discovered, with paved ways and wide streets, described by some authors as being similar to the back of a turtle. It also had a public bath house called the Great Bath and a fully developed sewer system underground, and each house had its own bathing area, drainage system, and water well. There were venues for public gatherings, and bullock-drawn wooden carts dotted the streets. Bazaars and buildings built with baked red bricks were some of the salient features of the city of Mohenjo-Daro. Tribes living upstream in the hills floated logs down the Indus River to the city, which helped the city dwellers of Mohenjo-Daro build multistory houses. Artifacts—such as beads, ornaments of gold, a half bust of a man called *King Priest,* and a statue of a dancing girl—confirmed that this civilization was of the pre-Aryan period.

Aldous Huxley, describing the newly found Indus Civilization, wrote:

> *Recent archaeological research has shown that this correlation between war and civilization has not been invariable. The civilization of the Indus Valley was as rich and elaborate as those of Sumer and Egypt. But it was a civilization that knew nothing of war. No weapons have been found in its buried cities, nor any traces of fortifications. This fact is of highest significance. It proves that it is possible for men to enjoy the advantage of a complex urban civilization without having to pay by periodical mass murder.*[35]

John Roach wrote in *National Geographic*:

> *The city lacks ostentatious palaces, temples, or monuments. There's no obvious central seat of government or evidence of a king or queen. Modesty, order, and cleanliness were apparently preferred. Pottery and tools of copper and stone were standardized. Seals and weights suggest a system of tightly controlled trade.*
>
> *A watertight pool called the Great Bath, perched on top of a mound of dirt and held in place with walls of baked brick, is the closest structure Mohenjo-Daro has to a temple. It suggests an ideology based on*

---

[35] K. R. Malkani, *The Sindh Story: The Immortal "Mound of the Dead,"* (Allied Publishers Pvt. Ltd., 1984).

cleanliness. Wells were found throughout the city. There was the intricately carved and colored statue of Priest King, so called even though there is no evidence he was a priest or king.[36]

Mohenjo-Daro was an egalitarian society with no religion. In the words of Possehl, "It seems cleanliness was their faith." Three types of artifacts not discovered in Mohenjo-Daro were those symbolizing monarchy, clergy, and weapons, proving that this society lacked the concepts of a tyrannical ruler, organized religion, or war. The most prominent building in this 5,000-year-old archaeological city was a public bath surrounded by streets and houses, all of same size. There were no palaces or quarters for the servants, as was common among other ancient civilizations. Thus, it would seem that since the beginning of time, inhabitants of Sindh have always been democratic, secular, and peaceful in nature. They were practicing the principles of egalitarianism and peaceful coexistence long before the rest of the world adopted these values.

Prior to the excavation of the sites of Mohenjo-Daro, no one in the world knew about the existence of a civilization prior to Aryans, which was a much later civilization. Credit goes to Banerji for discovering Mohenjo-Daro.

In 1901, Lord Curzon, then Viceroy, ordered a wide-ranging archaeological survey of India. A new department called Archaeological Survey of India was formed for this purpose,

---

[36] Gregory Possehl. *The Indus Civilization: A Contemporary Perspective.* (Boston: AltaMira Press, 2002).

and a young British archaeologist named Sir John Marshall was appointed as the first director general.

The history of civilization of Indus Valley remained unearthed until 1920. Discovery of a pre-Aryan civilization completely shattered the previously held myth that civilization on Indus began after the invasion of literate Aryans who transformed the illiterate indigenous people of Sindhu Civilization.

It all began when Governor-General Warren Hastings of India, who was familiar with the local languages of Urdu, Hindi, Persian, and Bengali, asked Judge William Jones of the Supreme Court of West Bengal to establish the Asiatic Society for tracing back origins of local Indian languages. Judge William Jones's curiosity emanated from his knowledge that some languages spoken in Indus Valley had Indo-European roots.

Nevertheless, it was Sir John Marshall who came to supervise and carry out operations of excavations on the Gangetic and Indus Plains. Previously, he was posted and took part in excavation of ancient Greece. But his work southwest of the Himalayas was a different experience than that in Greece, as the area was vast in comparison to his previous archaeological fields in Greece. Sir John Marshall came to India in 1902 to start excavating.

The Story of Excavation and Man of Mohenjo-Daro

Although the site of Mohenjo-Daro had previously been visited on multiple occasions by local archaeologists and district officials, it remained obscure until it caught the attention of R. D. Banerji, who began excavation at the site in 1922.

According to John Marshall, "R. D. Banerji had no idea the ruins he had dug were to reveal a prehistoric era. Instead, his focus was to dig out beneath or beside a Buddhist stupa-like monument erected on the site and made of bricks used from old ruins."

But indigenous Indian archaeologists of modern age contradict John Marshall's claims as downplaying the efforts of R. D. Banerji as pioneer of the discovery of Mohenjo-Daro. They allege that research, as well as the excavation work of R. D. Banerji, was stolen by John Marshall and credited to him.[37] They are of the view that the discouragement and inappreciation R.

---

[37] Lahiri, *Finding Forgotten Cities: How the Indus Civilization was Discovered.*

D. Banerji received at the hands of his colonial, British superior, along with his diabetes mellitus, may have led to his early death.

However, Sir John Marshall recalls the services of R. D. Banerji with the following accolades:

> *Nevertheless, Mr. Banerji discovered that those earlier remains must have antedated the Buddhist structures by some two- or three-thousand years. That was no small achievement. Another reason Mr. Banerji's work at Mohenjo-Daro is deserving of special recognition, for it was carried through in the face of very real difficulties due in part to lack of adequate funds, in part to hardship inseparable from the camp life in such a trying climate.*

These trial excavations confirmed archaeological evidence that the site contained remnants of an exceptional civilization beneath the earth.

The excavation team was divided into four groups, headed by:

I. H. Hargreaves, the then-superintendent of the Frontier Circle
II. M. S. Vats
III. K. N. Dikshit
IV. B. L. Dhama, assistant superintendent of Rajputana and Central India

They were joined by archaeological chemist Mohammed Sana Ullah. These heads of the four groups had a labor force of between 1,000 and 1,200 individuals. Most of them were Brahui tribe members of Dravidian origins.

Approaching the mounds at Mohenjo-Daro, Banerji writes:

> *The ruins consist of the vast mounds of burnt bricks surrounded by smaller ones. In the center of this area is a very high mound about eighty or ninety feet above the surrounding country. This is called Mohenjo-Daro. The top of the entire mound consists of debris and brickbats but here and there loose debris had slipped away exposing straight walls of burnt bricks. The mound is about six hundred feet in length and two hundred in breadth. In one place of this mound there is a drum of stupa made of sun-dried bricks. Only the shell of the drum remains, as the core has been excavated to a depth of some of thirty to forty feet by treasure seekers. The inhabitants of the surrounding village have dug out and removed bricks from this mound from time immemorial and do so even now. Some of the people who do not acknowledge to have excavated this mound for bricks within the last ten or twelve years state that when they dug for bricks previously, they found entire mounds to consist of huge platforms of burnt bricks on which water built numerous round, hemispherical objects of burnt as well as sun-dried. Close to this platform of stupa there is another high mound, which is the second largest in this place. This appears to have been a temple or monastery, as the old villagers state that they found rows of small, square*

chambers arranged around a square courtyard in this mound. Search among the ruins led to the discovery of a number of carved bricks, but no human figures or images were found. The villagers are unanimous in stating no coins have ever been found in any of these mounds. These two mounds are surrounded by numerous small mounds, which represent the ruins of the village or township that had grown around this stupa and temple in the heights of their glory. The stupa at this place is higher than the stupa at Depar Gangro or Mīrpur Khās and appears to have been the largest and highest Buddhist stupa in the country of Sindh.[38]

---

[38] R. D. Banerji, *Memoirs of the Archaeological Survey of India*, 1931.

C. R. Roy, who was the curator of the Victorian Museum in Karachi and a participant in the excavation of Mohenjo-Daro, wrote an article, published in the journal *Indian World*, in which he stated, "The discovery of Mohenjo-Daro proves that no Aryans came to this part. The inhabitants of Mohenjo-Daro were Aryans themselves in their own right. There existed a high-class, world-level civilization in Sindh, which was far superior to the civilizations of Egypt, Mesopotamia, Elam, and Babylonia."

Archaeologists, including John Marshall (1931), Stuart Piggott (1950), Mortimer Wheeler (1968), and Bridget Allchin (1982), have concluded that the advent of Aryans in the second millennium BCE came long after the building of Mohenjo-Daro. It was not the horse, but the bull whose inscriptions were found at the ruins of Mohenjo-Daro. John Marshall concluded, "The horse seems to have been unknown in the Indus Valley Civilization but was prominent in the culture described in the Vedas." In addition, the people of Mohenjo-Daro used to bury their dead, while the Aryans cremated theirs. Twenty-one skeletons of humans were found at Mohenjo-Daro.

Excavations of Mohenjo-Daro were carried out in five winter seasons from 1922 to 1927. R. D. Banerji was the main archaeologist under whose supervision most of the artifacts were discovered. He was succeeded by M. S. Vats and K. N. Dikshit.

The areas of the archaeological sites were demarcated in alphabetical order. For instance, Sir John Marshall himself unearthed the Great Bath, a landmark in the city of Mohenjo-Daro. As the work of excavation progressed, by 1925 and 1926, the services of two more outstanding officers of the Survey of

India were employed from other areas. Those outstanding officers were Ernest Mackay and Rai Bahadur Daya Ram Sahni, both assets of the Survey of India office.

Discovery of elegantly built buildings, brick houses, paved streets, and even city blocks, all reminded Sir John Marshall of the city of Lancashire. "Anyone, walking for the first time through Mohenjo-Daro, might fancy himself surrounded by ruins of some present-day working Lancashire."[39]

Researchers assume the city was built after the inhabitants along the River Indus in present Sindh carved the red brick from the silt that the River Indus brought every year in its seasons from the Himalayas all the way down to the tail end of the Indus. Sir John Marshall estimated the volume of silt brought by Indus to be of significant quantity. "The amount of the silt carried down by the river at Sukkur during the monsoon season is calculated at nearly a million tons a day."

In the monsoon season of 1929, when dangerous floods visited Sindh, Marshall wrote, "The violent floods of this year (1929) and havoc caused by them have afforded a striking, if terrible, illustration of the dangers which must always have threatened the dwellers in the Indus Valley, even though the river may not have been as turbulent then as now."

Marshall wrote further of the brick that was a base to the foundation of Mohenjo-Daro. "Crude brick was well-known to

---

[39] Marshall, *Mohenjo-Daro and the Indus Civilization*.

the builders of Mohenjo-Daro but was never used as it was in Mesopotamia and Egypt. In the espoused part of the buildings, it was reserved for foundation or for the packing of terrace and the like, where it could not be affected by the elements."

That is how the bricks of Mohenjo-Daro, used in its foundation, still lie at ground zero for the first megacity of the world. The whole city was founded on baked or sun-dried brick structures.

Yet it still remains a unique wonder to the world, even in the twenty-first century, just how good the city planners of the Indus Valley Civilization were in the third millennium BCE. With meticulously planned utilization of water, Mohenjo-Daro dwellers were the first people to use underground drainage systems beneath the well-paved, bricked streets of the city.

Sir John Marshall wrote of the inhabitants' reverence for water, "Of the sanctity of water, no tangible evidence has yet been found, but that water was held in great reverence, and it played a highly important part in the daily lives and religions of the citizens of Mohenjo-Daro, as demonstrated by elaborate bathing establishments."

The city itself, in the words of Indus scholar Gregory Possehl, was "pretty faceless." Instead of palaces or temples, archaeologists found collective baths, assembly places, and grain depots.

According to Mortimer Wheeler, "This [grain depots] served both as a state bank and treasury of the ancient city of Mohenjo-Daro, used as great granary (storage of grains)."[40]

It means the city was a democratic state, rather than a monarchy or theocracy.

According to Wisconsin University archaeologist Jonathan Mark Kenoyer, who spent a great deal of time researching the post-Mohenjo-Daro era in Sindh, "Of greater interest to me, though, are a few stone sculptures of seated male figures, such as the intricately carved and colored *Priest King*, so called even though there is no evidence he was a priest or king." The sculptures were all found broken, Kenoyer says. "Whoever came in at the very end of the Indus period clearly didn't like the people who were representing themselves or their elders."

In Sir John Marshall's words, "Like the Minoans, the Indus people may have had no public shrines at all, or if they had them, the shrines may have been totally like their ordinary residences. Among the buildings of Mohenjo-Daro are several whose purpose we have not yet succeeded in discovering, and any of these might have been a shrine, as well as anything else." Marshall saw Mohenjo-Daro as unique, compared to its contemporary Egyptian, Euphrates, Sumerian, and Mesopotamian civilizations.

As described by John Roach in a *National Geographic* article, "The city lacks ostentatious palaces, temples, or monuments.

---

[40] Mortimer Wheeler, *The Indus Civilization*, (Cambridge University Press, 1962) 14.

There's no obvious central seat of government or evidence of a king or queen. Modesty, order, and cleanliness were apparently preferred. Pottery and tools of copper and stone were standardized. Seals and weights suggest a system of tightly controlled trade."[41] It had trade relations with distant civilizations like Mesopotamia and Egypt. The discovery of seals, weights, jewelry made of ivory, shells, and bronze prove that the city had a flourishing mercantile class.

According to British archaeologist Jane R. McIntosh:

> *Four examples of graduated rules had been found made of terra-cotta, ivory, copper, and shell; they came respectively from Kalibangan, Lothal, Harappa, and Mohenjo-Daro. They were marked into divisions of about 1.7 millimeters, the largest unit marked on the Mohenjo-Daro rule being 67.056.*
>
> *The system of stone weights was similarly standardized throughout the Indus realms and was also used overseas where it was known to Mesopotamians as the standard of Dilmun, adopted as far away as Ebla.*

The houses had upper floors, courtyards with staircases, and solid terraces. The total area of Mohenjo-Daro was constructed on 500 acres and had a population between 20,000 and 40,000. The city lasted for 600 years, which was significantly longer

---

[41] John Roach, "'Faceless' Indus Valley City Puzzles Archaeologists," *National Geographic*.

than the cities of any of its other contemporary civilizations, including Sumar, Egypt, and Mesopotamia, where the average lifespan of a city was about one hundred years.

The city of Mohenjo-Daro was one of the first urban centers in the world where trade was conducted based on modern principles of business. Its society was a realm of inner and outer peace. The marketplace of Mohenjo-Daro was connected with all major business metropolises of the time—Mesopotamia and Egypt—through the Indus River. Its seals and weights were recognized and respected in these markets as currency.

A highly prosperous urban life thrived in the megacity of Mohenjo-Daro, with an evolved way of living consisting of meticulously organized social events and special reverence for the River Indus. Artifacts discovered from the city, including statues of the dancing girl and intricately woven fabrics of cotton and wool, prove this society held women in high esteem and had a special love for fine clothes, testifying to the elegance of the city and their way of living.

The society of urban Mohenjo-Daro was egalitarian and peaceful. As H. T. Lambrick stated, "It may reasonably be inferred that the Indus people were never involved in a war with a formidable enemy until, perhaps, the very end of the many centuries of their rule."[42] Thus, Mohenjo-Daro, one of earliest city-states and urban centers built by humankind, was an entirely egalitarian, weapon-free society.

---

[42] H. T. Lambrick, *Sind, Before the Muslim Conquest (History of Sind series, v. 2)* (Karachi: Oxford University Press, 1973).

It is still not entirely clear as to who the builders of Mohenjo-Daro were. Were they migrants from a foreign land who had settled here, or did this highly organized urban society evolve from the indigenous populations?

Evidence from the archaeological site suggests that Mohenjo-Daro wasn't built by a single race, as skeletons belonging to four different groups were found at the site:

1. *Mongoloid*
2. *African*
3. *Proto-Australoid*
4. *Mediterranean*

All the aforesaid groups trace back to the present populations in the north and south of the present subcontinent of South Asia, as discussed in the preceding chapter. The roots of ethnicity of the modern Sindhis cannot definitively be traced back to the Mohenjo-Daro era. Scholars working on the script of the ancient Indus civilization, through seals and tablets recovered from the sites, have come to varying conclusions. It is still unclear if the people of Mohenjo-Daro were of Aryan origin who had migrated from the north or of local Dravidian origin.

Dr. Ghulam Ali Allana, the renowned linguist and scholar on Sindhi language, concluded that the people of the Indus Valley were called *Sindhui* (ones who were inhabitants of Sindhoo—the present Sindhi people), and they had lived in the Indus Valley long before the arrival of Aryans. Advancing his argument on the basis of his lifelong research, Allana stated:

Now the question arises when the Indus Civilization, claimed to be the pre-Aryan Civilization, and the ancient cities such as Mohenjo-Daro, Harappa, Lothal, and many other cities were already in existence much before the arrival of the Aryans, then how could it be possible that the seals which have been found from the ancient sites be considered to have any relationship with the Indo-Aryan Civilization of the Indus Valley? On the contrary, these seals belong to the civilization which was in existence much before the arrival of the Aryans.[43]

According to my research the Indus Valley was inhabited by the people who were known as Sindhui (from the Sindhu, the name of the River Indus) and the language they spoke was also known as Sindhui. Abū Rayhan Al-Bīrūnī, the well-known scholar of the eleventh century, has also referred to Saindhava, an alphabet used in Sindh. This Saindhava or Sindhuvi was the parent language of the Proto-Dravidian as well as of Sindhi, Dardic, Lahnda, Kashmiri, Rajasthani, Gujarati, Brahui, and other languages of the people who presently live in various regions of the Indus Valley.[44]

---

[43] Parveen Talpur, G. A. Allana, Foreword. *Indus Seals (2600-1900 BCE) Beyond Geometry: A New Approach to Break an Old Code* (BookBaby, 2017).

[44] Talpur, Allana, Foreword. *Indus Seals (2600-1900 BCE) Beyond Geometry: A New Approach to Break an Old Code.*

Other scholars and archaeologists who agree with Dr. Allana's conclusion that that these people were of Dravidian roots include John Marshall, Mortimer Wheeler, Dr. Ernest J. H. Mackay, Jonathan Kenoyer, Sirajul Haq Memon, Parso Gidwani, M. H. Panhwar, and N. A. Baloch.

Jonathan Mark Kenoyer, who is considered an authority on fresh perspectives on the Indus Valley civilization, suggests:

> *In order to decipher an ancient script, it is necessary to establish certain parameters or assumptions. If the Indus script is logo-syllabic, it cannot be deciphered as an alphabetical or a syllabic script. A logo-syllabic script can only be deciphered if the language that it represents is known. At present, no modern language can be directly traced to the Indus script, but most scholars agree that it belongs to the Dravidian language family. Over twenty-five Dravidian languages are presently spoken in the subcontinent, including Tamil, Telugu, Kannada, and Malayalam. Most of these languages fall in the categories of central and southern Dravidian and are found in peninsular India and northern Sri Lanka, areas that were never part of the Indus culture. A branch of north Dravidian, called Brahui, is still spoken in Baluchistan and southern Afghanistan, a region at the western edge of the Indus Valley in the form of the river. Names and many Dravidian loan words are found in the ancient Sanskrit, the Indo-Aryan language of the Rig Veda.*

A three-member team of world experts worked on the language of the lower Indus Valley and ruled out the possibility that the Indus Civilization's inhabitants had a written language. This team of experts included Steve Farmer, a historian; Richard Sproat, a computer linguist; and Michael Witzel, an expert on Indology. They found trade relations between the people of the Indus and Mesopotamia, through the cuneiform script, rather than a writing system based on a language. These experts reached the conclusion that the people of Indus Valley did it intentionally because they feared their knowledge would be stolen.

There are many theories about what destroyed the biggest city of the Indus Civilization, the most famous being the Massacre at Mohenjo-Daro theory formulated by Mortimer Wheeler in 1950. This theory is now dismissed by nearly all archaeologists and scholars.

Most academicians now link the fall of the 8,000-year-old Sindhu civilization with natural catastrophe and other social and economic upheavals that brought life in the first megacity of the Indus Civilization to a tragic end. "Mohenjo-Daro itself may have been destroyed by an epidemic, or by natural phenomena such as floods, an earthquake, or a shift in the course of the River Indus."[45]

---

[45] William J. Duiker and Jackson J. Spielvogel, *World History, 9th Ed.* (Cengage Learning, 2018).

Urban decay and shrinking of trade with the outside world seem to be other major factors that contributed to the downfall of Mohenjo-Daro in the last period of the metropolis of the Indus Civilization. Per Jane R. McIntosh:

> *At Mohenjo-Daro, the last period of the occupation of the city shows a serious decline in civic standards, with poorly constructed houses, pottery kilns in what had previously been residential areas, the neglect of the civil amenities such as drains, and corpses thrown into the abandoned houses or street instead of being buried with due rites. Important public buildings such as Great Bath went out of use. Some stone sculptures were deliberately broken.*[46]

However, the Indus Civilization continued, and so did the journey of the human population of Sindh through the ages.

---

[46] Jane R. McIntosh, *The Ancient Indus Valley: New Perspectives (Understanding Ancient Civilizations)* (ABC-CLIO, 2007).

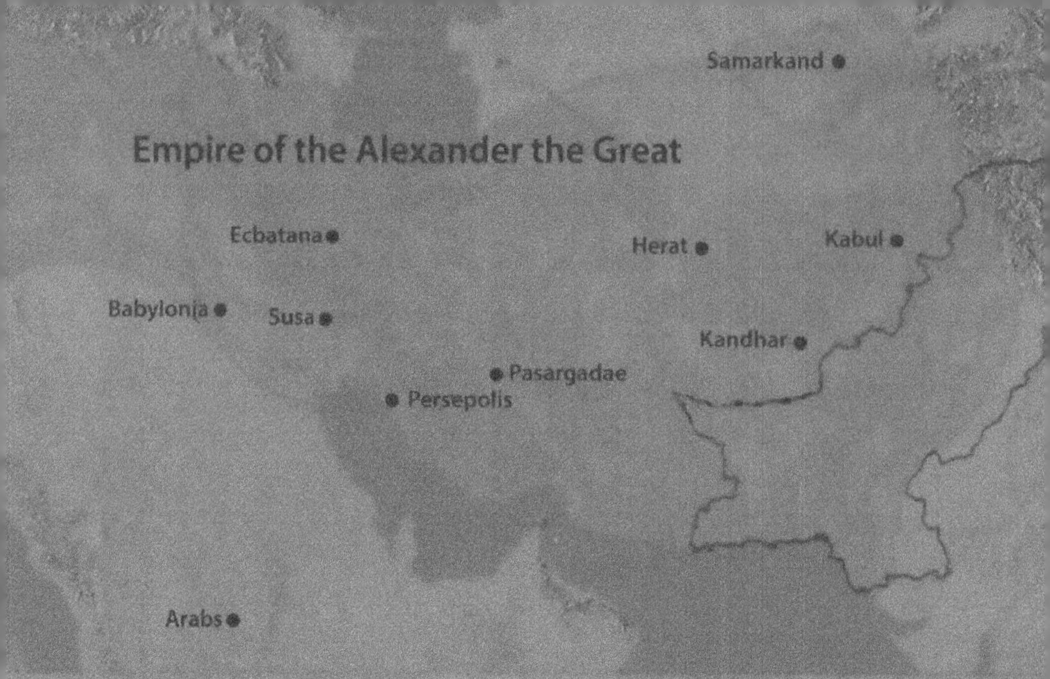

Empire of the Alexander the Great

Samarkand

Ecbatana

Herat

Kabul

Babylonia

Susa

Kandhar

Pasargadae

Persepolis

Arabs

Vedic Era

*How many of Sindhis know that the Sumerians
derived their culture from Sindh?
How many know that Sindh has a share in
checking Alexander's march in India?
How many remember that once Sindh carried on commerce with
Rome and Greece, with Asia Minor, Babylonia, and Egypt?
How many know that Sindh sent out her sons to colonize Java?
How many know that Buddha blessed Sindh by his meditation and
personal teachings?
~Sadhu T. L. Vaswani*

*The Sindhi mind is a free mind, a tolerant mind, a mind surcharged
with spirit and equality, patriotism and urge for freedom...
~G. M. Syed*

There seems to be a huge gap where very little, or almost nothing, is recorded of the history of this part of the world, from the end of the Indus Valley Civilization to the start of the Persian and Greek invasion in year 515 BCE, when Persian King Darius occupied Sindh and annexed it to his Achaemenid Empire.

According to the research of prominent Sindhi scholar Ali A. Jafarey, "This is the first time on the record that the name Sindhi was employed to designate the people of the valley. The Sindhu in Sanskrit is a plural, meaning 'men from Sindh,' first recorded Mahabharata." That is why the word *Sindh* is found among the inscriptions on the tomb of King Darius I, which mentions Sindh as one of the states of the Aryan Kingdom.

According to historian Suhail Zaheer Lari:

> *The Persians replaced the letter S of the Sanskrit word Sindhu for the river with H and the Greeks with I. Therefore, Sindhu became Hindu to the Persians and India to the Europeans.*

"Sindh lives by the Indus, which has indeed given its name not only to the province but also to the subcontinent," wrote O. H. K. Spate and A. T. A. Learmonth in their book, *India and Pakistan: A General and Regional Geography*.[47]

---

[47] O. H. K. Spate and A. T. A. Learmonth, *India and Pakistan: A General and Regional Geography* (Methuen, 1967).

There is no archaeological evidence that another megacity was built on the subcontinent of South Asia, and certainly none that would come close to Mohenjo-Daro for more than 2,000 years after its downfall.

According to scholar Phiroze Vasunia, "Sindh is derived from the Persian, which adopted the Sanskrit word *Sindhu* (river), but Sindh is connected linguistically via Sanskrit, Avesta, Old Persian, Greek, and Latin…"[48]

Although the language of the Indus Civilization has not so far been deciphered, the journey of the indigenous Sindhi people through the ages offers ample evidence that their ancestors were those who built the Indus Civilization and ancient Sindh while constantly having to adapt to the great variations seen in the flows and directions of one of the mightiest rivers known to mankind, the Indus.

It is said that history repeats itself—so does the story of Sindh. It is a saga of invasions, one after another, conquests, and migrations. With each were introduced new cultures, religions, languages, and genetic pools. But there has always been a distinct energy and resilience of Sindh. It absorbed what they brought and still managed to survive through millennia.

In the words of contemporary historian Suhail Zaheer Lari of Sindh, "Whereas the Himalayas formed an effective barrier

---

[48] Phiroze Vasunia, *The Classics and Colonial India (Classical Presences)* (Oxford University Press, 2013).

against the large-scale migration from the north, the mountain ranges ended to the north of Kandahar in Southern Afghanistan allowing large-scale migration though Sistān and Khorasan into the Indus Valley placed Sindh on the most convenient route of mass infiltration into South Asia."

Aryan Age

The biggest wave of migration to Sindh occurred with the Aryans. The era of hymn-singing Aryans with their iron tools, chariots, horses, and agricultural skills began in 800-900 BCE. Priestly tribes or Rishis (sage men) of the Aryans were said to have composed Vedas around the banks of the River Indus:

> *Flashing, whitely gleaming in her mightiness,*
> *She moves along her ample volume through the realms,*
> *Most active of the active, Sindhu unrestrained,*
> *Liked to a dappled mare, beautiful, fair to see.*
> *Rich in good steeds is Sindhu, rich in cars and robes,*
> *Rich in nobly fashioned gold, rich in ample wealth,*
> *Rich in lunch grass, rich in lovely wool, rich in sweet syrup.*

According to M. H. Panhwar, chronologist and modern historian on Sindh, the wave of Aryans began in the post-Harappa period. In the words of Bherumal Meharchand Advani, an authority on Ancient Sindh:

> *The Aryans were not born genius people. Like other nations, the source of their livelihood was first hunting. They later excelled in farming skills. Among them*

> *Rishis, people of their priestly clan, were of original thinkers, who founded the religion of Hinduism. Thus, Sindh is the land where the foundation of Hinduism was laid. The Aryans settled in ancient Sindh where, according to Bherumal Meharchand Advani, the founders based Hindu sociology on sixteen rituals.*

They settled in villages. They were hunting tribes, so the Aryans naturally happened to be meat eaters. It took them centuries to become vegetarians. The poor Aryans would live in straw-made huts, while the rich settlers would live in mud- or clay-made houses. Sindhi society seemed to have completely fallen to Aryan ways.

Linguists and historians recognize Sanskrit as the language of the early Aryans in the Indus region.

> *Nevertheless, a study of Sanskrit, old Persian, and Avesta shows that in the early Aryan age, Aria was the interprovincial language and that a Sindhi could converse as easily with a Persian, Parthian, or Sogdian as he could do today in a dialect with Jadgal in Southern Iran or a Kachhi in Western India. Aniya was as uniformly extensive in that age as its offshoots are diversely limited today.*[49]

Asko Parpola, a universally renowned scholar and historian on the Aryans, recognizes the Sindhi language spoken

---

[49] Hamida Khuhro, *Sindh Through the Centuries* (Oxford University Press, 1982).

by Sindhi people in present Sindh as a compilation of different Indo-Aryan languages. David Ross, the nineteenth-century English scholar on Sindh, in his book, *The Land of the Five Rivers and Sindh*, said, "The Sindhi language has pure Sanskrit basis and is closely related to the ancient Prakriti."[50]

Rigveda records thirty names of Aryan tribes. Among them were King Purukutsa and King Divodasa of Bharta, who were the leaders of the Aryan immigrants crossing over the Hindu Kush Mountains into the Indus Valley (Parpola).[51]

---

[50] David Ross, *The Land of the Five Rivers and Sindh: Sketches, Historical and Descriptive* (Chapman and Hall, Ltd., 1883).

[51] Asko Parpola, *The Roots of Hinduism: The Early Aryans and the Indus Civilization.* New York: Oxford University Press, 2015.

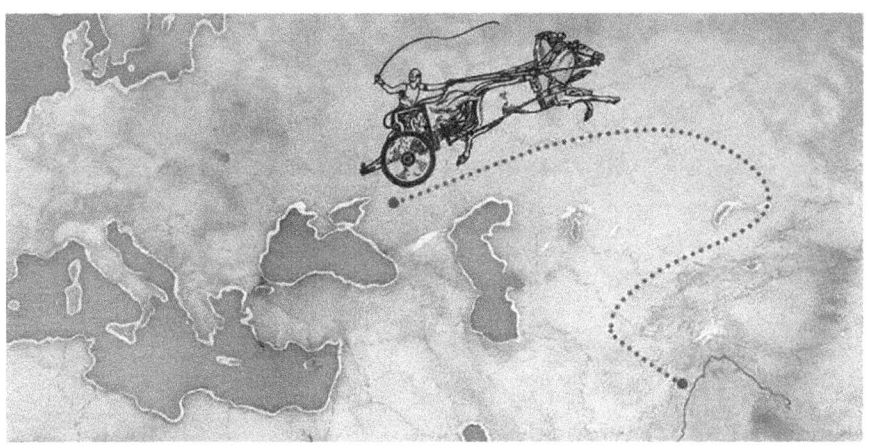

The Rigveda also praises the countries, mountains, and rivers. Among them, River Indus and its tributaries have a special place as they have been described as *Sparta Sindhava*, meaning the Seven Streams, or *SaPata Sindhoo*, as many historians interpret it.

According to Bherumal Advani:

> *In Rigvedic age, Aryan people were mostly settled in the Sindoo Valley (Indus Valley). In the Yajur Vedic period, many among them migrated and settled in the United Province of Agra and Oudh.*
>
> *They founded their kingdoms stretched from the Himalayas to the Sandhya mountain range in the name of Madhya Pradesh (midland). In Yajur Veda they built a united kingdom consisting of Sindh and*

> Punjab. They conquered Sindh later and founded
> the Aryan Kingdom.[52]

This is recognized by historians as the Rigvedic era. In a way, Aryans were the founders of sociology, as their primary focus was on the home; second, clan; and then, class, tribe, and religion. However, a large number of historians and scholars vehemently reject the theory of Aryan invasion of the Indus Valley or any other part of the Indian subcontinent. Instead, they believe that Aryans were merely mass migrants.

A strong voice among such scholars is David Frawley, who terms the theory of the Aryan invasion "a myth." He also dismisses the belief that the Indus script was predominantly developed by the Aryan culture. According to Frawley, "Current archaeological data do not support the existence of Indo-Aryan or European invasion into South Asia at any time in the pre- or historic periods. Instead, it is possible to document archaeologically a series of cultural changes reflecting indigenous development from the prehistoric to historic periods." On the arguments, debates, and discourse of Aryan-Dravidian conflicts in which many scholars have been engaged, Frawley emphatically suggests that it never happened.

And it was not the Saraswati River, but the banks of River Indus, where Rig Vedas were written, since the Sarasvati River had dried up thousands of years before the Aryans arrived.

---

[52] Bherumal Advani, *History of Hindus in Sind* (Bombay: Sharda Prakashan, 1991).

Thus, the banks of the Indus became the place where the foundation of Hindu religion was laid.

Ali A. Jafary sums up the Aryanization of Sindhis in the following words: "I believe that all the Sindhis did was to join the confederation of the Aryans as their allies, to create the first international union. And they defended it to the last."[53]

---

[53] Khuhro, *Sindh Through the Centuries*.

Sindhis Under Persians (519-400 BCE)

It was through the writings of fifth-century-BCE Greek historian Herodotus that the outside world found out that the Persian King Darius had dispatched Scylax of Caryanda to survey the Indus River and the Sindhi sea.

Herodotus named it Sindimanaand. This dynasty had originally been founded by Cyrus the Great and was under the rule of King Darius during this era. The inscription on the tombstone of Darius reads as follows:

> I am Darius, the great king, king of the kings, of the lands peopled by all the races, for long, king of this great earth, the son of Vishtāspa (Hystaspes), the Achaemenians, a Persian son of Persians. An Aryan of the Aryan descent.

Darius put a great number of his trustworthy men in command of Scylax to survey the River Indus. According to the Herodotus account, "Darius the Great wanted Scylax to discover where the River Indus ended in the sea."

Scylax and his leading Greek men, selected by Darius himself, gathered at the Kabul River and started their journey by sailing a fleet all the way down to the end of the River Indus, where it merged into the oceans. It was an expedition of thirteen months. Scylax and his team also voyaged farther to Egypt for six months. According to Herodotus, as soon as Scylax returned and reported to him, "Darius annexed Sindh in circa 519 or 518 BCE as the twentieth satrapy of the Achaemenian Empire. And used the sea."

According to Bherumal Advani, Darius forced Sindh to pay taxes equal to 360 maunds (14.4 metric tons) of gold annually. None of the other occupied territories of the era were asked to pay taxes even close to that amount, which confirms that Sindh, even under the Persians, was one of the richest provinces. Darius enforced Aramaic as the official language of all the Achaemenian Empire's provinces, including Sindh. According to Suhail Zaheer Lari, "It gave birth to the oldest Urdu script, known to Persian people as Kharosthi." Darius also built an intricate web of highways throughout his empire to connect all of his provinces.

The relationship between Persian occupiers and the indigenous people of the Indus Valley seems to have been tumultuous at times, resulting in pitched battles between the two. It seems that though the local monarchy was eliminated quickly, a mass resistance continued for most the 200 years of Persian rule, until Alexander the Great launched attacks on India and defeated Darius the III on October 1, 331 BCE.

Sindhis Under Greeks

The richness of Sindh and its resources, including the mighty River Indus and its ocean, attracted many Greek adventurers, strategists, explorers, historians, warriors and others from the West.

According to contemporary historian Manan Ahmed Asif, when Greek historians and Persian explorers mentioned "the wonders of India," they meant the richness and wealth of resources of Sindh.

> *It is largely the region of Sindh (tagged as India) which emerged as land of marvel from these earliest Greek resources. These sources in turn influenced the bulk of future accounts. The fifth-century-BCE treatise on India by Ctesias of Cnidus, and the fourth-century-BCE Indica by Megasthenes both fall into this category.*[54]

Carators, a commander of Alexander, saw the province of Sindh as the richest province in India. In 325 BCE, Alexander, the Emperor of Macedonia, invaded Sindh. His naval fleets first landed at Patala in Lower Sindh. The Greek armies were unfamiliar with the tropics of Sindh, the extreme variations in the flow of the River Indus with its high-flooding seasons, and the troubled waters of the Sindhi Sea. The Greeks suffered significant losses as a result, many of their ships sinking.

---

[54] Manan Ahmed Asif, *A Book of Conquest: The Chachnama and Muslim Origins in South Asia* (Cambridge: Harvard University Press, 2016).

According to M. H. Panhwar, Sindhi men dressed in cotton were seen in the armies of Darius III to resist the Macedonian emperor. Likewise, Dr. Hamida Khuhro seconds the presence of Sindhis resisting the Greek armies of Alexander the Great:

> *A contingent of Sindhi soldiers fought in the army of Xerxes during the invasion by Greeks. Sindhis also fought in the last battle of the Persian Empire against Alexander at Arabella, where they provided men and elephants.*

Alexander the Great, along with his Greek army of 100,000 soldiers, also brought doctors, scholars, and historians. Megasthenes was among those who accompanied Alexander the Great to India. Others included Arrian, Q. Curtius, Diodorus, Plutarch, and Justin. Some among them were the scholars who documented Alexander's campaigns in India and Sindh.

Alexander started his campaign on the banks of the Indus River at a kingdom called Musicanus. At the time of the invasion by Alexander the Great, Sindh was divided into several *parganas* (provinces).

In the north, Upper Sindh was the country called Sogadi, which stretched from Uuch Sharīf (Bahawalpur) to Sukkur, Khairpur, and Nawabshah, with Aror as its capital, ruled by the Musicanus. Sindimana was a central province with Sehwān its capital under King Sambus. And the third province was Patala, which covered present-day Laar, or Lower Sindh, with its capital at the junction of the River Indus and the sea, probably modern-day Thatta.

Interestingly, even at that time, none of the rulers of these three provinces of Sindh were at peace with each other. But Alexander's invasion and use of brute force united the rulers and people of Sindh, and they put up their valiant resistance to one of the most brutal generals in the history of humankind. When Alexander occupied Musicanus, Sehwān, and Paral, his armies killed 80,000 Sindhis. Sindhis defended their motherland to the best of their capabilities.

According to M. H. Panhwar:

> *Alexander the Great was badly wounded by the arrow of a Sindhi soldier at Arabella. The arrows were draped in a venom taken out of specific snakes in Sindh.*
>
> *Greek historians specially mentioned the Sodhas of the deserts from Amarkot, Bahawalpur, who gave Alexander and his armies tough times as they fought fierce battles against them.*[55]

The Sodhas were the warrior caste of the indigenous population. They were the first responders to Alexander's invasion on the banks of the River Indus near Multan. Their distinct weapon was an arrow between five and six feet in height. They had mastered the science of directing these arrows with extreme accuracy and force at their enemies. This proved to be a lethal weapon against a much larger and better-equipped army.

---

[55] Popati Hiranandani, *Sindhis: The Scattered Treasure* (Malaāh Publications, 1980).

Greek historians described the Sindhis as fully conversant in the medical sciences and with an average lifespan of one hundred years. Sindhi parganas functioned largely as autonomous units, each with a highly developed welfare system and local governments providing food, clothing, and shelter for all its citizens. Sindh had mines of gold and silver that attracted foreign invasions, including that of Alexander. Greek historians were spellbound by the fertility of Sindh, the good governance of its rulers, and the prosperity of its people.

The killing of 80,000 Sindhis is stark evidence of the level of resistance Alexander met in Sindh. It also shows the resilience of the Sindhis in defending their motherland. Not a single Sindhi ruler of any of the provinces of Sindh stretching from Multan, Shorkot, to present-day Karachi were spared. The Musicanus ruler was crucified.

Thus, Sindh, the realm of peace and prosperity, came under occupations like these time and time again because of its wealth, resources, river, and sea. Facing such great resistance and being injured personally, Alexander the Great and his generals were left with no choice but to retreat. They decided to escape via the naval route. But this was the high-flood season, which resulted in great losses to their fleet, due to the sinking of their ships. It was as if the mighty Indus River, the eternal giver of life, was sending a message that those who come to Sindh in peace will forever be blessed by it, but those who come with ill intentions will face its wrath.

Even after Alexander's invasion, the subjugation of Sindh continued over millennia, one after another. Foreign invaders, tyrants, and military adventurers have tried to conquer and subjugate Sindh and Sindhis, each of them plundering and looting its natural resources, especially the mighty river, along with its natural harbors and long coastline.

But at the same time, Sindhis, without ever invading any foreign territories, have been influencing the cultures of the neighboring regions including Western, Central, and Southern Asia.

Sindhis Under Maurya Dynasty

Alexander the Great died in 323 BCE. Following his death, the Greek forces, under his successor, Seleucus, began to weaken and lose control of most of the territories occupied by them, giving rise to the Nanda dynasty. But even this did not last very long, as it became unpopular with the people and was overthrown by Chandragupta Maurya. "Maurya founded the first Indian Empire in subcontinent, consisting of Northern India, with its capital Magadha (in present-day Bihar). The Maurya Empire included Sindh as its principality."[56]

Young Chandragupta Maurya, who was the commander-in-chief of the armies of the Nanda dynasty, overthrew his master and brought Sindh and Punjab under his control. He annexed Sindh into his empire; thus, not only did he establish the Mauryan dynasty, but he was the first ruler to unify the whole

---

[56] Bherumal Advani, *Sindh Je Hindu Ji Tarekh (History of Hindus in Sindh)*. Bombay: Shardha Prakashan, 1991.

Indian subcontinent as one empire. This is recognized as one of the most prosperous and peaceful eras for Sindh. It is said that this was a time of such tranquility that there were no locksmiths in the country, as no one needed a lock to protect their homes and belongings. "Two thousand years after the fall of the Indus Civilization a new and first empire in subcontinent was built in northwestern India with Sindh in its peripheries" (Talpur, Parveen)[57].

Ashoka the Great, known in Sindh as Asoka, was the grandson of Chandragupta the Great, who introduced Buddhism in Sindh. He built many stupas with elaborate inscriptions on the stones. Asoka was an ardent follower of Buddha and a great promoter of nonviolence in the whole subcontinent, including Sindh.

When Gautama the Buddha died, Asoka decided to distribute his remains equally among eight of the provinces under his empire, including Sindh. These eight provinces were specifically chosen because Buddha, during his lifetime, had visited each of them. Sindhis built stupas over the remains of Gautama the Buddha. Most of these stupas had to be rebuilt multiple times due to seasonal floods and changing courses of the mighty Indus.

Bactrians (Bahktarians) and Other Foreign Invasions in Sindh

Between the end of the Mauryan dynasty and the beginning of the Rai Sahasi era, a native Sindhi dynasty, Sindh remained under

---

[57] Talpur, *Indus Seals (2600-1900 BCE) Beyond Geometry: A New Approach to Break an Old Code.*

the yoke of foreign invaders and rulers. Dr. Hamida Khuhro sums up the history of foreign invasions and onslaughts on Sindh and the aftermaths in the following words:

> *Following the meteoric invasion of Alexander, Sindh experienced various changes of fortune. It was subjugated by the Greeks, then by the Chandragupta Maurya. It was a part of Asoka's domain when it became Buddhist. It was also a part of the great Kushan ruler Kanishka. Kanishka was Mahayana Buddhist, and he strengthened the Buddhist tradition in Sindh. In the fourth and fifth century AD, the White Huns established their dominion and this period saw the beginning of Brahmanism. By the middle of the third century AD, Sindh came under Persian hegemony for the second time in the Sassanid Empire. During the sixth century AD, Sindh became independent once again and remained so under the Rais and the succeeding Brahmans until its annexation by the Arab Muslim dynasty of Umayyads.*[58]

Interestingly, the erection of the Great Wall of China in 220 BCE due to the expansionist intentions of Chinese Emperor Qin Shi Huang uprooted nomadic tribes from their pasturelands (Lari) and brought trampling hordes of invaders and conquerors to Sindh.[59] Any looter, plunderer, and conqueror

---

[58] Khuhro, *Sind Through the Centuries*.

[59] Suhail Zaheer Lari, *A History of Sindh* (Oxford University Press, 1995).

driven out of Central Asia, Persia, and Afghanistan found their way to the country of Sindh. Sindh absorbed many of them in its distinct culture and language, giving rise to an old Sindhi folk quote: "Where are Alexander and Darius? But Sindh and Sehwān are still there." So are the Sindhis.

In the words of Sindhi scholar Subhadra Anand:

> *Sindh has seen many shifts in her history. Her geographical position made her vulnerable to foreign contacts in the form of invasion as well as trade. Her physical environment arising out of contiguity with South Asia as well as the approximation with West and Central Asia made the region susceptible to two-way "assaults" by contemporary societies. Thus in the process of apparition and affiliation, Sindh has played an axial role as an anchorage, as well as a catalyst agent to all forms of "drifts," racial and cultural, that seeped through the region.*[60]

Rai and Chach Dynasties

In the modern-day territorial geography of South Asia, the kingdom of Sindh under the Rai Sahiras era expanded from Karachi in the south to Peshawar in the north. To the west, it included most of the modern-day Balochistan province of Pakistan, including all its coastal regions. Its domains included

---

[60] Subhadra Anand, *National Integration of Sindhis* (Vikas Pub, 1996).

Multan, Bahawalpur, Cholistan, Thar, Rajasthan, Rann of Kutch, and Kashmir.

Mirza Kalich Beg, founding father of Sindhi literature, drew a map of Sindh under the Rai and Chach Dynasties in his translation (the only English version of *Chach Nama* so far):

> *East: Rajput states in Jodhpur and Jaisalmer, West Kelat, North Kelat, parts of Punjab and Bahawalpur state; and South: Arabian Sea and the Rann of Kutch, Debal the port city, Brahmanand (near Nerun, present-day Hyderabad-Shāhdādpur), Siwistan (today's Sehwān), Iskandar (near Rawalpindi and present Islamabad and Dhadhot), and Multan were the main principalities of the kingdom of Sindh.*

Rai dynasty was Buddhist by faith. Later, Chach established a Brahman dynasty. The population of Sindh at that time was a mixture of Buddhists, Jains, and Hindus.

Rai Sahiras II, the truly most indigenous Sindhi king in recorded history, laid down his life for the sovereignty of his country, defending his motherland against an invading army of the Persian King Nimroz. This battle was reportedly fought near the city of Kerman, not too far from the current Iran-Pakistan border.

King Nimroz invaded Sindh. On hearing this, Rai Sahiras II went up to face the invaders halfway and launched a fiercely pitched battle. In battle, the Sindhi king fell, but he forced the invading Persian king to retreat. After the martyrdom of Rai Sahiras II, his son, Rai Sahasi III, ascended the throne of Sindh.

One day, the king was presiding over his court with his most trusted *wazir*, or Minister Ram, when a stranger was presented to the king. He introduced himself as Chach, a son and brother of local Brahman ascetics, in the temple of the capital town, Aror.

Chach Nama, considered the most authentic book on the history on Sindh, describes the dialogue between Ram and the stranger Chach, as excerpted below:

> *"My name is Chach. My father's name is Selaji, and my brother is Chandar, who live in a temple in the outskirts of Aror. I have come to seek favor to grant me an opportunity to serve you as assistant in your office," the visiting Chach told Ram.*
>
> *On this, Ram quizzed Chach, "What skill do you possess to serve in the court?"*
>
> *"I have all the four books of Hindu religion memorized on my fingertips" was Chach's answer.*
>
> *Ram asked him to recite from the Vedas. Chach followed, and he recited with such eloquence that Ram was spellbound. Then he asked him in what other subjects he excelled.*
>
> *"I have learnt laws and ethics," Chach said.*
>
> *Ram asked him to draft an answer to a letter. He wrote the letter with a beautiful choice of words and language. Ram appointed him as his assistant.*

One day the king needed an urgent response to some correspondence, so he sent for his wazir, Ram. Ram was on leave, so Chach appeared before the king.

"Who are you?" asked the king.

He said he was assistant to his wazir, Ram. With flattery and verbosity of writing, he impressed the king as well.

King Sahasi made Chach his assistant secretary and awarded him with robes. He helped the king in matters of governance, letter writing, and other affairs of the kingdom. One day, King Sahasi summoned Chach into his private quarters and his queen, Suhandi, was present. In her presence, King Sahasi dictated some letters to Chach and sought his counsel.

As narrated in the Chach Nama, about Chach, over the course of time, Queen Suhandi fell in love with Chach but found Chach uninterested in her gestures of affection toward him. He told her that he was an orthodox Brahman, and his father and brother were ascetics in the temple of Aror, and that to him having an affair with the queen of his king would not only be ungrateful but also a sin. But the queen continued her romantic pursuits and was eventually able to win him over.

When King Sahasi fell ill, Queen Suhandi kept the news of the king's illness secret. She summoned the potential claimants to the throne, to his private apartment, one by one, telling them that the king wanted a private audience with each for their advice. She would then have each of them locked in the dungeons by her loyal servants. And then she would order her guards to kill each of the potential heirs.

She then summoned all the feudal lords, ministers, and notables of the kingdom and announced the illness of the king. She also proclaimed that the king was not able to see anyone because of his serious illness, and ill treatment by his close relatives. Therefore, he had appointed Chach, his viceroy, to take over the day-to-day governance of the court.

As the king did not have a child of his own, and Chach was now in full control of the affairs of the government and state, Chach, with the full support and backing of Queen Suhandi, declared himself the new sovereign when King Sahasi was finally declared dead. Thus, King Chach became successor to Rai Sahasi II, bringing an end to the Rai Dynasty, and establishing the Chach Dynasty, the first and last Brahman Dynasty to rule over Sindh.

Rana Maharath of Chittor, and brother to King Rai Sahasi, on learning of the above, invaded Aror to dethrone Chach but was killed by the wickedly clever moves of Chach. It is said that Chach told Maharath, "I am Brahman. I can't fight while mounted on horse. So please, majesty, get off the horseback, so that we can fight, one to one."

But when Maharath got off the horse, Chach handed his own horse to one of his soldiers and told another soldier to kill Maharath.

When Chach died in 672 CE, his brother, Chandar, whom he had made a minister, declared himself his successor. But later Chandar was dethroned by Raja Dahir. Thus Dahir Sen, a son of Chach, ascended as successor to his father as king of Sindh.

The Arab Era

راجا ڈاهر
تنهنجون نياڻيون
سهڻيون سياڻيون
ڪنهن هيئن آنديون
مانديون بانديون
چيلهه ۾ رسا
چڪبا چوڻا
اڳتان گهوڙا
پنتان پياريون
راجڪماريون
ننگيون ساريون
ها پر آهي
پوءِ به انهن جي
منهن تي نفرت
عزت حشمت

(شيخ اياز)

Raja Dahir!
Your daughters
Beautiful, wise
Who dragged them here
Anxious, tied,
Ropes around their waists
Tight and short,
Horses in front
Your beloveds behind,
The princesses
All naked,
But with heads held high,
There is defiance on their
faces,
With honor, and courage.

~Shaikh Ayaz

This poem is one of the most vivid descriptions of how two daughters of Raja Dahir were presented to the Caliph Walid Bin Abdul Malik, Bin Marwan. These verses were written approximately 1,400 years after the actual event, by Shaikh

Ayaz, considered the second-greatest poet in the history of Sindh after Shah Abdul Latif Bhittai.

The most quoted source on the period around the Arab conquest is *Chach Nama*. This book is said to have been originally authored by an anonymous Arab historian soon after the Arab conquest of Sindh. It was originally called *Fatehnama* (*Book of Conquest*). Five hundred years after the Arab invasion, this manuscript was discovered by a Persian historian named Ali Kufi, who translated it into the Persian language and renamed it *Chach Nama*. Kufi, from Bhakkar, Sindh, was descended from the original Arab families who had come to Sindh with Muhammad Bin Qasim. Mirza Kalich Beg, the founding father of Sindhi prose, translated the complete text of *Chach Nama* into English in 1900.

The Persian text was republished by legendary Sindhi scholar Umar Bin Muhammad Daudpota in 1939. A refined version of that text was published in 1981 by another great Sindhi scholar, Dr. Nabi Bakhsh Baloch. According to one of the highest-regarded experts on the history of modern and medieval Sindh, Manan Ahmed Asif, "The oldest extant manuscript of *Chach Nama* is dated 1651 CE and is currently in Punjab University's collection in Lahore. There are copies of the manuscript in Talpur's collection in Hyderabad, Sindh, in the Rampur collection in Bankipur, and in the British Library in London."

According to *Chach Nama*, Raja Dahir heroically fought to defend Sindh but fell to the Arab army, led by their dynamic teenaged general, Muhammad Bin Qasim, on June 20, 712 CE. His severed head and his two daughters were sent as trophies to the Caliph Walid Bin Abdul Malik, Bin Marwan, the Umayyad ruler at Baghdad.

With the fall of King Dahir came the end of the Rai dynasty and the independence of Sindh at the hands of Arab conquerors. Every Sindhi who would have witnessed the sun setting over the mighty Indus River that evening must have assumed that to be the last day for Sindh and Sindhis.

It is narrated that the place where Raja Dahir fell in the battlefield was called Wadhu Wah, near Nerun, and close to the current city of Hyderabad, not far from Doaba, where the Mehran River flowed in two streams. Many historians narrate Raja Dahir was killed on a Thursday in June 712 CE, in the of the month of Ramadan, in the ninety-third year of the Islamic calendar.

Maharaja Dahir, along with his army of brave Sindhi soldiers, had put up a valiant effort to defend Sindh. This king of Sindh received an arrow in his chest from an Arab hitman; then he fell from the elephant into the River Indus and died. Thus, once again, Sindh, the land of peace and harmony, was conquered and subdued by sheer military might. With a strike of an arrow and then a sword, the head of the Sindhi king was severed from his body, along with the freedom of Sindh.

The Arab army, led by Muhammad Bin Qasim, had a significant edge over the defenders. They had mastered the techniques of naval warfare, along with propelled explosives, thus, rapidly expanding their rule both east and west by conquering territories previously considered unreachable, from Spain to Indonesia.

It is debated whether the Arab forces reached Sindh by sea or land, but it is clear that they were equipped with naval, infantry, and artillery capabilities. They had the latest catapult stone-throwing machines, a primitive version of modern-day tanks, which they fondly called *uroos* (the bride), also known as *manjaneeq* in Arabic.

Even after the fall of Raja Dahir, his queen, Ladee, continued to resist in the hope of receiving reinforcements. Historians disagree on her fate. Some suggest that she was captured alive, later converted to Islam, and given in *nikah* (marriage) to Muhammad Bin Qasim. Others believe that she made herself *sati* (pious) by immolating herself along with her six female servants, a common practice among widows in the region in those times.

Her two daughters were taken as slaves, along with 30,000 other men, women, and children. According to the prevailing norms of the time, they were divided as war booty, or *Maal-e-Ghanimat*, among the Arab soldiers.

Following the death of Raja Dahir, his son, Jaisiah, fortified himself along with other family members in Brahmanabad, the capital of Lower Sindh. Historian Zahir Lari depicted the resistance of Raja Dahir's heirs and army as follows: "He [Jaisiah] had defied the Arab army for six months before they were captured. The men were put to the sword and women and children enslaved."

Muhammad Bin Qasim then marched on to Aror. Its people defied him for several months, but capitulated after he agreed to spare the lives of its inhabitants. This was a significant departure from the usual practice, as the norm was that any people who were defeated or surrendered were given two options only—convert to Islam or face death—unless they belonged to one of the other Abrahamic faiths, or *Ahl al-Kitāb* (people of the Book), as it was believed that the *Quran*, the holy book of Muslims, was a continuity of the previous celestial revelations to the descendants of prophet Abraham. But in this case, those who surrendered were allowed to keep their faith in return for paying *jizya*.

Muhammad Bin Qasim then advanced to Askalanda (Uch). After having captured it, he crossed the Chenab River and went on to besiege Multan. The fortress of Multan was forced to surrender after a long siege, as its water supplies were cut off. Multan, one of the richest cities in the region, lost an enormous amount of gold and wealth as a result of being captured.

Al-Hajjaj Bin Yusuf, then governor of the province of Iraq and the person who had assigned Bin Qasim to lead the expedition on Sindh, proudly wrote to Caliph Walid that the invasion of Sindh was an unparalleled financial success. He reportedly said, "We have appeased our anger and avenged our injuries, and we have gained sixty million *dirhams*, as well as the head of Dahir."

The daughters of Raja Dahir, princesses Surya and Premala, were captured and sent as a gift to Caliph Walid for his personal harem. According to *Chach Nama*, when princesses Surya and Premala were presented to Caliph Walid, they tricked him and told him that they were not virgins, as they had been violated by Muhammad Bin Qasim. On hearing this, the caliph became enraged and ordered for Muhammad Bin Qasim to be placed alive in a bag made out of an oxen's hide and brought to him.

Though, according to Ahmad ibn Yahyā al-Balādhurī, a ninth-century Muslim historian, Bin Qasim's death was due to palace politics that resulted after the death of Caliph Walid. After Walid's death, his brother, Sulayman ibn Abd al-Malik, took over as the new caliph. And he became hostile toward Bin Qasim, as Bin Qasim's primary allegiance was with Al-Hajjaj Bin Yusuf, the governor of Iraq, who had refused to accept Sulayman's right of succession in all territories captured by Al-Hajjaj. Thus, Sulayman had all the generals and top administrators who had ties with Al-Hajjaj, including Bin Qasim, eliminated to consolidate his rule.

The latter appears to be a much more plausible explanation of the untimely demise of Bin Qasim at a very young age of nineteen or twenty. Muhammad Bin Qasim was in the middle of preparing further expansions when Al-Hajjaj died. The new governor, Yazid ibn al-Muhallab, had Bin Qasim arrested.

According to Al-Balādhurī, Bin Qasim and his family were tortured to death by the new fiscal manager of Sindh, Salih ibn Abd al-Rahman, as revenge for his brother's execution by Al-Hajjaj. The Arabs had had an eye on Sindh since the beginning of the rise of the Islamic Empire. They had wanted to reach and control the trade route from the Indian Ocean to the River Indus.

Sindh was an independent country with its capital at Aror in the hills of Rohri along the River Indus, then called Mehran. Its last dynasty had been founded by Rai Dewaji of the Rai dynasty.

Quoting and redefining *Chach Nama*, the earliest historiographic account on Muhammad Bin Qasim and his conquest, modern historian Manan Ahmed Asif narrates about the kingdom of Rai Sahiras and his capital Aror as follows:

> *His kingdom of Sindh with capital Aror. It was a grand and lively city, ornamented with palaces of various kinds, wide and colorful roads, streams, fountains, gardens, and orchards. It was founded by the shore of Sehwān, called River Mehran. The king of this lovely city was Rai Sahiras bin Rai Sahasi, whose treasury was full and coffers plentiful. His justice and generosity were known around the world. The limits of his polity extended to the north until Kashmir, to the east until Makran, to the south until Daybul, and the shore of the Great Sea, to the west until the mountains of Kikanan. To his four provinces he assigned four governors.*

The rising Islamic Empire, with its capital initially in Medina, and then Damascus, had enjoyed trading ties with Sindh via land and sea. But even before that, the seaports of Sindh were frequented by Arab traders and considered some of the most lucrative in the world.

Mariah bin al Saqafi, cousin of the governor of Bahrain, was the first Muslim commander who unsuccessfully launched a military campaign against Sindh. According to historian and scholar Derryl MacLean, the Arabs had been trying for seventy-three years to conquer Sindh before the invasion under Muhammad Bin Qasim.

Finally, in the year 711 CE, an army of 6,000 soldiers was organized, the largest to date, for the biggest offensive on Sindh. Though they were faced with pitched resistance by the defending forces of Sindh, in the end the local army was defeated. The Arabs, a purely tribal society who had for centuries been involved in intertribal/clan wars, blood feuds, disputes over inheritance and control of preciously limited resources were finally united under the ideology of Islam.

After the departure of the Prophet of Islam, for a brief period, a semi-democratic system of governance was established under the rule of Khulafa-e-Rashideen, the rightly guided successors, whereby the ruler at the time was elected by a *shura* (council) of elders in the community. But disputes started to arise during the time of the third Khulafa, Uthman. And the conflict got significantly worse by the time the prophet's cousin and son-in-law, Ali, took over the reign of the Islamic state after the assassination of Uthman.

Old dynastic and clan disputes between Banu Umayya and Banu Hashim, the two main tribes of Mecca, boiled over into open civil war until Muawiyah bin Abi Sufyan, then governor of Syria, established the Umayyad Caliphate in Damascus. Muawiyah was the son of Abi Sufyan, the ruler of Mecca before Islam. His rule had been abolished by the Prophet. Abi Sufyan later converted to Islam when Mecca was captured by the Islamic army led by the Prophet himself.

The Islamic Empire continued to expand rapidly under the Umayyads. Thus, it was natural they started to strategize about capturing the lucrative ports of Sindh, along with its mercantile routes and fertile agricultural lands. This was strategically extremely important in gaining control over the Indian Ocean.

The commonly held myth is that the reason for the military campaign on Sindh was solely due to the fleet of cargo ships being attacked and some Arab women and children being abducted by pirates from one of the ports of Sindh.

It is said that when Hajjaj Ibn Yusuf, the legendary governor of the eastern half of Umayyad Khulafa, was informed of the above, he demanded the return of all the women and children and compensation for the looted material. But Raja Dahir, then ruler of Sindh, refused to comply. Thus, Hajjaj was left with no choice but to send his forces to avenge them.

This appears to be a myth, however, or at most an excuse by the rising superpower of the time to expand territorial control. According to historian Manan Ahmed Asif, the alleged pirating of an Arab ship would have been at least fifteen years before the invasion of Sindh led by Muhammad Bin Qasim. As this happened in 711 CE, whereas the Arabs, due to their rising military and naval powers, had secured their naval routes to as far as Ceylon and the far east by the end of the previous century.

The tragedy of Karbala, which resulted in martyrdom of Imam Husayn, along with most of the male descendants of the prophet, and imprisonment of female members of his family, resulted in widespread resentment against the Umayyad rulers, which, in some instances, boiled over in open resistance and rebellion. This was crushed mercilessly by Yazid, the second

Khulafa of the Umayyad dynasty and son of the founder of the Umayyad Khulafa.

After the unexpected death of Yazid, his son Mu'awiya II became Khulafa, but he could only hold on to rule for little more than a few months. He had to relinquish his rule after failing to control the rebellions against him, thus bringing an end to the Sufyan line of caliphs of Umayyad's rule.

After him, the Marwanid sect of Umayyad took over the Khulafa, and Abdul Malik, son of Marwan, became the Khulafa. He sent in an army under Hajjaj Bin Yusuf to dislodge Abdullah Bin al-Zubair, who had declared a rebellion against the new Khulafa and had sought refuge in Mecca. Hajjaj besieged Kaaba and demanded an unconditional surrender, but when this happened, he attacked Kaaba. Abdullah Bin al-Zubair and his companions, who had taken refuge inside Kaaba, were killed. This was strictly against the injunctions of the prophet, as he had sternly prohibited the killing of even an ant or destruction of any property inside the holy Kaaba. It is said that the Kaaba itself was destroyed by heavy bombardment with catapults. But Hajjaj was able to crush the rebellion. As a reward, Caliph Abdul Malik appointed Hajjaj as governor of Iraq.

Hajjaj Bin Yusuf s full name was Abu Muhammad al-Hajjaj ibn Yusuf ibn al-Hakam ibn Aqil al-Thaqafi, called al-Thaqafi, as the family was originally from Taif, a city in current-day Saudi Arabia, approximately forty miles from Mecca. The city is known for relatively cooler weather due to its elevation of around 6,000 feet; its highly fragrant roses; the quality of fruits such as pomegranates, figs, and grapes; and the sweetness of its honey.

But the city is also considered the epicenter of the destruction of the family of the prophet, as it is believed to be the place where the Umayyads secretly hatched their sinister plan to get rid of the descendants of the prophet so that they could regain their rule. The Umayyad dynasty had started to set their eyes much farther than just the Arab peninsula. As the boundaries of the rapidly rising Islam Empire expanded farther, they wanted to gain control of the seaports of Sindh as a foothold for further expansions At the same time, a number of family members of the prophet Ahl al-Bayt, along with their companions and sympathizers, tried to escape the persecution of the Umayyad rulers and began to seek asylum and find refuge in Sindh.

Descendants of these members of the family of the prophet are held in extremely high esteem and revered all over Sindh to this day. They are called Syeds as a mark of high respect. G. M. Syed, the father of the modern Sindhi Nationalist movement, a descendent of the prophet himself, when asked why he praised Raja Dahir so much, said, "I would be most ungrateful if I did not praise my benefactor who had given asylum to my ancestors."

Among one of the earliest to seek asylum in Sindh was Muhammad Alafi, who was not only given asylum, but was also granted privileges in the royal court, reserved for only a select few, by then Brahman King of Sindh, Raj Dahir, after the fall of Damascus, which was then the capital of the eastern region of the Byzantine Empire. The Arabs had gained control of most of the trade routes connecting the known world, making them the biggest imperial and trade power in the Indian Ocean and Mediterranean. According to historian Hasan Zahir Lari:

> *This made Arabs the sole power linking the Indian Ocean to the Mediterranean and dominating maritime commerce between Europe and South Asia. They were being resisted by the Indian seafarers, especially the Medes of Sindh, who were backed by the merchants of Debal. Thus, conquest of Sindh was essential for the Arabs if they were to control the seaports and maritime trade routes of Asia.*

After Abdul Malik, his son Walid ascended to the caliphate. Manan Ahmed Asif, in his critical review of *Chach Nama*, described his assessment of the reasons behind the Umayyad's military campaigns to capture Sindh:

> *Judging from Balādhurī's reconstruction of late seventh-century and early eighth-century Muslim campaigns in Sindh, we can conclude that the Umayyad state was interested in the region for several reasons: to secure frontier regions against rebels, to address the financial affairs of the Marwanid branch of Umayyad, and to consolidate mercantile routes.*

As a matter of historical fact, the first Arab military campaigns on Hindh and Sindh had started as early as the rule of the second Islamic Caliph, Umar I (634-644 CE).[61]

Caliph Umar sent naval expeditions to Debal and other ports and trade centers along the coastline of Sindh and rest of the

---

[61] Lari, *A History of Sindh*.

Indian subcontinent. With their rapidly evolving maritime sciences, they pretty much gained full control of the naval routes between the Middle and Far East and were eyeing lands as far as Indonesia and the Maldives. They had also overpowered the two superpowers of the time called Qaisar O Kisra (Caesar and Khosrow) and the Byzantine and Sassanid Empires of Rome and Persia to their east and west.

Uthman, the third caliph, also ordered an expedition by land to current-day Baluchistan. He sent in his governor al-Hakim Bin Jabal al-Abwi to survey the area. But Caliph Uthman did not pursue further military expeditions to Sindh after his governor reported, "Water is scarce, the fruits are poor, and their robbers are bold. If few troops are sent there, they will be killed. If many soldiers are sent, they will starve."

The fourth caliph, Ali, son-in-law of the prophet, also ordered a military expedition to Makran and other coastal areas of Baluchistan and Sindh, under the command of Al-Harith al-Abdi. The Arab army was faced with a powerful counterattack and suffered a large number of casualties on the Sindh-Makran border and had to retreat. According to famous Sindhi historian Bherumal Advani, at the time of the Arab invasion, Sindhis were mostly of Buddhist and Jain faiths, both based on pure nonviolence.

> *Most probably they had lost the element of militancy. Arabs had the latest army and equipment like catapults or manjaneeqs, by which they destroyed forts and garrisons. Thus, there ran fear among the Sindhi population, so they easily converted themselves into Islam.*

But most other historians believe a vast number of Brahmans and Buddhists, including monks and the common population, cooperated with the Arabs because Muhammad Bin Qasim made an exception from the rules of his predecessors and allowed the local Hindus to keep their faith if they agreed to pay jizya. This exception was previously reserved for other Abrahamic faiths only.

Among the earliest to accept Islam were many chiefs of Rajput origin, the warrior sect in the indigenous Hindu population. These tribes then acquired new tribal names ending with *pota*, a tradition that still goes on, with last names like Halepota, Daudpota, and more.

Nevertheless, Dahirsiya, son of Raja Dahir, with thousands of his loyal army, continued his resistance. He intensified his resistance after the death of Muhammad Bin Qasim but was eventually captured by the Arab army and executed. Umar Ibn Abdul Aziz, also known as Omar II and considered by many as one of the best and most just rulers in Islamic history, went a step further and allowed the local Buddhists and Hindus to retain their lands, prompting Raja Dahir's youngest son, Jaisiah, to convert to Islam.

Umar II is still today considered by many Muslim scholars as one of the only true caliphs of Islam, alongside the first four caliphs. *Khulafa-e-Rashideen*, literally translated, means the Rightly Guided. Like the first four caliphs, Umar II was chosen to be the caliph based on his merit and righteousness, instead of purely on his lineage. Many Muslim scholars consider the rest of the caliphs of Islamic history to be nothing more than worldly rulers who happened to inherit their rule instead of being Rightly Guided, as were the first four caliphs of Islam and Umar II.

However, when Junayd ibn Abd ar-Rahman al-Murri became governor of Sindh in 723 CE after the death of Khulafa Umar Ibn Abdul Aziz, he demanded jizya from Jaisiah. Jaisiah refused to pay the jizya on the grounds that he had converted to Islam, and thus should not have to pay. His refusal enraged the new governor, and after the death of Umar II, the new caliph, Yazid ibn Abd al-Malik, and his governor did not show the same generosity and leniency as their predecessors. Thus, Jaisiah was captured and killed for his refusal, despite having become a Muslim.

According to M. H. Panhwar, Jaisiah sent his nephew to Baghdad to apprise the governor of the above breach of contract, but his nephew was captured and killed. Hearing of his nephew's execution, Jaisiah abjured Islam and decided to resist al-Murri.

Panhwar estimated the site of the above battle to be Chotiari, close to Brahmanabad in the present-day Sanghar District. According to Bherumal Advani, many Hindus refused to convert. Instead of giving up the faith of their forefathers, many Hindus migrated to Kutch and Punjab, where they were recognized as Arora Bansi, meaning inhabitants of Aror. It is said the fortress city of Debal had a large temple in the middle of the town. On top of the temple was a tall flagpole that flew a red flag, which was visible from miles away. The local belief was that as long as the red flag stood over the temple, no invader would be able to conquer the city.

But the Arab army, with their newly acquired skills of targeting fortresses with their *manjaneeqs*, were able to knock the red flag down, even before breaking into the fortress. On seeing the flag being dislodged, the local priests and monks told the army to surrender, as the fallen flag was considered an omen that the city was lost.

Debal later became the first Arab colony established in Sindh. It is said that about 4,000 Arab families migrated to Debal. This was also the city where the first *masjid* was built in Sindh. The newcomers brought with them new languages and customs, including foods, flora, and fauna, the most famous being the date palms that still flourish all over Sindh, especially around the historical cities of Khairpur and Sukkur.

Arabs recognized Sindhis as people of intellect and craftsmanship. Sindhi Hindus and Buddhists found their place in the new Arab administration. And it did not take them long to be adjusted in good offices in Sindh under the Arabs. Thus, a new era of cultural exchange was ushered in at Sindh.

> *The Arab conquest could not be sustained too long. Umayyad rule stretched too far, and any further consolidation proved futile. Qasim was recalled to Baghdad. Muslim rule shrank in Sindh and southern Punjab. But coastal trade and presence of Muslim colony in Sindh permitted significant cultural exchange and introduction of Islamic teachers. In Sindh, Arabs consolidated their power, and conversion was widespread especially amongst the Buddhist majority. Multan became the center of Ismaili sect of*

Islam and many adherents of this sect even now live in Sindh.[62]

Dahir—Hero or Villain?

I am going to meet the Arabs in the open battle and fight them as best as I can. If I crush them, my kingdom will then be put on a firm footing. But if I am killed honorably, the event will be recorded in the books of Arabia and India and will be talked about by great men. It will be heard by other kings in the world, and it will be said that Raja Dahir of Sindh sacrificed his precious life for the sake of his country, in fighting with the enemy.
~Raja Dahir

History is seldom kind to the vanquished, and Raja Dahir, the most famous ruler of Sindh, was obviously one of its biggest martyrs. In his thirty-two-year rule over Sindh, Raja Dahir established a welfare system and a decentralized government with rules similar to those found in present-day governance. His era is reported to have been one of prosperity and wealth.

In recent textbooks in Pakistan, he is portrayed as an infidel with extremely low character, one who married his own sister. He is also described as a ruthless, murderous ruler. However,

---

[62] B. S. Ahloowalia, *Invasion of the Genes: Genetic Heritage of India* (Eloquent Books, 2009).

Muhammad Bin Qasim, the man who opened the doors of the Indian subcontinent for Islam, is idolized as a valiant, young general, a pious young man with an impeccable character, and a savior of Sindh.

G. M. Syed, the founding father of modern Sindhi nationalism and a proud descendent of the earliest Arab Muslim immigrants to Sindh, was one of the first Sindhi scholars to challenge this rhetoric. He worked effortlessly to correct the historical records. He described Raja Dahir as a hero king of Sindh, one who defended its sovereignty valiantly and was martyred. Syed also challenged the commonly taught myth in the textbooks that the sole reason behind the Arab invasion of Sindh was to save Muslim women and children who were being kept hostage by Sindhi pirates.

Syed very poignantly raised the question, "If this was the case, then what was the reason behind their military campaigns with other countries from as far west as North Africa, to as far north as Central Asia, to as far east as Indonesia?" He also questioned the other factually incorrect notion propagated by the clergy that Raja Dahir was a ruthless Hindu tyrant who mercilessly suppressed Buddhists and followers of other religions. He countered the teaching with the fact that Buddhism actually flourished in Sindh during the rules of Raja Dahir and Chandar Sen.

As a matter of historical fact, two of Raja Dahir's governors were of Buddhist faith. Buddhism, despite being pushed out of most of the Indian subcontinent by fundamental Brahman priests, was prosperous in Sindh during Raja Dahir's rule, and Raja Dahir granted many privileges to Buddhist monks and temples.

Contrary to common teachings, Dahir was known for his valor and benevolence. Sindh, under his rule, was a country in which oppressed people from far lands found refuge. One of those was an Arab dissident named Muhamad Alafi, who sought to escape the oppression of the Umayyad rulers. Dahir not only granted him refuge, but also issued a coin in his honor. It is said that when Sindh was attacked by Muhammad Bin Qasim, Raja Dahir asked Alafi to go with him to face the invading army. He said to Alafi, "You are best acquainted with the ways of the Arab army, and it is advisable that you should go with my forces in advance."

Muhammad Alafi replied, "O King! We are grateful to you, but we cannot draw our swords against the army of Islam. If we are killed by them, we will earn a bad name, and if we kill them, we will burn in hell. We agree that in return for the favors you have shown us, we must at least give you some advice on how to fight these invaders, even if we do not draw our swords against them. But if we give you advice, then, again, this army will never forgive us. Please be kind to us and allow us to depart quietly."

Upon hearing this, Raja Dahir valiantly excused Alafi and his companions and allowed them to leave his kingdom. In the words of G. M. Syed, "Raja Dahir became martyred while fighting to defend Sindh; that is why every Sindhi must be proud of him. I value him at the top of the list of the Sindhi heroes."

G. M. Syed, with his logic and historical facts, was able to change the mindset of many Sindhis, thus clearing the tarnished image of Raja Dahir. Following him, many contemporary Sindhi writers and poets have written extensively on Raja Dahir; most prominent among them is Shaikh Ayaz, the great national poet of Sindh who introduced King Dahir as a symbol of Sindhi patriotism and heroism in his poetry. In the words of one of the most prominent modern-day historians of Sindh, Manan Ahmed Asif:

> *During my visits to Hyderabad and Thatta, I had many chances to sip tea and speak about Sindh's glorious past with those who keep the cultural memory alive. Chach Nama was often invoked, as were Muhammad Bin Qasim and Raja Dahir. Yet three women from Chach Nama, Dahir's wife, Queen Ladi, and Dahir's daughters, Surya and Premala, carry equal weight in the cultural memory of Sindh's past. Their stories are recited to explicate the nationhood of Sindh and to argue against imperial aggressors.*

With the fall of Raja Dahir, Sindh again came under the yoke of foreign occupation, which lasted for the next 340 years, until the establishment of the Soomra dynasty in 1050 CE.

Sindh: The Melting Pot of Faiths

Sindh, Beloved Country of the God

Sindh, besides being the gateway to India, was the birthplace of many faiths and ancient religions, including Religion of the Indus (as coined by John Marshall), Vedas, Hinduism, Jal Panthis, and Jarpoojaras (water worshippers). Sindh has been a fertile ground for many established religions, such as Jainism, Buddhism, Islam, and a special brand of Sufism that is a unique blend of Hindu Vedanta and Muslim Tasawaf. The greatest Sufi poet of humankind, Maulana Jalaluddin Rumi, in one of his most well-known poems, "Moses and the Shepherd," described how different people of the world supplicate to the Almighty in their unique ways. "For their own goodness comes every command. Hindis in their own tongue God will praise. Sindhis, in prayer, their arms will raise. I do not become cleansed from counting beads."

It is said that among those who made pilgrimages to Sindh were Jesus and Gautama Buddha. According to some traditions, Prophet Mohammed once said, "I can feel the cool winds blowing from Sindh, similar to the winds from heaven."

Sindh has always been the melting pot of all faiths; as such, it has developed its own brand of Sufism based on principles of pluralism, tolerance, and peaceful coexistence. Here, the perfect mix of Abrahamic Kabballah and Vedanta of Hindu faiths has been practiced daily for thousands of years.

That was the reason Buddhism and Hinduism survived in Sindh hand in hand. Even today, many Sindhi Hindus happen to practice both Hinduism and Sikhism simultaneously. Thus, Bhagavad Gita and Granth find their places side by side in Sindhi temples (*tikanas*).

Religion of the Indus

Before the advent of Aryans in Sindh, the people of the Indus Valley Civilization had a unique religion with its own individuality. John Marshall, who led the first excavation of Mohenjo-Daro, found no religious relics that could indicate the faith of the people of Indus Valley Civilization. Among the relics he did find were several female figurines, but it was not clear in any way that these represented divinities. He believed that these female figurines represented nature as a maternal form—in other words, Mother Nature.

Sir John Marshall was also the first researcher who discovered that there was a civilization that existed before the Indo- and Euro-Aryan era in Sindh. He called it the pre-Aryan, or Vedic, civilization.

One of the statues discovered in Mohenjo-Daro was that of a priest king with a cloth worn around his right shoulder; it had trefoil inscriptions similar to the modern-day Sindhi Ajrak. These inscriptions are considered the earliest version of Ajrak, and it is believed that these trefoil inscriptions signify a sacred symbol.

Jane R. McIntosh, quoting Asko Parpola, believes that the multilayered symbolism of the trefoils inscribed on the garment indicated that it "was worn by both gods and the priest kings and was a heavenly garment later mentioned in the Vedas."

Unlike other contemporary civilizations, like those of Egypt, Mesopotamia, and Sumer, Mohenjo-Daro did not have any buildings that could be identified as places of worship. But it is believed that the Great Bath and adjoining buildings were used as places of physical and spiritual purification. "Scholars seem by and large united in considering that this was a religious structure connected with ritual bathing," says McIntosh about the temple and the nearby Great Bath.[63]

The Great Bath was accessible only through one grand staircase, which connected it to the grand citadel in the center of the city, indicating that the people of Mohenjo-Daro and the rest of the Indus civilization had great reverence for water. Though, otherwise, they were a faithless and weaponless people.

Water and the Indus River have remained the lifeline of the people of Sindh—from Mohenjo-Daro to Vedas, to the composers and rhyme-reciting Rishis, to the concept of Jhoolay Lal (Odero Lal) or Khwaja Khizr. Water has always been a central focus in most indigenous sacred places. Still today, there are descendants of Jarpoojaras in Sindh; though, unfortunately, their numbers are diminishing rapidly.

According to scholar Parveen Talpur:

> *In Lower Sindh, about two-hundred miles from Mohenjo-Daro, is the shrine of the long-dead saint.*

---

[63] Jane R. McIntosh, *The Ancient Indus Valley: New Perspectives (Understanding Ancient Civilizations)* (ABC-CLIO, 2007).

But his legend is still alive, which can very well be the epitome of the ancient river. Hindus and Muslims alike revere this saint, whose name is Odero Lal, also known as "Darya Shah" (the river king).[64]

Daryapanthis are the followers of Odero Lal, who was known as Shaikh Tahir among Muslims. The Daryapanthis beliefs have their origin in the Hindu desire to find some answer to the challenge of Islam. The Hindu regarded Odero Lal as a champion against Islam, as he is reported to have stopped proselytization of Muslim rulers. It has to be noted that even though Hindus accepted Sufism they did not adopt the orthodox principles of Islam.[65]

The greatest Sindhi poet Shah Abdul Latif Bhittai, in the eighteenth century, devoted a whole chapter titled "Sur Samundi" to the water-revering maritime traders of Sindh.

اُبِيُون تَرَ پُوڃِينِ، وَهُون وَتِجارِن جُونِ؛
آٽِيو اَکا ڏِينِ، ڪَٿُوري، سَمُونڊَ ڪي۔

Standing, they worship the wharf, wives of the sailors
Offering benefactions with musk, to the mighty sea

---

[64] Talpur

[65] Anand

In another verse, he urges the traders to pay homage to the sea.

سيوا كَرِ سمندَ جِي، جِت جَرُ وهي تو جالَ؛
سَئِين وَهَن سِيرَ مِ، ماٹَڪَ، موتِي، لالَ؛
جي ماسو جُرِّيئِي مالَ، تہ پُوچارا! پُرِ تِئِين.

Revere the sea, where water flows in abundance
In the waves, are precious pearls, and rubies
If the ocean blesses you, abundance will be yours

Today, Sindhi Hindus as well as Muslims worship the River Indus by throwing their *arzis* in the river. These are messages written on pieces of paper and then inserted into a small ball of dough. These notes are thrown in the river as a way of giving back to Mother Nature by feeding the fish. The basic idea is to please the deity by taking care of her creations, and thus it was believed that your prayers would be fulfilled, especially around the holy days of all faiths. The fact that this practice has been going on since time immemorial is proof enough that there might be some truth to the belief.

Rigveda and Sindhu

Moreover, Hindu is not a native word, but comes from a word for the river (Sindhu) that Herodotus (in the fifth century BCE), the Persians (in the fourth century BCE), and the Arabs (after the eighth century CE) refer to everyone who lived beyond the great river of the northwest of the subcontinent, still known locally as Sindhu, and in Europe as the Indus.[66]

The hymn-reciting priestly tribes of Aryans composed Vedas on the banks of the River Indus. They praised the Sindhu and its tributaries. In verse 1-IV of the Rig Vedas, it says that "Aryans migrated to South Asia from Central Asia in about 2000 BCE. Rishis settled and lived on the banks of the River Indus and called it Hind. Thus, the word *Hind* is derived from Sindhu."[67]

Sindhi writer Popati Hiranandani describes the intertwining of the etymology of *Sindhu* and *Hindu* as follows:

> *There is a similarity between the word Indus and India and the Sanskrit word Indu (moon). Whether Indu has become Hindu, or Sindhu has changed into Hindu, whether people of the region were called moon-faced ones, or because the Iranians could not spell Sa, we do not know. We can only decide about the facts that there was no religion or faith called Hindu or Hinduism and the people of that particular region have been worshipping water since ages.*[68]

---

[66] Wendy Doniger, *The Hindus: An Alternative History* (Penguin, 2010), 30.

[67] Pon Kulendiren, *Hinduism; A Scientific Religion and Some Temples in Sri Lanka* (iUniverse, 2012), 11.

[68] Hiranandani

According to the Finnish Sindhologist Asko Parpola, "These foreigners, probably of West Iranian descent, entered the subcontinent from the west via Sindh, Gujarat, and Rajasthan."[69]

Parpola is of the opinion that holy Hindu bathing places, called *ghats*, probably originated from the Indus Civilization, the prime example being the Great Bath of Mohenjo-Daro. Parpola also believes that the great Pandavas—the five sons of the King Pandu and their allies described in the Mahabharata—came to South Asia via Sindh, Gujarat, and Rajasthan around 800 BCE. According to Gidwani, the word *om*, the primordial sound used to describe ultimate reality, was first used by inhabitants of the Sindhu valley. Asko Parpola, tracing the origin of the word *om*, came to the same conclusion. He said, "This conclusion is supported by many Dravidian loan words in the Vedic language, including the oldest available source. Thus, Sindh was the birthplace of Hinduism and the holy land where the word *Hindu* was driven from."[70]

In his book, *The Roots of Hinduism*, Asko Parpola categorically states:

> *The etymology of Hindu goes back to about 515 BCE when the Persian King Darius the Great annexed the Indus Valley to his empire. Sindhu, the Sanskrit*

---

[69] Parpola

[70] Asko Parpola, *The Roots of Hinduism: The Early Aryans and the Indus Civilization* (Oxford University Press, 2015).

name of the Indus River and its southern province, the area now known as Sindh, became Hindu in the Persian language. The Ionian Greeks serving the Great King did not pronounce the words' initial aspiration (like French speakers today), and so in the Greek language, Persian Hindu became Indos and its surrounding country became India.

It prompts the question, "Where did the many, indeed dominant, elements of Hinduism that are non-Vedic come from?" No doubt many local religious cults were absorbed into and assimilated by Hinduism in the course of its millennial development and expansion and a lot of ideological evolution took place, yet even so the Indus Civilization seems the likely original source, in spite of its antiquity. Classical Hinduism is considered to be of post-Vedic date, beginning around 400 to 200 BCE, and epitomized in the epics the Mahabharata, Ramayana, and Puranas.[71]

In Puranas, a story narrates the pilgrimage of Lord Ram, Sita, and Lakshman to Hinglaj. Lord Ram was said to have meditated in the oyster caves of present-day Keamari at Karachi. He encamped near a pool, which was surrounded by an orchard. That is why the area was called Ram Bagh until the Partition of India in 1947. Sindhi historian Bherumal Meharchand Advani

---

[71] Parpola, The Roots of Hinduism: The Early Aryans and the Indus Civilization.

writes in his *History of Hindus in Sind*, "So it proved Sri Ramachandra set his holy feet in Sindh."[72]

But unlike the rest of India, Sindhi Hindus were never rigid in their religious rituals or caste system. Sindhi Hindus have always been mostly merchants and craftsmen. They consisted primarily of goldsmiths (sonoras) and traders (lohanas). Much later, a new class was added—amils—during the Talpur dynasty.

According to Subhadra Anand:

> *The Lohanas presented a picture that was very antithesis of the caste system. This laxity in the socioeconomic setup was again due to the fact that Sindh oscillated between western contact and the subcontinent. A society becomes rigid only when it isolates itself from all external influences. Exposures led to flexibility. The Hindus of Sindh had, out of necessity, to be less rigid, for otherwise it would have led to completely wiping out of their religion from the province.*[73]

A Sindhi is simultaneously a Hindu, Sikh, and Sufi Muslim. An average Sindhi has no problem in keeping Masnavi from Maulana Rumi, *Shah Jo Risalo*, Bhagvati Gita, Guru Nanak Sahib, and the Quran, all with the same reverence. Sindhi Sufi Mian Mir was invited by the Fifth Sikh Guru Arjan Dev to lay the

---

[72] Advani, *History of Hindus in Sind*.

[73] Anand

foundation stone of the Golden Temple of Amritsar. Guru Nanak, the founder of Sikhism, is considered a prophet by many Sindhis. In the words of Dr. Motilal Jotwani:

> *The Mul Mantra of the Japji Sahib by Guru Nanak, who is popularly described as Guru of the Hindus and a pir of the Muslims, opens with a highest mystic syllable "Ek Onkar Satnam, Karta Purakh."*

A lot of Sindhi Hindus are known for their mixed faith. They practice Hinduism while following the teachings of Guru Nanak. Their annual religious pilgrimages include most of the holy places of the Sikh faith. Until the Partition of India, a great number of Sikhs, including Labana Sikhs, lived in Central and Northern Sindh.

Quoting members of the Sindhi community in Lucknow, the scholar and author of the book, *Hindu, Sufi, or Sikh,* Steven W. Ramey, writes:

> *There is a misconception in minds of local people. Even after fifty years they are not recognizing us as Hindus. They don't because we worship Guru Nanak. "So you are Sikhs," (they) say. We worship Guru Nanak because we think Guru Nanak is part of Hinduism.*
>
> *In Sindh, there are multiple places where Hindus and Muslims both worship together. These are called dargahs (shrines built around a burial site of a Sufi saint).*

There are annual festivals, which are secular, and open to followers of all faiths.[74]

Sindhi sage, Sufi master, and well-known humanitarian Sadhu T. L. Vaswani wrote "Nuri Granth" in Sindhi. This is recited and revered equally with Gita and other texts in Sadhu Vaswani centers. Sadhu T. L. Vaswani himself, a Sufi master, started a unique brand of Sindhi Sufism based on compassion and human service—a special blend of the teachings of sages and great Sufis such as Guru Nanak, Shah Abdul Latif Bhittai, and Sachal Sarmast. The teachings of Guru Nanak, Sai Baba, Kabir, Bhittai, Sarmast, and Saami are highlighted in the message, which was later refined and popularized by Vaswani's nephew, a great Sufi scholar in his own right, Dada J. P. Vaswani. The Vaswanis are actually a continuation of a long-standing list of Sindhi Hindu Sufi masters and saints, including Bhagat Kanwar Ram, also known as Amar Shaheed (Eternal Martyr); Sant Lilashah; Maharaj; Swami Harnam Das; Sufi Sant Dr. Sain Teoonram; and many others.

Sadhu T. L. Vaswani founded Mira High School for Girls, as well as the Ladies Club, in Hyderabad, Sindh. During the riots after the Partition of the India, when Hindu properties and businesses were being looted by incoming migrants from India, he asked his disciples, men, and women to stay in Sindh and continue serving their new country and the people there.

---

[74] Steven W. Ramey, *Hindu, Sufi, or Sikh: Contested Practices and Identifications of Sindhi Hindus in India and Beyond* (Palgrave Macmillan, 2008).

Tolerance and pluralism were the essence of Sadhu Vaswani's message as he himself fasted while reciting the Quran after Muhammad Ali Jinnah, the founder of Pakistan, died on September 11, 1947. Sadhu T. L. Vaswani was forced to leave his native land of Sindh because of political persecution and a witch hunt of Sindhi Hindus, Sikhs, and Sufis by the newly established government soon after creation of the country.

Rochaldas, a Sindhi national, came to India in 1948 and settled in Shanti Nagar, Ulhasnagar. He carried on charitable work and celebrated Sindhi mysticism by organizing a procession celebrating Lal Shahbaz Qalandar every year in Ulhasnagar, India.

Hindu Bhakti and Muslim Tasawwuf coexist in Sindh and influence the very fabric of the Sindhi populace. Be they Hindus, Muslims, or Sikhs, all Sindhi hearts and souls have been penetrated to the core. Sindh is also a spiritual melting pot that has the infinite energy needed to absorb outside philosophies, thoughts, cults, and religions. Sindh has always had the capacity to absorb and influence outsiders to merge into the essence of Sufism. That is why the Greek historians who accompanied Alexander the Great called the region the Land of Sophy, or Land of Learning.

According to Dr. Motilal Jotwani:

> *Tasawwuf originally roots back to the teachings of the Prophet Mohammed. But the Indian Sufism is a combination of prophetic teaching and original Indian thoughts. When Tasawwuf reached India, through Sindh, it became a combination of Brahma and Haq (truth).*

Sufis found Haq (truth) or Brahma in each and every object, living or dead. From leaves blowing in the wind, to twigs or bubbles floating on the surface of the water, to unsurmountable peaks of Himalayas.[75]

Shah Abdul Latif Bhittai says:

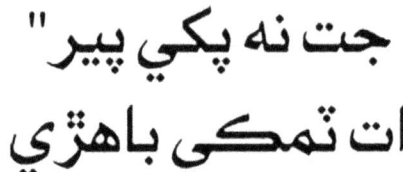

*Where even a bird can't set its foot
There flickers the fire of the divine*

Dr. Michel Boivin, French Sindhologist and scholar on Sufism, traces origins of Sufis in the Sindhu Valley from medieval times to after the Arab conquest between the eighth and twelfth centuries AD. Boivin claims that Sufism started in Sindh in the ninth century AD and rose to prominence in the tenth century. Ismaili missionaries also came to Sindh in the ninth century to spread the message of their Fatimid Imam from Cairo. They converted Hindus to Ismailis.

In 1843, the Imam of Ismaili, Hassan Ali Shah, Aga Khan I, emigrated from Iran to Sindh. Jhirk, a small town north of Karachi, became a major center for the Ismaili community. According

---

[75] Motilal Wadhumal Jotwani, *The Sindhi Through the Centuries* (Aditya Prakashan, 2006).

to highly reliable sources, this was the birthplace of Pakistan's founder, Muhammad Ali Jinnah, who was born an Ismaili.

Nooruddin Satgur was the first Ismaili missionary who wrote Ismaili prayers, or *ghinana*, in Sindhi. Ismaili Khojas are settled mainly in Lower Sindh, and they have shrines of Pir Amir and Pir Turel in Thatta and Badin (Boivin, 2015). Even long before these, a series of Sufis came and settled in Sindh, including some Ismailis. According to Dr. Ghulam Ali Allana, an original scholar on Sindh and its language, Qalandar Shahbaz was also an Isma'ili Sufi.

Quoting Dr. Ghulam Ali Allana, Michel Boivin writes:

> *Lal Shahbaz Qalandar was Pir Hasan Kabiruddin's son, making him an Ismaili. Allana also cites the ritual of dhikr as evidence of Sufism's origins in Iran. These were the times when great Sufi Mansur Al-Hallaj was also said to have visited Sindh in 896-97 CE. No wonder nineteenth century's great Sindhi Sufi and poet of seven languages, Sachal Sarmast, was influenced by the former.*[76]

Sachal Sarmast was called Mansur the Second because of open defiance of the authority of rigid mullahism and religious puritanism. In one of his most famous verses, he declares:

---

[76] Michel Boivin, *Historical Dictionary of the Sufi Culture of Sindh in Pakistan and India* (Oxford University Press, 2015).

مذهبن ملڪ ۾ ماڻهو منجهايا
ملن پنڊت شيخن بزرگن بيحد پلايا
ڪي نوڙي پڙهن نمازون
ڪن مندر وسايا
اوڏا ڪين آيا عقل وارا عشق ڪي
(سچل سرمست)

Religions, have the people confused, in many a countries
Mullahs, Pandits, Shaikhs, and those of knowledge,
have misguided countless souls
Some offer salah by bowing their heads in humility
Others establish temples
But the savvy ones, have never met love

Among his followers were people of all faiths, including Muslims, Hindus, and Sikhs. The burial grounds in the compound of his shrine include the graves and ashes of his disciples of all faiths. One of his most well-known disciples was Yousif, whom he had affectionately nicknamed Yousif Nanak, a name he is still known by because he had made multiple pilgrimages to the Golden Temple at Amritsar as a token of respect to Guru Nanak.

Boivin calls the spreading of Tasawwuf in the Sindhu Valley the "vernacularization of Tasawwuf." He termed Shah Abdul Latif as the Zenith of Sindhi Sufism, in old as well as modern times. Shah Latif Bhittai is considered the eternal poet of Sindh, as his message of universal love is not limited by the dimensions of time and space, as exemplified by one of his most famous verses.

سائينم سدائين كرين مٿي سنڌ سڪار
دوس مٺا دلدار عالم سڀ آباد كرين

O my Lord, shower abundance over Sindh
Sweet Beloved, may you prosper the whole universe

Shah Abdul Latif Bhittai was a universal Sufi. His collection of poetry called *Shah Jo Risalo* is considered by all Sindhis to be the ultimate culmination of universal love and harmony. In the words of Dr. Ernst Trumpp, a German missionary and the first scholar to translate *Shah Jo Risalo* and introduce Shah Abdul Latif to the world, "Sindh had been the first Indian Province that had succumbed to the fury of Muslim invaders. That is now a country without caste or Brahmans."[77] Shah Latif had been in the company of yogis with whom he undertook his arduous pilgrimages to Hinglaj and Lahore. He meditated with them for years.

---

[77] Ernst Trumpp, *Grammar of the Sindhi Language: Compared with the Sanskrit-Prakrit and the Cognate Indian Vernaculars* (Legare Street Press, 2023).

بک وڍائون بگرين جوڳي کندا جج
طلب نہ رکين طعام جي اوتيو پين اج
لاھوتي لطيف چئي، من ماري کيائون مچ
سامي جھاڳي سچ وسنئن کي ويجھا ٿيا

The yogis pack their bags with hunger And prepare themselves for Ananda
They desire not for the food
And lustily pour the thirst in their cups and sip it.
They flog their mind
Until they be like beaten flax.
Thus, they wade through the wasteland
And at last get close to the regeneration and fertility.[78]

Inayat Shaheed is considered the Crown Jewel of all Sufis in Sindh. Some call him a socialist Sufi because of his struggle to establish the concept of collective farming in Sindh, where he organized peasants against local feudal landlords and the clergy, much like during the French Revolution. His village, Jhok Sharif, became the epicenter of Sufi awareness against the puritanism of mullahs and oppression from feudal lords in Lower Sindh.

This infuriated the Mughal ruler of India, Farrukhsiyar. At the time, Sindh was ruled by the Kalhora dynasty. Kalhorans were subjugated by the Mughals and were obligated to share

---

[78] Jotwani, Trans. *Sufis of Sindh.*

a part of the taxes they collected with the Mughal emperor in Delhi. The emperor had his court mullahs pass a fatwa against Shah Inayat, citing him as a deviant from Islam, and used the fatwa to crush the peasant movement with brutal force. Shah Inayat, along with hundreds of his disciples, both Hindus and Muslim, were put to sword. Since then, his shrine has become a center of Sufi and Sindhi political pilgrimages. The annual congregations at his shrine on the eve of his Urs is the biggest example of Sindh's pluralism. At the shrine, Hindus and Muslims from all over the world, especially from Sindh, India, and the Far East, are seen shoulder to shoulder, regardless of religion, gender, or class. Sindhis of all faiths stand and sit in rows for prayers and meditative music in the compound.

Chainrai Sami is considered a proponent of the Bhakti movement in Sindh; he is a scion from an affluent Hindu family from Shikarpur. He became a disciple of swami Maharaj, from whom he learned Vedanta, originally in Sanskrit. Sami is one of the most prominent poets of Sindhi literature. He wrote poetry in Gurmukhi script and is said to have put his poetry in a clay jar to remain anonymous. According to Michel Boivin, the diction of Sami's poetry was different from other Sufi poems, as the metaphor of *ishq*, or love, was surprisingly missing from his poetry, an element that was conspicuous in works of other Sufi poets. Rather, Sami emphasized the *maya*, or illusion, of life and the world. However, his love for Lord Krishna was a central idea of his collection of Sindhi works titled *Sami Ja Salok*.

The shrines of Rama Pir, Pir Pithoro, Uderolal, Shah Inayat of Jhok, Sachal Sarmast, Shah Abdul Karim, and Karim's grandson, Shah Abdul Latif Bhittai, are all places of pilgrimage.

Indigenous Sindhi Hindus from Dravidian origins like Kohli, Bheel, Meghwal, Jogi, Shikari, and many other tribes congregate with Hindus of other castes and Sindhi Muslims.

The liberal ideas of Mahamati Prannath were an inspiration to Indian secularism. He was also born of a Sindhi mother. Mahamati Prannath authored *Shatritu & Sindhi Vani: Agony of Separation*. One of the greatest Sindhi Sufis of modern times, G. M. Syed, was the father of the Jeay Sindh Freedom Movement. A contemporary of Mahatma Gandhi, he, like the Mahatma, was a great believer of peaceful resistance.

In his masterpiece, *Paigham-e-Latif*, Syed's portrayal of the heroes, and especially heroines, originally described in Shah Latif's poetry gave birth to the modern Sindhi Sufi renaissance. He used these characters as symbols of Sindhi patriotism, humanism, love, tolerance for all, and pluralism. Through his published works and written speeches, Syed influenced and galvanized a whole generation of Sindhis to ignite a Sindhi nationalist movement. He had to spend most of his adult life, until his last breath, incarcerated by successive governments as a prisoner of conscience. He formed Bazm-e-Sufia-e-Sindh, an organization of the Sufis of Sindh, in 1966, but this was banned by the military regime under General Ayub Khan. G. M. Syed challenged the decision in court, but his petition was dismissed.

Prior to the ban, Syed aired his modern Sindhi Sufi thoughts by organizing gatherings, literary festivals, and literary congregations at the shrines of Sindhi saints and Sufi masters. He combined Sindhi Sufism and nationalism to introduce the concepts of the religion Sindhyat.

Syed described Sindhis as sharing the following common characteristics:

- *Attachment to social tradition and sense of social pride*
- *Loyalty*
- *Hospitality*
- *Nonviolence*
- *Love*
- *Altruism*
- *Patriotism*
- *Tolerance*
- *Sentiment for liberty*
- *Spirit of resistance*

Archaeological evidence from the excavation of Mohenjo-Daro and other sites of the Indus Valley Civilization, as old as 6,000 years, shows primitive artifacts suggestive of the beginnings of an organized religion. The leaves of the *peepal* (banyan) tree inscribed on the tablets recovered from the sites of Sindhu civilization and a deity similar to Lord Shiva suggest early Yogic and Yaksha cults.

The peepal tree is as essential as the bodhi tree in Buddhism. It is considered to have originated from the Mohenjo-Daro Civilization. It is believed the site of Mohenjo-Daro was visited by Buddha himself. Later, in memory of Buddha's visit, the great Buddhist King Ashoka ordered a stupa to be built over the ruins of this ancient city. As a matter of fact, this stupa was the first to be discovered by R. D. Banerji before his crew dug deeper to uncover the great archaeological metropolis underneath the stupa.

The Chinese Buddhist Mahayana traveler, Hsuan-tsang, while traveling to trace the origins of Buddhism in India also came to Sindh during the rule of King Raj Sahasi II in 650 CE. He mentioned in his travelogues that Sindh was a Buddhist country ruled by a Sudra King:

> *All the Gujarat-Rajasthan region had only a few or no Buddhists. But Sindh described as a land producing an abundance of wheat and millet, suitable for breeding of oxen, sheep, camel and other animals, and with men whose disposition is "hard and impulsive, but honest and upright," was a Buddhist country. The people study without aiming to excel; they have faith in the law of Buddha. There are several (monasteries) occupied by 10,000 priests.*

Historian Bherumal Advani, quoting the ancient book of the Jain religion, *Bharateshwar Bahubali Verti*, wrote about a king, named Udayin, who ruled Sindh. Among his sixteen provinces were Kutch, Kathiawar, and Sauvīra, and his capital was Vitabhaya Patan. The territories he ruled stretched over thousands of miles and consisted of 363 cities and towns with a population of 1,000,000 people. To keep his empire intact, he ruled through tyranny.

In the last days of his rule, Swami Mahavira came to Sindh. His sermons had such an influence over King Udayin that he renounced his throne and became ascetic. He gave the same advice to his son—never become king. Thus, his nephew Keshi Kumar took over the reign of his empire. Keshi Kumar's rule lasted for a decade and proved more oppressive. But his rule was brought to an end in 630 BCE by a devastating earthquake that destroyed most of the cities and towns, opening the doors to foreign invasions.

Bherumal Meharchand Advani has documented the presence of at least ten Buddhist stupas throughout Sindh, including those at Nagarparkar, Hala, Mīrpur Khās, and Larkana. So did modern-day Sindh historian and archaeologist Parveen Talpur, citing Chinese Mahayana traveler Hsuan-tsang, who visited Sindh in 642 CE:

> *When Tathāgata was in the world, he frequently passed through this country, therefore Asoka has founded tens of stupas in places where the sacred traces of his presence were found.*

In the words of the greatest Sindhi poet of modern times, Shaikh Ayaz:

اجان بہ ٽل تي هيا ٺکاٺا, اجان بہ ڪي سنک سار مرها
سڳي وڄي تي سنئين لڳين ڪي ٻہ چار يڪشو وهار مرها.

> *Yet there were rendezvous on the Stupa, yet there were some ashes in the memory*
> *Yet the conch shells being blown, yet there were some monks in yogic posture*

According to one of the most well-known Sindhi chronologists and scholars, M. H. Panhwar, "Long before, Buddha, Mahavira, the founder of Jainism, and his Swami Upagupta had visited Sindh. But Jainism could not flourish in Sindh, because of the rapid spread of Buddhism."[79]

Nevertheless, there were some Jain temples and pockets of Jain population in Tharparkar and Karachi. Bherumal Meharchand Advani was of the opinion that the Jain population consisted of immigrants to Sindh, while Buddhists were the indigenous Sindhis. British explorer Richard F. Burton believed that Sindhi mysticism originated from Zoroastrianism, and Sindh was one of the "fifteen good lands and countries" that Ahura Mazda created.

Although the Iranians had begun settling in Sindh during the second century CE, when Sindh was under the Sassanid kings, the major Iranian emigration to Sindh took place at the beginning of the seventh century CE. Iran came under the occupation and rule of Muslims in the thirteenth century CE; this led to the emigration of Zoroastrians, first to Khorasan and then into Gujarat and Sindh. According to G. M. Syed, "Jews and Zoroastrians were given asylum in Sindh."

Similarly, the scriptures of Judaism have never been new to Sindhi literati, as the Old Testament was first translated into Sindhi by Abhay Chand, one of the favorite pupils of the famous Armenian-Jewish Sufi, Sarmad. Calling Sindh the "beloved country of the God," Nicolas Notovitch, the author of the book *The Unknown Life of Jesus Christ*, states, "In the course

---

[79] Panhwar, *The Chronological Dictionary of Sindh.*

of his fourteenth year, young Issa journeyed beyond Sindh and settled among the Aryans and beloved country of the God."[80]

According to Notovitch's book, Jesus, with some traders from Jerusalem, traveled at a very young age to Sindh.

> *The fame of his name spread along Northern Sindh. When he passed through the country of the five rivers and Redjipoutan (Rājputana), the worshippers of the god Jain begged him to remain in their midst.*[81]

The authenticity of this account is questioned by many modern Christian scholars. But if true, the most probable major destination of his party would have been Shikarpur, which was the main trade center of the time, between Banaras and Jerusalem. It is believed that the traders in whose company Jesus came to Sindh were Sindhi Hindus, who have always been known for their global trading ties.

This could explain why Shikarpur was the first city in which a Sindhi Bible society was established in the nineteenth century and the first Sindhi version of the Bible was published. Jesus is said to have spent about six years in Sindh and the rest of the Indian subcontinent. According to Notovitch's book, "They

---

[80] Nicolas Notovitch, Trans. Alexina Lorianger. *The Unknown Life of Jesus Christ, by the Discoverer of the Manuscript.* Chicago: Indo-American Book Company, 1916.

[81] Notovitch, *The Unknown Life of Jesus Christ, by the Discoverer of the Manuscript.*

taught him to read and understand the Vedas, to heal by prayer, to teach and explain holy scriptures, to cast out evil spirits from the body of man, and to give him back his human semblance."[82]

Besides Sindh, Jesus spent some time in Rajgarh, Banaras, and other holy cities with Khatris and Sudras. The book also stated that:

> *It was then that Issa clandestinely left the father's house. He left Jerusalem, in the company of some traders. He travelled toward Sindh so that he might perfect himself in divine word and study the laws of the great Buddha.*

---

[82] Notovitch, *The Unknown Life of Jesus Christ, by the Discoverer of the Manuscript.*

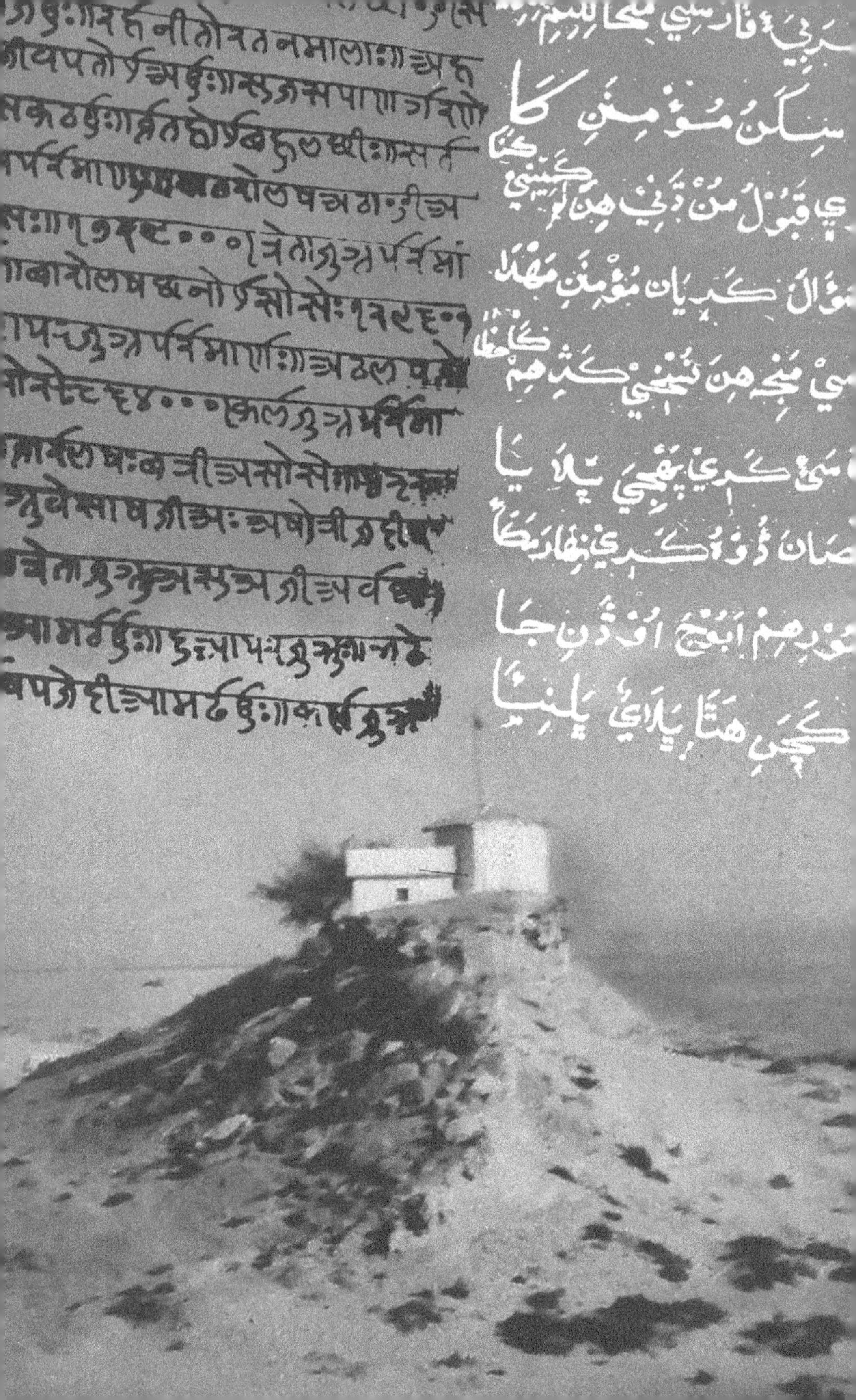

Reclaiming Sindh: History of Haakims, Native Sindhi Rulers

One of the biggest icons of the modern-day megalopolis of Karachi, the current capital of Sindh, is the mausoleum of Abdullah Shah Ghazi, which is perched on top of a hill overlooking Clifton Beach. According to local folklore, Abdullah Shah Ghazi is the saint who protects the city of Karachi and its inhabitants from the ocean. And as long as the mausoleum exists, Karachi will never be hit by a hurricane or a tsunami. But the real history is very different.

The man buried under the mausoleum was a descendent of Imam Husayn; he escaped from Baghdad and sought refuge in Sindh. The Umayyad chased and finally caught him. After his capture, he was executed and buried at his current resting place. Later, a mausoleum was built over his grave, and the site became a place of pilgrimage for Sindhis of all faiths.

Increased conflict within the Umayyad's rulers led to further weakening of its control over its peripheral territories, including Sindh. The local rulers were joined by rebel groups and warring tribes of Sindh, including nomadic Jat tribes who resisted the Arab governors and gave them hard times for twenty years. For the next hundred years, Sindh saw bad governance, breakdowns of law and order, and blood feuds among Arabs. In the last years of the Umayyad caliphate, the tenth governor of Sindh, Yazid Bin Umar, was assassinated by a rebel named Mansur al-Kalbi. Mansur al-Kalbi was a rebel against the khalifa of Damascus and had escaped to Sindh. Mansur al-Kalbi besieged the city, took Yazid bin Umar as prisoner, and reportedly buried him alive. Mansur al-Kalbi then declared himself the sovereign ruler of Sindh. Thus, the Umayyad rule that was established in 711 by the fall of King Dahir came to an end in 749 CE.[83] The new governor, Musa Ka'b al-Tamimi, was sent to Sindh with a strong contingent of army. Musa then chased Mansur al-Kalbi into Thar Desert, captured him, and beheaded him.[84]

In 792 CE, by the time Harun al-Rashid began his reign as the caliph of Baghdad, the tribal wars among Hijazi and Yamani rebels and rivals had intensified. The Abbasid rulers could not properly concentrate on administering Sindh. Their control over Sindh was reduced to a minimum.

The Habbari Dynasty

The year 854 CE was the beginning of a new period for Sindh. Umar ibn Abdul Aziz al-Habbari, a local Arab resident of Sindh,

---

[83] Panhwar, *The Chronological Dictionary of Sindh*.

[84] Lari, A *History of Sindh, 1994*.

became the governor of the easternmost province of the Abbasid caliphate. At the same time, the caliphate was in crisis due to internal rifts, which minimized its control over the peripheral territories.

Habbari, taking advantage of the situation, established his rule over Sindh with minimal interference from the caliphate and created a dynasty that ruled Sindh for the next two centuries; its capital was the city of Mansura. The Habbari called themselves Emirs of Sindh, but they continued to pledge allegiance to the Abbasid caliphs. The Sindhi language has the unique distinction of being the first language that the Holy Quran was translated into, which was done during the Habbari rule.

Soomra Dynasty in Sindh

Al Khafif was the last emir of the Habbari period and the founder of the Soomra dynasty, which continued its allegiance to the Abbasid caliphates until the bloody siege of Baghdad in 1258 by Mongols led by Hulagu Khan. Al Khafif was originally from Samarra, Iraq, and acquired the title Khafif Soomra. He ruled for fifteen years, from 1011 to 1026 CE. Some scholars, especially G. M. Syed and Bherumal Meharchand Advani, dispute this and believe that the Soomro were of Rajput Hindu origin.

The Soomra dynasty is described in Sindhi literature, both prose and poetry, as the best and worst of human qualities. Members of this dynasty have become mythical symbols of heroism and treachery, courage and cowardice, chivalry, and chauvinism. While Chanesar is despised for his cowardice and treachery, his younger brother Dodo Soomro and his sister Baghul Bai have become the ultimate symbols of Sindhi honor, chivalry, courage, and patriotism. Their names are used as common metaphors not only in Sindhi poetry and prose, but also by most Sindhis on a daily basis.

Most historians believe that the Soomra era in Sindh was a golden period for evolution of Sindhi language and literature. Sir Malcolm Robert Haig, in his famous book *The Indus Delta Country*, describes the beginning of the Soomra dynasty.

> *The first seat of Sumra power was the town of Thari. There is more than one place of this name in Lower Sindh, but the Sumra capital was most probably the Thari township on the right bank of western Puran, where the ruins of the old town still exist about six- and a-half miles from the present town of Mohabat Dero. In the India office copy of Mir Ma'sum's history, and also in the Sindhi version, Thari is one place described as "on the bank of the river," meaning, of course, Puran, and it may be that in early Sumra times, the river was still flowing.*[85]

Sindh under Sumros had trade links with countries as far as Egypt, which was at that timed ruled by Fatimid Ismailis. So Sumros were said to have embraced the Ismaili influence. The

---

[85] Malcolm Robert Haig, *The Indus Delta Country: A Memoir Chiefly on Its Ancient Geography, History, and Topography*, (Walton Press, 2010).

delta from Thatta to present-day Karachi was predominantly populated by Ismaili communities. G. M. Syed described the rule of Sumros as the golden age of Sindhi civilization, culture, and national autonomy. But Bherumal Meharchand Advani saw Sumro rulers as oppressors who were obsessed with luxuries. He claims that many indigenous tribes had to leave Sindh and settle in Kutch due to atrocities at the hands of Sumro rulers in Sindh.

According to Richard F. Burton, "Sumros were of unknown extraction, influential landholders who maintained their authority even when Mahmud Ghaznavi lost to the son of Ghori. Sumros exercised their authority and declared their rule as independents in many parts of Sindh, extending up to Kutch, spanning for sixty years."

The Soomra dynasty ruled Sindh for almost 400 years. Some of the most iconic characters of the history of Sindh belong to this era, including Dodo, Chanesar, and Baghul Bai Soomro, as well as the famous tale of Umar Soomro and Marvi, which was immortalized by the poetry of Shah Abdul Latif.

According to commonly narrated folklore, after the death of Khafif Soomra, his wazirs and the elders of the court elected Khafif's younger son, Dodo, to become the next emir. This was done because the crown prince and elder brother, Chanesar, was not considered fit to rule due to his debauchery and disinterest in the running of the state. This decision angered Chanesar, who sought help from Delhi's ruler, Alauddin Khalji, to overthrow his younger brother. It is said, among other concessions, Chanesar promised the hand of his sister Baghul Bai in marriage to Alauddin Khalji. Allauddin Khalji, leading his armies, stormed and encamped on the borders of the Soomra kingdom. He sent a message to Dodo Soomro, giving him the choice of abdicating his throne, giving his sister's hand in marriage, paying war expenses, or going to battle with the much larger army of Khilji.

Dodo convened a meeting of his wazirs, advisors, and elders of the court, and shared with them the demands of Alauddin Khalji. The overwhelming majority agreed with Dodo that the demands were unacceptable and against historical traditions of the nation. Thus, Dodo accepted Khalji's challenge to go to battle.

Baghul Bai, along with other womenfolk, were sent to Kutch under the shelter and protection of the neighboring king of Kutch, Abro. Dodo, along with his undermanned and underarmed army, fought valiantly to save Roopa Mari, which is near today's Badin. But he and all his top generals were killed. Shaikh Ayaz, in his epic ballad describing the martyrdom of Dodo Soomro, described the words of Baghul Bai after Dodo shared the demands of Khalji with her.

دودا تنھنجو ساھہ تہ ویندو ماٹھو جو ویساھہ نہ ویندو

"O, Doda, you will lose your life, but restore the faith of the people."

G. M. Syed termed Dodo Soomro the second-biggest Sindhi hero. Dodo's martyrdom at Dahir made him a core element of Sindhi nationalist ideology. Still today, almost a millennium after his death, traditional Sindhi folk singers, called *faqeers*, sing of the heroic bravery of Dodo Soomro. Dr. L. H. Ajwani, author of *History of Sindhi Literature*, views the Dodo-Khalji war story from a different angle.

> *During the reign of Chanesar II (AD 1283-1300), Allauddin Khalji, Sultan of Delhi (AD 1296-1316) sent his army into Sindh to evict the Mongols who had occupied Sehwan. The Delhi army also invaded Lower Sindh and Kutch and adjudicated between two warring factions of the Sumras. That gave birth to the ballads or folk lyrics of Dodo Chanesar, which, if genuine, contain the oldest extant verses in the Sindhi language.*[86]

The Sumra rule that was established in 1010 CE came to an end by the fall of the last Sumro King, Hamir, at the hands of the Sammas in 1352 CE.

The Sammas

The Sammas were an indigenous tribe of Sindh; because of their persecution during the Soomra dynasty, they fled and sought refuge with the rulers of Kutch. Besides taking them in by granting them asylum, the rulers of Kutch allotted them large tracts of land and other perks. Sammas are highly respected Sindhi tribes that live on both sides of the current

---

[86] L. H. Ajwani, *History of Sindhi Literature* (Sahitya Akademi, 1970).

Indian-Pakistani border. The most well-known Samma tribes are the Jarejas and Junejas. Some historians suggest that the Sammas betrayed the raja of Kutch and tricked him to deprive him of his throne.

In *Chach Nama*, the Sammas are mentioned as the members of the local population who went to greet Muhammad Bin Qasim soon after the fall of Debal. It is believed that the Sammas were also the first converts to Islam after the Arab conquest of Sindh.

The Sammas were of Rajput origin, as they hailed from the Lower Sindh. The earliest known Samma ruler was Lakho, son of Jakhro. He founded Samma rule in Kutch. His son, Unar, extended the rule over Sindh. He took on the title of Jam and was known as Jam Unar.

The famous North African traveler Ibn Battuta, in his travelogues, describes an incident that occurred when he reached present-day Sehwān. He narrates that, the day before his arrival, a local Hindu trader, who also was in charge of keeping the tax-collection accounts for the sultan of Delhi, was killed by a local bandit by the name of Unar. This prompted a swift response from the security forces of the sultan of Delhi, who hanged in the streets of Sehwān anyone they suspected of helping Unar. Ibn Battuta witnessed the hanging and promptly decided to move to his next destination.

Ibn Battuta traveled to Sindh in 1333 CE and chronicled the Samma rebellion against the sultanate of Delhi, which was ruled by the Tughlaq dynasty at that time, with Jam Unar as the chief of the Samma tribe. Battuta took advantage of the feud between

Soomro rulers of Sindh and the sultan of Delhi. He started a revolt against the Soomros, defeated them, and established his own rule, which ushered in the Samma dynasty.

After Jam Unar, Sindh again came under the direct rule of Delhi. Tamachi, son of Jam Unar, assumed the title of Jam in honor of his elder brother. This was the same Jam Tamachi who later became the main character of one of the most frequently retold romantic folktales of Sindhi, "Noori Jam Tamachi." Soon after becoming the Jam, he and his family were taken prisoner and forced to live in exile in Delhi for many years. However, the people of Sindh continued to be loyal to the Samma rulers.

This epic love story "Noori Jam Tamachi" is about the love of a prince for a common fisherwoman, Noori, and how she won his heart by her humility and the purity of her soul. This famous tale was forever immortalized by Shah Abdul Latif, who devoted a whole chapter in his *Shah Jo Risalo* to describing their tale of love on the banks of Keenjhar Lake.

Khairuddin, son of Jam Tamachi, who, as a child, along with his father and the rest of his family, had been forced to live in exile in Delhi, was eventually allowed to return to Sindh after his father died in captivity. On his return, he took over the helm of affairs and became the second Jam of the Samma dynasty. Later, Babinah, the younger brother of Jam Tamachi, took over as their tribal chief, but he never acquired the title of Jam.

Sindh at that time was a battleground between the Tughlaq rulers of Delhi and the Turkic groups from the northwest, including those led by Timur (Tamerlane), who sacked Delhi in

1398. Muhammad bin Tughlaq invaded Sindh in 1351 CE. Historians differ on the reason for this invasion. Some claim that the purpose was to restore the Soomra dynasty, while others claim that Sultan Muhammad Tughlaq came to Sindh in pursuit of a rebel named Taghi but died during the expedition.

It is said that Muhammad bin Tughlaq expressed the desire to meet Jam Khairuddin. But the Jam, having remained the sultan's prisoner, refused to do so. This infuriated the sultan, who then decided to attack Sindh, but he died before a battle could ensue.

After Muhammad Tughlaq's death, his nephew, Firuz Shah Tughlaq, took over the reins. He buried the body of Muhammad Tughlaq in Sehwān, close to the mausoleum of Shahbaz Qalandar. This remained a conspicuous monument in the city until 1967, when the government of Pakistan bulldozed it.

The Samma rule that was founded in 1351 ended in 1520 CE. It lasted for about one and a half centuries, during which there were a total of fifteen Samma rulers over Sindh. Many of their descendants, still today, very proudly continue to use titles such as Jam, Jakhra, Unar, etc. Jam Nizamuddin and his commander-in-chief, Dollah Darya Khan, are revered as national heroes of Sindh. Like their predecessors, these Samma rulers employed and maintained only indigenous Sindhis in their army and administration.

Jam Nizamuddin was the most well-known Jam of the Samma dynasty; the territories he ruled consisted of modern-day Sindh, southern Punjab, and parts of Balochistan. He was fondly called Jam Nindo by his subjects. The Samma dynasty reached the peak of its power under his rule, which is recalled as one of the golden ages of Sindh. He and his legendary commander-in-chief are known as scholars and gentlemen who ruled with absolute power. His rule lasted longer than that of any other Samma ruler.

Darya Khan's original name was Mubarak Khan Qaboolio. According to G. M. Syed, Darya Khan hailed from the Lashari tribe. Immediately after taking over the reins, he had to go to battle, in Bhakkar, against dacoits and rogue tribesmen who had been looting the innocent people of the area. This campaign lasted for a year. But after defeating these rogue elements, he is said to have ruled for almost half a century in peace and prosperity.

In 1490, North Sindh was invaded by a Kandahar army led by Shah Beg Arghun. Jam Nindo responded by sending a large contingent under the command of his trusted general, Dollah Darya Khan. The Sindhi army thoroughly defeated the invaders near present-day Sibi. Shah Beg's brother, Abu Muhammad Mirza, was among those killed on the side of the invaders, after which they were forced to retreat back to Kandahar.

During Jam Nizamuddin's rule, many Sufis from the Middle East and India came to take refuge at Thatta. Under his rule, Thatta became one of the greatest centers of learning and scholarship, akin to those in Samarkand, Bukhara, Cairo, Damascus, and Baghdad.

Jam Nizamuddin died in 1508 CE. This proved to be the beginning of the end of Samma rule and the start of a long period of crises for Sindh. His death resulted in a tug-of-war for power between his son Jam Firuz and a cousin, Jam Salahuddin.

Jam Firuz was the last ruler of the Samma era. He became a ruler at an early age. Though he was officially the sultan, most control of the government was taken over by his father's trusted vazīr and commander-in-chief, Dollah Darya Khan. Jam Firuz spent most of his time in his harem and seldom went to his court out of fear that he would be killed by Darya Khan. In order to counter the influence of Darya Khan, Jam Firuz joined forces with his father's staunch enemies, namely the Arghuns. He appointed Kibak Arghun as his advisor and settled a large number of Mughal soldiers in Thatta to try to increase his power.

Unfortunately, this shortsighted policy was the cause of his eventual downfall, as these same people induced Shah Beg Arghun to invade Sindh again in 1519 CE. Shah Beg Arghun, this time, was able to conquer Sindh, bringing an end to the Samma dynasty.

Jam Nizamuddin and his commander-in-chief, Dollah Darya Khan, were said to be highly influenced by a great Sindhi scholar and saint, Makhdoom Bilawal, who is one of the most revered national martyrs in the history of Sindh. "The popular belief in Sindh is that he was ordered to be crushed alive in an oil press, after the Battle of Talti, for opposing the conquest of Sindh by the Arghuns. This legend, however, does not receive confirmation from any of the known historians of Sindh."[87]

---

[87] Lari, *The History of Sindh*.

Makhdoom Bilawal was a cousin of Jam Nizamuddin. He was also the spiritual leader of Hyder Shah Sannai, great-great-grandfather of G. M. Syed at San. Over the next decades, Makhdoom Bilawal put up great resistance to the Arghuns' invasion of Sindh. He and his followers opposed the foreign usurpers tooth and nail. He led a stiff opposition by declaring the Arghuns cruel tyrants.[88] In Sindhi literature, both prose and poetry, and in the minds of most Sindhis, he is revered and sung about as one of the greatest Sufis, heroes, and martyrs of Sindh. Sindhi poet Khaki Joyo pays tribute to Makhdoom Bilawal in the following words:

مون جنگ وطن لاء جوڻي آ مخدوم بلاول موڻي آ
کا ويرين سان ويڙهاند ڪيون
تو رها تڪي پيو پيو يت ڏٽي

I have waged a war for the motherland
Come back, Makhdoom Bilawal,
Let us fight our war against the enemies of our land
The lord of Bhit is waiting for us

Arghuns and Tarkhans

During Jam Nizamuddin's reign, invaders from Central Asia increased their advances on Sindh, but were forced to retreat by Sindh's army under Darya Khan. Arghun armies set on fire Thatta City, and Darya Khan was captured after a pitched

---

[88] Michel Boivin, *Sindh Through History and Representations: French Contributions to Sindhi Studies* (Oxford University Press, 2007).

battle. He was said to be killed by a sword at the hand of Shah Beg Arghun himself. After his death, however, Darya Khan's successor, Jam Firuz, was unable to maintain control, and Jam Firuz's wrong decisions resulted in Thatta being conquered by Shah Beg Arghun.

Many historians believe Darya Khan is buried in his native village. But others believe he is buried at Makli Necropolis. Modern-day Sindhi historian Ghulam Muhammad Lakho quoted Sada Rangani on the state and structure of the tomb supposed to be Darya Khan's. "He is buried on Makli Hill in a stately tomb. Which is supposed to possess the peculiar merit of fulfilling the desires of the people who walk around it seven times."

After Darya Khan's death, Sindh again came under foreign rule for the next 200 years. After the fall of Thatta and the defeat of the Samma rulers, the plunder, looting, and arson of the city continued for ten days. Thousands of Thatta inhabitants fled to Kutch and Gujarat to escape death by starvation and revenge. Shah Beg Arghun ordered the whole city to be completely burned to ashes, destroying hundreds of thousands of unique books and manuscripts, very much in line with the burning of Baghdad by the Mongols.

The historical city of Thatta has similarly been destroyed three times throughout its long history. First, by Shah Beg Arghun. A second time when Mirza Isa Khan Tarkhan engaged in war with Shah Beg Arghun and sought help from a Portuguese naval ship anchored on the Sindhu delta. The Portuguese, led by Pedro Barreto Rolim, carried out the grandest plunder and arson. According to the *Gazetteer* of Sindh, "Then, the plundering and arson on such a scale was unprecedented in the Asian continent."

Thomas Postans writes in his *Personal Observations on Sindh*:

> *Mirza Isa Khan Tarkhan engaged Portuguese mercenaries to assist him, who, during his absence from Thatta, fired and pillaged the city. This is the only mention made of these, the first European conquerors of India, as seeking this degrading employment under native power. This state of things continued in Sindh until the year 999 Hijri, the Islamic calendar (AD 1590).*[89]

Akbar, the most illustrious emperor in the history of the Indian subcontinent, put a stop to the internal wars and disputes between his governors by subjugating the whole of Sindh under Khan Khanan and annexing it to the throne of Delhi. Thatta was burned and plundered a third time under the order of Isa Khan Tarkhan in order to preempt Akbar's invasion.

Akbar was born near Amarkot in Sindh. His father, Humayun, was defeated by Sher Shah Suri and driven out of India. Humayun had to take refuge first in Rajasthan and later with Ranas of Amarkot. Until 1736 CE when Kalhorans took over control of Sindh, Arghuns, Tarkhans, and Mughals continued to plunder Sindh under the direct and indirect governance of their deputies.

---

[89] Thomas Postans, *Personal Observations on Sindh* (Legare Street Press, 2023).

Kalhoras

Kalhoras ruled at the mercy of Persian and Afghan kings and usurpers like Nader Shah, Ahmad Shah Abdali, and Madad Khan Pathan. The two most well-known Kalhora rulers were Noor Muhammad Kalhoro and Ghulam Shah Kalhoro. It was during the rule of Ghulam Shah Kalhoro that Sindhi poetry reached its zenith in the form of Shah Abdul Latif Bhittai, considered by most Sindhis to be the greatest poet mankind has ever seen. Other great poets of the time include Shah Inayat, who was followed a little later by Sachal Sarmast.

The Kalhora rulers claimed to be descendants of Abbās, the uncle of the prophet Muhammad; their genealogy is said to go back to their great-grandfather Odhana, whose origins trace back to Makran. Adam Shah Kalhoro was buried on a hill near Khairpur Mirs; he was known as Adam Shah Ji Takri and highly popular among his followers. His popularity created jealousy among his local rivals, inducing them to complain to the Mughal rulers of Delhi. Adam Shah Kalhoro was arrested, jailed, and tortured to death. But during his incarceration, his jailer also became his disciple; it was he who buried the shah on a hill as a mark of high honor.

Yar Muhammad Kalhora won the favor of Mughal Prince Moizuddin, grandson of Emperor Aurangzeb. Yar Muhammad Kalhora was appointed governor of Sibi and was given the title of Khudayar Khan. Yar Muhammad Kalhora established the Kalhora dynasty in Central Sindh, its seat of power at Khudabad near Dadu. He died in 1718.

The tragedy of Jhok, which included the martyrdom of Shah Inayat and his fakirs, took place during the rule of Mian Yar Muhammad Kalhoro. Yar Muhammad Kalhoro was succeeded by his son, Noor Muhammad Kalhoro, who declared his loyalty to the Mughal Empire of Delhi. In return, he was appointed as *subahdar* (governor) of Sehwān and Bhakkar.

In 1731, the Brahuis of Kalat invaded Sindh but were defeated by Mian Noor Muhammad Kalhoro. Noor Muhammad Kalhoro captured the city of Shikarpur from the Daudpotas, thus consolidating his rule over most of Sindh.

In 1736, the Safavid Empire in Persia came to an end, and Nader Shah declared himself the shah of Iran. Nader Shah invaded India a year later and annexed Sindh. Noor Muhammad Kalhoro fled to Thar in the hopes that the desert of Sindh would prove to be inaccessible by the Persian king and his army. But Nader Shah's guards caught up with Noor Muhammad Kalhoro in Amarkot before he could escape into the desert. He was captured and brought before Nader Shah, who spared his life in exchange for 1,000,000 rupees. Nader Shah also kept two of Noor Muhammad Kalhoro's sons as ransom until the payment was made.

Noor Muhammad Kalhoro, in turn, increased taxes on the population and encouraged the slave market to raise the necessary funds to pay off Nader Shah and save the lives of his sons. Nader Shah was assassinated in 1747 CE. Ahmad Shah Abdali, leading his strong army of Central Asian descent, raided Persia and plundered what the former had looted from India. Ahmad Shah Abdali invaded Sindh and captured the Kalhoro capital town Mohammadabad, which forced Noor Muhammad Kalhoro to flee once more to the desert.

Diwan Gidumal succeeded in persuading the Afghan king to pardon Kalhoro. But Noor Muhammad, meanwhile, died in Jaisalmer. Ahmad Shah Abdali appointed Muradyab Khan, the eldest son of Mian Noor Muhammad Kalhoro, as the new ruler, bestowing on him the title of Sarbuland Khan. This left Muradyab Khan with the obligation of having to pay exorbitant taxes to the Afghan king. Unable to meet the demands, he tried to flee to Muscat.

On suspecting his intentions, other Kalhora emirs foiled his plans, arrested him, gave the throne to his brother, Ghulam Shah, and angered Afghanistan. Ghulam Shah had to retreat to Udaipur, and then Bahawalpur, to reinforce his army and fight against the invading Afghans. He later recaptured Sindh with the support of his new, loyal army, which resulted in forcing the Afghan king to negotiate with him. He was bestowed the title of Shah Wardi Khan and later sent by the Afghan king to quell the rebellions of Dera Ghazi Khan and Dera Ismail Khan on separate occasions.

Mian Ghulam Shah Kalhoro was the architect of the current city of Hyderabad. Diwan Gidumal supervised and managed the construction of the new city. He brought chief mason Muhammad Shafi from Multan, with his artisans, who built the historical Pucca and Katcha Qilas (fortresses) on the hills of Hyderabad. These, unfortunately, are on the brink of collapse due to the utter neglect of subsequent governments over the last many decades. The old city was called

Nerun Kot. Ghulam Shah Kalhoro built the new city as his capital and named it Hyderabad.

> *Kalhoras also built Shikarpur City in the times of Noor Muhammad Kalhora that was taken away by Afghan King Ahmad Shah Abdali. Abdali annexed Shikarpur to Sibi. Hindus, Afghans, and Pathans came and settled in the city during Kalhoras with an Afghan as governor of Shikarpur.*[90]

According to Bherumal Meharchand Advani's account, "Shikarpur in fact was *shikargah* (hunting ground) of Daudpotas. Daudpotas defeated Mahars of Lakhs. To celebrate their victory, they built the new city of Shikarpur."

Shikarpur rose to become one of the most significant trade centers of the region, which included Bukhara, Peshawar, and Kabul. By the eighteenth century, Hindu Sindhi traders had established multiple trade offices in Qandahar during the Kalhora period. Ghulam Shah Kalhoro died suddenly in 1771 CE and was buried in Hyderabad. Mian Ghulam Shah Kalhoro is considered one of the greatest Sindhi kings; he is credited with unifying Sindh and with being the architect of the city of Hyderabad,. After the death of Ghulam Shah Kalhoro, his son, Mian Sarfaraz Kalhoro, succeeded to the throne. He was the last ruler of the Kalhora dynasty.

---

[90] Bherumal Advani, *Sindh Je Hindu Ji Tarekh (History of Hindus in Sindh)*. Bombay: Shardha Prakashan, 1991.

Talpurs

It is said that Mian Sarfaraz Khan Kalhoro, sensing a revolt against him, had his commander-in-chief, Bahram Khan Talpur, and his son, Sobdar Khan, killed. In retaliation for these acts, Sarfaraz Khan Kalhoro was deposed, arrested by the Talpurs, and replaced by his brother, Mian Ghulam Nabi, as the new ruler in the Kalhora dynasty. When Mir Behram Khan was murdered with one of his sons, his other son, Behram Khan, was on a pilgrimage, or *hajj*. On his return, the battles between the Kalhora king and the Talpur chiefs ensued, which led to the killing of Mian Ghulam Nabi in the battlefield. Abdullah Khan, the son of slain Mir Bijar Khan, became the new ruler of Sindh. According to historian Suhail Zaheer Lari, "The infighting between the Kalhoras and Talpurs, combined with attempts by Afghan kings to extract as much money as possible from contending parties, led to the end of the era of prosperity in Sindh."[91]

In the final round of war between the Kalhoras and the Talpurs, the Talpurs, led by Mir Fateh Ali Khan, were victorious. Afghan King Timur Shah issued *sanad* in favor of the Talpurs. On the death of Afghan King Timur Shah, his son, Zaman Shah, took over the throne of the Afghan kingdom. In 1793 AD, Zaman Shah renewed the *Sanad* for the ruling of Sindh by Mir Fateh Ali Khan. Mir Fateh Ali Khan divided the ruling of Sindh into seven parts. He gave Khairpur to his uncle Mir Sohrab Khan. And to his cousin, Mir Tharo Khan, he assigned Mīrpur Khās. Mir Fateh Ali Khan and his brothers Ghulam Ali, Karam

---

[91] Lari, *A History of Sindh*.

Ali, and Murad Ali retained vast rule over Hyderabad—called then Choyari, or Kingdom of the Four Rulers.

Mir Fateh Ali Khan died in 1801 CE. He was succeeded by his brother, Mir Ghulam Ali Khan, who was killed by a deer hog while hunting. Mir Karam Ali Khan succeeded Mir Ghulam Ali Khan. Mir Karam Ali Khan did not have any biological children, so he adopted two sons. They were reportedly orphans of the Georgian-Persian war and named Mirza Khusro Beg and Mirza Sydney Beg. Mirza Sydney Beg became a close aide of Mir Karam Ali Talpur in affairs of his governance and court, as well as in palatial matters.

The British Raj

*Sindh has now gone, since the English have
seen the river, which is road to its conquest.*
~A faqeer on seeing James Burns in 1830

The urban legend for a long time was that after conquering Sindh, Charles Napier, the general leading the British forces, sent a one-word telegram to his boss, Lord Ellenborough. The telegram reportedly said, "PECCA-VI." Decoded, it was supposed to mean, "I have Scinde." It was thought to be a pun whereby Napier was conveying to his boss that he had conquered Sindh. Or it could be that what he really meant was that he had sinned by taking over territory to which the British had no claim.

However, the current consensus is that there was no such telegram. But irrespective of whether or not the telegram was sent, most scholars consider the British conquest of Sindh to be one of the greatest sins committed by the British colonizers.

Charles Napier became a household name overnight. He reportedly was rewarded with 70,000 British pounds and was knighted three years later, thus becoming Sir Charles Napier. However, he stepped down after he developed differences with Lord Dalhousie, the governor-general of India.

Wendy Doniger describes Charles Napier's conquest of Sindh in her book, *The Hindus: An Alternative History*: "In 1843, Napier maneuvered to provoke a resistance that he then crushed and used as pretext to conquer the territory for the British empire."[92]

As portrayed in a play published in 1852: "What exclaim, the gallant Napier proudly flourishing his rapier! To the army and the navy, where he conquered Sindh."[93]

The first Europeans to reach Sindh were the Portuguese and Dutch, which prompted Shah Abdul Latif to warn the fisherman of Sindh in the eighteenth century:

معلم ماڳ نه اڳئين قلنگي منجهه قريا
ملاح تنهنجي مڪڙي اچي چور چڙهيا

Navigator has no knowledge of the foreigners ahead
O' Fisherman, the thieves are about to attack your boat

The first contact of the British-Indian administration with Sindh was in the days of Kalhora ruler Ghulam Shah Kalhoro in 1758.

---

[92] Wendy Doniger, *The Hindus: An Alternative History* (Penguin, 2010).

[93] *The Nation's Weekly* Vol. 96 (January 1913): 595.

He signed a treaty with the East India Company, granting permission to open up a factory in Thatta. The treaty became unenforceable when Sarfaraz Kalhoro succeeded Ghulam Shah.

Later, during the Talpur dynasty, when the Talpur ruler Mir Murad Ali Khan fell sick, the governor-general of India was contacted to send a physician to treat him. The British demanded a treaty between the government of British India and Talpur rulers of Sindh before they would send a medical team via the naval route to Hyderabad. The Talpurs had no other choice but to agree to the demands of the British in order to save the life of their emir. He was suffering from malaria, and the British were the only ones with the newly discovered cure for it.

Dr. James Burns, with a medical team, was dispatched to treat the emir of Sindh. The country was under an epidemic of malaria, and the medicine that cured the Talpur king and a number of his subjects was seen as a miracle cure. Overnight, Dr. James Burns became a living legend in Sindh.

> *It was on the evening of the 8th, that I arrived at Bunna, and saw for the first time the River Indus. In my impatience to view this famous classic stream, I had become so excited that I left all of my luggage behind, and riding nearly forty miles during the day, reached its bank at sunset, quite exhausted and fatigued. The feeling with which my curiosity was at length gratified, I will not attempt to describe; but I question whether my Hindoo attendants, who began to mutter their prayers to the river as an object of adoration, and who considered immersion in its sacred*

> *waters a nearer step to everlasting bliss, felt a stronger or more overpowering emotion than I did, in contemplating the scene of Alexander's glories. Never before than had the worship of water, or water gods, appeared to me so excusable, as on observing the blessings diffused everywhere by this mighty and beneficent stream.*[94]

It is said that on seeing a Britisher along the River Indus, a faqeer said, "Since now an Englishman has seen the river, there will be no peace." The saying in Sindh: "The British rulers begin with friendship and end with enmity."

By the beginning of the nineteenth century, the British Empire had already decided to invade Sindh to counter the competing economic and political powers, including France and Czarist Russia. It was imperative that the British gain control of the coastal areas of Sindh in order to create access for their troops to Afghanistan.

According to Richard F. Burton, "In 1809, the views of Napoleon upon our Indian Empire rendered it necessary to send the embassies to the crowned heads of Persia, Kabul, and Sindh."[95]

---

[94] James Burnes, *A Narrative of a Visit to the Court of Sinde: A Sketch of the History of Cutch, From Its First Connexion With the British Government in India Till the…Remarks on the Medical Topography of Bhooj* (Palala Press, 2016).

[95] Richard F. Burton, *Sindh and the Races That Inhabit the Valley of the Indus* (Oxford University Press, 1973) p. 27.

In 1830, Alexander Burns surveyed the River Indus. He was a brother of Dr. James Burns, who had successfully treated the Talpur ruler of Sindh for malaria. With the growing threat of the rising power of Sikhs in Punjab, under their dynamic leader Ranjit Singh, the Talpurs of Sindh feared being attacked by the Sikhs. Thus, they were cornered into signing a treaty with the British.

This treaty between Colonel Pottinger of the British and the Talpurs allowed permanent deputation of British soldiers, in addition to army and civilian officers in Sindh. It also allowed for an unhindered supply of fuel, weaponry, and other supplies to the British steamers in the cities of Sukkur, Bhakkar, Thatta, and Hyderabad. Prior to that, an existing treaty had given the East India Company exclusive trading rights on the River Indus, specifically excluding the French, but no arms or ammunition was to be ferried within the boundaries of Sindh by English representatives.

Major Outram and Charles Napier were posted as residents in Sindh. According to accounts mentioned in *History of Modern India*, "Pottinger forced the ameers of Sindh to pay Rs: 25,000,000 as arrears in tributes to Shah Shuja. He also asked them to pay Rs 300,000/yearly for British forces to establish their residents at Bhakkar and Shikarpur in the Sindh."[96]

It is clear from the now-declassified Dalhousie reports, originally prepared in 1830, that the British had devised expansionist plans for Sindh more than a decade before it actually occurred.

---

[96] Bipin Chandra, *History of Modern India* (Orient Blackswan Pvt. Ltd., 2020).

By far the greater portion of Sindh is a level country whose rich soil, and the wonderful facility of irrigation which the Indus affords, would be equal in value to gold. A great part of the country is taken up by the Shikargah, other parts are covered with Tamarisk and Babul Jungle, one-fourth of the country is cultivated. On the left bank of the Indus, the only irregularities that occurred between Khyrpoor and Kotri are two low ranges of hills, one extending from Ruree southward beyond Khunderah and the other called Gunja Jabool near Hyderabad, which extends as far as Takoor, a few miles near Hyderabad. Besides these, there is low range (on which the Fort and City of Hyderabad are situated), which is about two miles in extent. The country on the west of the Indus or right bank is more irregular, particularly from the Swan Southwards, as far as Jhirk. It appears from all accounts to be an unproductive wasteland, except in the immediate vicinity of the river. In the country north of Sehwān are the rich districts of Larkana and Shikarpur, which are by far the most fertile spots in Sindh. Shikarpur is said to yield a yearly revenue of five lakhs of rupees, of which one-third goes to Mir Murad Ali Khan and the remaining two are divided between the members of the Khyrpoor family.[97]

---

[97] Matthew A. Cook, Ed., *Observing Sindh: Selected Reports* (Oxford University Press USA, 2008) p. 17.

In his laboriously edited book, *Observing Sindh*, Matthew A. Cook gave his findings.

> *Pottinger's 1832 negotiations not only sought to bring Sindh's neighbors into treaty agreements, they also included Talpur's principality under the control of Hyderabad's chief, Mir Murad Ali Khan, on 4 April 1832, with Mir Rustam Khan, the Talpur ruler of Khairpur, which contained much of the same language, not many of the same clauses, as the one concluded with Mir Murad Ali Khan. For example, the article four promises that "traders shall suffer no let or hindrance in the transacting." Article three opens the Indus to free travel (as long as Talpurs of Hyderabad agree to this policy). It, like the treaty with Hyderabad, also opens the road to free.*[98]

Karl Marx, analyzing the rapidly changing political economy of the European empires of the times, commented, "Traders of India turned into servile tools at the hands of British despotism."

According to Manan Ahmed Asif, "Sindh had a long gestation in the company's imagination; some of the company's earliest concerns were with competition from Sindhi as well as Portuguese and Dutch merchants."[99]

---

[98] Cook, *Observing Sindh: Selected Reports*.

[99] Manan Ahmed Asif, *A Book of Conquest: The Chachnama and Muslim Origins in South Asia* (Harvard University Press, 2016).

In the famous words of Charles Napier, "We have no right to seize Sindh, yet we shall do so, and a very advantageous, humane, and useful piece of rascality it will be."[100]

He seized Sindh on February 17, 1843. Fear ran across Hyderabad and neighboring towns and villages. On the second day of the fall of Hyderabad, his troops a Bengal regiment, Napier entered Pucca Qila, the fortress that served as the capital and living quarters of the ruling family. Mir Muhammad Khan and Mir Sobdar were taken as prisoners without any resistance. The Union Jack was hoisted for the first time on the highest tower of Pucca Qila.

Mir Sher Muhammad Khan was the only one of the Talpurs who resisted. He continued to reinforce his troops for future battles. He later gained the title of Lion of Mīrpur Khās for his bravery and courage.

---

[100] Muhammad Qasim Soomro, Ghulāmu Muḥammadu Lākho, Eds., *Sindh, Glimpses into Modern History: Proceedings of PHIRC on the History of Sindh, 1843-1999* (Department of General History, Faculty of Social Sciences, University of Sindh, 2008).

Charles Napier was appointed the new military governor of Sindh. He initially established his office in Hyderabad, but later moved to Karachi. As historian Manan Ahmed comments, "Napier saw the liberation of Sindh from its despotic Muslim rulers as his Christian duty. With added benefit that achieving his goal would demonstrate his brilliance as a tactical commander."

In his own words, Napier said:

> *I made up my mind that although war had not been declared (nor was it necessary to declare it), I would at once march upon Imamgarh and to prove to the whole Talpur family of both Khyrpoor and Hyderabad that neither their deserts nor their negotiations can protect them from the British troops. The ameers will fly over the Indus, and we shall become masters of the left bank of the river from Mitenkote to the mouth, peace with civilization will then replace war and barbarism. My conscience will be light, for I see no wrong in so regulating a set of tyrants who are themselves invaders and have in sixty years destroyed the country. The people hate them.*[101]

Among those tribes who fought valiantly to try to save their motherland were the Nizamanis, Kathians (Pathans), Changs, Chhilagris, Rind Lagharis, Thorhas, Soomra, Khokhars, Hindus, and Syeds. According to local folklore, one of the most famous heroes of the battle was Hosh Muhammad Sheedi, who has since been immortalized by his forever-famous cry to battle:

---

[101] Asif, *A Book of Conquest: The Chachnama and Muslim Origins in South Asia.*

مرسون مرسون سنڌ نه ڏيسون

We will die again and again, but not give up Sindh.

Quoting Napier, Qadir Nizamani writes:

Mirs were sitting at home while Sheedis were fighting in the battlefield. An elegant sword was discovered in the field that was probably of Nadir Shah lying beside a fallen Sheedi soldier.[102]

Quoting the British, Nizamani writes:

About 10,000 brave men had gathered to fight against British, the night before the battle. But most of them returned home, after being disappointed by seeing the lack of interest in fighting against the invaders, on the part of the ruling elites. Later they joined forces with Mir Sher Muhammad, known as Lion of Sindh, to fight against the British invaders, at the Battle of Dubbo.[103]

Another war fought between Talpurs and Napier was Miani. The British did not fight any battles against the Talpur rulers of Khairpur; instead, the British allowed them to maintain a semi-autonomous status under British rule in return for cooperation with the invading British Army.

---

[102] Qadir Bux Nizamani, *Jang-e-Miani* (Baloch Adabi Society, 1947) 8.

[103] Nizamani, *Jang-e-Miani*.

Sindh was the last state in the Indian subcontinent to come under British rule. Before that, Sindh had existed as a sovereign country. After the British conquest, the *riasat* (princely state) of Khairpur was allowed to continue its semi-independent status. The rest of Sindh was annexed to an administrative division of the British province of Bombay, the rapidly developing port city of Karachi its new divisional headquarters.

A building boom began in the previously sleepy fishing village, till then known as Kolachi. Among the many newly built palatial government residences was a commissioner's house, the residential quarters of the newly appointed British commissioner of Sindh. This building now serves as the governor's house for the governor of Sindh and is still one of the most iconic buildings of the city of Karachi. The ruling Talpur ameers of Sindh were taken into custody and initially moved to Bombay and then later to Calcutta.

> *The fallen ameers, cousins of Mir Nasir Khan, and his nephew Shahdad and Hosain Ali, with Mir Mohammed, and Sobdar of Hyderabad, Mir Rustam Khan, and his nephew Nasir Khan and Wali Mohammed of Khairpur, with others were sent in captivity to Bombay, whence, in 1844, they were removed to Bengal, where a few of them still exist in a kind of state prison, the melancholy spectacle of fallen greatness.*[104]

---

[104] Burton, *Sindh and the Races That Inhabit the Valley of the Indus*.

In May 1843, Charles James Napier issued a *firman* (proclamation) to all feudal lords and tribal leaders of Sindh, whereby any landlord or tribal chief with 2,000 or more men at his disposal was given the option to either pledge their allegiance to the court or lose their estates. The meeting was convened at the historic Darbar Hall of Hyderabad.

In 1850, Charles Napier's conquest of Sindh and his overall conduct came under heavy scrutiny. Famously known as the Sindh Question, this scrutiny was brought not by his Sindhi victims, but instead by his fellow British officers, specifically Major James Outram and Captain Eastwick. James Outram, who had served as a political agent in Sindh before the Miani Battle, warned Napier "that every life that might hereafter be lost, in consequence, will be a murder."

Likewise, Captain Eastwick, who had served under Outram and was fully conversant with the local culture and language, vehemently differed with Charles Napier and his conduct in Sindh. Matthew Cook writes, "Eastwick argued that actions of Napier's in Sindh were reckless."[105]

---

[105] Cook, *Observing Sindh: Selected Reports.*

Hur Movement for Freedom of Sindh
The Hero King and His Valiant Hurs

Persian Pir Pagaro Soreh Badshah, hero king, wrote in a letter to Shahnawaz Bhutto from jail:

> Sibghatullah was growing into a large man, black-bearded, handsome, with eyes as calm as planets. He had suffered from smallpox in his childhood and the disease had left his skin pitted with the scars of it. But already he had a majesty of presence that was commented upon even by those who claimed to be unafraid. He had an agile mind, and, unlike his forebears, he gloried in his godhead. He was God! Let those ridiculous little Englishmen over in Sukkur, those Collectors and District Magistrates and Superintendents of Police, pore over their files and shake their heads! His world was his own to do with as he pleased.

It's all alike whether a man dies on earth or on a throne. To me the death looks to be preferable to the present life.[106]

---

[106] Peter Mayne, *Saints of Sind*, (London: John Murray, 1956).

It is reported that in 1940, G. M. Syed, then president of the All-India Muslim League of Sindh, heading a delegation of his party leaders, went to meet Pir Sibghatullah Shah II and invite him to join their party. As reported by G. M. Syed himself in his book, *Sindh Speaks*, dialogue between G. M. Syed and Pir Sibghatullah Shah Pir Pagaro ensued as follows:

> G. M. Syed: "We have come with request that you should join Muslim League."
>
> Pir Pagaro, smiling: "Why?"
>
> G. M. Syed: "So that we should struggle for the independence of the country as laid down in the 1940 (Lahore) Resolution."
>
> The pir laughed and said, "The Muslim League and independence. Shah Sahib, I thought you were a shrewd politician, but it seems that you are unaware of the basics of politics."
>
> Syed (sarcastically): "Since you have been in several jails and have had the opportunity of meeting political prisoners, you have politics on your fingertips."
>
> Pir Pagaro: "I don't claim that I know everything about politics, but a party which acts under British instructions, a party which has all the Sirs, Khan Bahadurs, Waderas, feudal lords, and yet talks about independence, then there is nothing further I can say in the matter."

Syed (becoming more somber): "Sir, we shall soon have the Sindh Assembly pass a resolution demanding independence for Pakistan."

Pir Pagaro (smiling): "Yes, the moment you get the resolution through, the British will give you independence! Remember this, Shah Sahib. In the first place, the British will not grant you independence. And even if the demand for Pakistan is conceded, the new country will be a tailored affair where the British will call the shots for years."

G. M. Syed (heatedly): "We'll not allow the British to have any say in the affairs of our independent country."

Pir Pagaro (smiling): "Where will you be then? Will you hold the reins then? You forget, Shah Sahib, that while you fight, when victory comes, only those will be in the saddle who have been born British lackeys. You will be the fly in the ointment, and you will be thrown out of the ointment. Not only thrown out but possibly put in prison. If we live and if my predictions come true, then we'll know who is more adept at politics between the two of us. I will, by the grace of God, either get my country or my coffin, but you will be nursing your wounds."

At this, G. M. Syed said a quiet goodbye to the pir and left.[107]

---

[107] G. M. Syed, Sindh Galah-e-thi (Sindh Speaks—Case of Sindh), Deposition in Court, pp. 11, 16, 24, 196-210.

G. M. Syed was engaged in this dialogue with a man who was the leader of one of the most powerful and devoted groups ever seen in Sindh. His *murids* (disciples) considered him a divinely appointed leader. They would willingly sacrifice their lives and belongings without raising an eyebrow. Pir Pagaro and his Hurs had been a force to be reckoned with in the history of Sindh.

Who knew then that the predictions of Pir Pagaro about G. M. Syed and Pakistan would prove true? Pir Pagaro Syed Sibghatullah II would lead his Hurs in an armed rebellion against the British that, in the end, would result in his martyrdom and unleash one of the worst forms of oppression by the colonial British forces, a policy that was continued for decades, even by their heirs apparent after the departure of the British colonizers.

The term *Hur* literally means "men of freedom," and it is derived from the Arabic word *hurriyat* (freedom). Hur was a soldier in Yazid's army. He switched his loyalties over to Imam Husayn, the grandson of Prophet Muhammad, during the Battle of Karbala. He was killed in the battle and became a symbol of selfless sacrifice.

Hur is a title that Syed Ahmad Shah gave to disciples of Pir Pagaro. Syed Ahmed, popularly known as Syed Ahmad Shaheed, was a spiritual leader of the Sunni Barelvi sect, which opposed the Sikhs in the beginning of the nineteenth century.

Syed Ahmad came to Sindh during the Talpur era to seek help against the rising power of the Sikhs. The Talpur rulers of Sindh declined to help him, saying that they did not want to engage in a war based on religion. However, Pir Pagaro agreed to join him and provide help, both financially and in manpower.

In the 1830s, Punjab was ruled by a Sikh king, Ranjit Singh. The common belief was that it was only a matter of time before he would invade Sindh. But Talpur rulers of Sindh were divided within themselves and were in no position to defend Sindh. This left Pir Pagaro with no choice but to join forces with Syed Ahmad against the rising regional power of the Sikhs under the leadership of Ranjit Singh.

Pir Pagaro provided Syed Ahmad his 500 disciples, who, in turn, gave them the title of Hurs, a title that still persists today, three generations later. Hurs of Pir Pagaro mainly populated eastern region of the Nara Valley in Central Sindh, to Nagarparkar, Rajasthan, and Gujarat.

The ancestral lineage of the Pagaros can be traced back to Prophet Muhammad himself. Their original ancestor in Sindh was Shah Ali Maki, a Sufi who came to Sindh from Mecca in the eighth or ninth century to preach Islam. Some historians suggest Ali Maki came along with Muhammad Bin Qasim at the time of the conquest of Sindh. According to some oral historians, he came from Mecca to destroy the kingdom of one cruel King Raja Dalorai in Aror, now known as Rohri. Pagaros are the most influential pirs, or spiritual leaders, whose dynasty was founded by Syed Rashid Shah, thus their family title of Rashidis.

After the conquest of Sindh, when Charles Napier summoned all feudal lords and tribal chiefs to pledge allegiance to the British Queen, Pir Pagaro was one of the very few Sindhi chiefs who refused to obey. This was the first breaking point between the British and Pir Pagaro II, Pir Ali Gohar Shah. Instead, he instructed his disciples to prepare to resist the onslaught of colonial invaders.

After the defeat of Talpurs in the Battle of Dubbo, Mir Sher Muhammad Talpur, who had resisted the British, took refuge with Pir Pagaro. The Talpur rulers of Khairpur who had sided with the British informed the British rulers, who saw this as an act of resistance on the part of the pir and started retaliatory actions against him and his Hurs. This started the first Hur rebellion against the British colonizing forces.

According to Dr. Nabi Bakhsh Khan Baloch, the first Hur rebellion ensued in 1869 CE when Darya Khan Nizamani trained his comrades in arms in Mukhi forests and started actions against the British. The British exerted pressure on Pir Hizbullah Pagaro III to force the surrender of Darya Khan Nizamani. Pir Hizbullah Shah was framed in the murder of his own relative, Pir Fazlullah Shah, which later proved to be a purely fabricated case. The British authorities also put many curbs on the movement of Pir Hizbullah Shah, including a ban on his visiting or living in the Tharparkar and Sanghar Districts. Under the direction of the British, criminal cases ranging from murder to kidnapping were fabricated to frame Pir Pagaro.[108]

---

[108] Nabi Bakhsh Khan Baloch, ed. Clifford Edmund Bosworth and M. S. Asimov, *The Age of Achievement: AD 750 to the End of the Fifteenth Century: The Achievements (History of Civilizations of Central Asia)* (UNESCO Publishing, 1998) 307-308.

After many years of his activities against the British and their informants, Darya Khan Nizamani was finally captured with his partner, Qaaim Mochi, and imprisoned in the Fort of Kot Diji, under the control of the Talpur ruler of Khairpur, which had been granted the status of a princely state by the British.

Pir Hizbullah Shah was the one who organized his followers into a *jamaat*, or brotherhood, and divided them into twelve smaller groups called *chowkis* (sectors) along geographic lines. This system continues today, each chowki supervised under a khalifa who manages the day-to-day chores and business of running the jamaat locally. Presently, three of these chowkis are in India, the rest in Sindh.

Hurs have a uniquely close network of brotherhood. Since the first Hur rebellion, they have been known for maintaining a highly effective network of intelligence and information gathering. According to Nasir Aijaz:

> *He [Pir Hizbullah Shah] also wrote letter to Sultan Abdul Hamid of Turkey drawing his attention towards atrocities of British in India in general and Sindh in particular and urged him to play a role. Although he organized the Hur community against the foreign rulers but realized that fighting such a powerful enemy was not possible without foreign help. The letter to Sultan of Turkey was written in Persian language.*[109]

---

[109] Nasir Aijaz, *Hur: The Freedom Fighter* (Karachi: Culture and Tourism Department, Government of Sindh, 2015) 38, 40.

After the death of Pir Hizbullah Shah, his son, Pir Ali Gohar Shah II, assumed the *gaddi* (seat of the spiritual leader of the Jamaat). Contrary to most other gaddis, this one is unique in the sense that the next pir is actually elected by a majority vote among the khalifas from twelve chowkis.

During Pir Ali Gohar Shah II's leadership from 1890 to 1896, the rebellion against the British heightened and entered a new phase as new generations of freedom fighters joined the struggle. A group of disciples of Pir Pagaro, making their base in Mukhi Forest, declared an independent government led by Bachu Badshah (Bachu the King) and Piru Wazir (Piru the Minister).

Bachu Badshah's full name was Muhammad Bachal Khaskheli. He had originally joined a small group of peasant revolutionaries headed by Waryam Fakir. Waryam Fakir was an ardent disciple of Pir Pagaro, who still today is considered a legendary figure in the history of Sindh for his bravery and courage.

Mukhi was the largest natural lake, which, at its peak, stretched over approximately 1,000 square miles between Khairpur Mirs and Achro Thar (the White Desert). In the area, there are several villages in which the Hurs resided; it was surrounded by dense forests and spotted with at least 200 smaller lakes.

To crush the Hur rebellion and clear the area of the Hur presence, the British destroyed and erased thousands of square miles of natural forest and evacuated hundreds of Hur villages. In their place, they created what were termed as *chaks*, newly built villages, in which new inhabitants were settled. The new inhabitants, who had proved their loyalties to their British Colonial masters, were mostly from Punjab.

Among the new settlers were Pathans, Kabulis, and Bugtis. They were allotted lands and villages that previously belonged to Hurs. The new settlers were recruited as militias to fight and repress the Hur movement in the area. Bugti Sardar Shahbaz Khan was rewarded with large tracts of land in the Sanghar area. Sardar Shahbaz Khan was the grandfather of Nawab Akbar Bugti, governor of Baluchistan after the creation of Pakistan; he was ironically killed in a missile attack by the armed forces for leading an armed struggle for Baluch autonomy.

According to journalist and author Nasir Aijaz:

> *Waryam Fakir was such a brave person that once he saved the life of Raja of Jaisalmer and killed the lion with his sword. Raja had rewarded him with a gold bracelet and a sword. The British were scared of Waryam. They implicated him in a false murder case along with his two other friends, Laiq Dino Shah and Syed Muqeem Shah. After trial in a local court, he was sent to Hyderabad Jail where he was poisoned to death. The jail officials claimed Waryam Fakir committed suicide.*[110]

Pir Bux, alias Piru Vizir, was locally known as Hothi Jam. In his village, he was considered to be intelligent. Piru and Bachu

---

[110] Aijaz, *Hur: The Freedom Fighter*, 98.

both formed parallel governments and inducted their group members as their cabinet to deal with everyday public affairs in the area controlled by Hurs. Fatlo Faqeer Wasan was assigned as *qazi* to adjudicate disputes. Khamiso Wasan was deputized as *kotwal*, or police officer, in the area. The other team members were Gu-loo Machi and Bhalo Gaho.

Sarah F. Ansari writes:

> *The crisis of 1890, which took the form of a "rebellion" on the part of the Hur followers of Pir Pagaro, challenged British authority on a scale which rocked the province as a whole: while the actual disturbances more or less confined to the areas stretching from Hyderabad to Sanghar in the east, the implication of threat to the law and order were felt throughout the province. The administration was unable to control the problem on its own, so the crisis pulled the system sharply into focus by highlighting the limits of the British authority when it was not accompanied by the cooperation of influential local elites.*[111]

The British government's all-out repressive efforts failed to capture Bachu Badshah. Hur villages were seized, their men were rounded up, crops were burned down, and livestock were forfeited. But the British government could not extract any information that could lead to the arrest of Bachu Badshah,

---

[111] Sarah F. Ansari, *Sufi Saints and State Power: The Pirs of Sindh, 1843-1947* (Cambridge University Press, 1992) 18.

as he and his cabinet had immense support, cooperation, and sympathy from the local Hur populace.

Bachu Badshah and his companions started targeting those suspected of being British informants. The British administration and police officials branded Bachu and his group as criminals and outlaws and increased pressure on Pir Pagaro, Syed Ali Gohar Shah, to make Bachu and his companions surrender to the colonial authorities. But the Hurs led by Bachu Badshah and Piru Vizir continued their actions against British officials and the British machinery in their areas. A senior police official, Jawala Singh, was killed in an attack in 1896.

A local sage and poet of that time, Mehmood Pali, a singer of praises for the bravery and courage of Bachu Badshah and his companions, wrote:

انگريزن جي صاحبيءَ مِ چوڏهين صدي سير
پر ڊر اچي پيدا ٿيا, بانڪا بي نذير
بارنهن جٽا ڀرو ٿيا, هئا مڪيءَ پاسي مير
بچو ان جو بادشاهه پيرو اڳيان وزير
ڪر ڏاڪي سان دلگير, تن ڊيهه ڏڪائي ڇڏيا.
ڊيهه ڏڪائي ڏيا سان, ڪيائون زير زبر
اڪ نه هين انگريز تي, ٻيو ڪنهن مٿي ڪلٽر
ماري سو سپاهين جا, ٿي لوڙهيائون لشڪر
ڏسي هيبت حرن جي, ٿي گهٽن ڇڏيا گهر
پورا ٿي ويا افسر, تن جي ٽاٽن پئي ٽڪون جهليون

> *The rule of the English continues in fourteenth-century Hijri,*
> *But Brave Men are finally born,*
> *Youthful and Matchless Twelve men have risen,*
> *The heroes of Mukhi Bachu is their king, Piru is the Vizir*
> *With their force They have shaken the countryside*
> *They have no fear of the English, neither the collector*
>
> *They killed the invading soldiers and defeated the army. Many left their homes out of fear of Hurs. The British Officers have run away, leaving police stations deserted. After the killing of Jawala Singh, the British became more brutal against the Hur population. They killed scores of Hur men, brutally tortured women and children, reduced houses and crops to ashes. Local criminal gangs were given free hand to loot and kill civilians, for which Hurs were blamed.*[112]

William Henry and Deputy Collector Lucas were at the forefront of operations against Hurs after Jawala Singh was killed. They tried to persuade Pir Pagaro to effect the surrender of Bachu Badshah and his partners, but the pir refused.

According to Hur historian Professor Mubeen Wassan:

> *Pir Syed Ali Gohar Shah called Bachu Badshah and Piru Vizir and ordered them to "go and fight unto death."*

---

[112] Aijaz, *Hur: The Freedom Fighter*, 143.

> "Get the people rid of the British atrocities and till then food and water is forbidden to you," he had asked them.

> "Yes, Murshid! We are lions and lions never leave the field," was Piru's response to Pir Pagaro.

Bachu Badshah visited Rajasthan to spread the message of Pir Pagaro. His other comrades, led by Piru Vizir, entrenched themselves near village Faqeer Bhanbhro and put up a fierce battle with police. After the death of his trusted friend and aide, Piru Vizir, Bachu Badshah surrendered on May 7, 1890. He was later convicted of treason and hanged to death in November 1896.

It is reported that after the killing of his close comrades in arms, Bachu was sad and heartbroken. Meanwhile, he received a handkerchief from his murshid, Pir Pagaro, which was reportedly a signal from the pir to surrender. He kissed the handkerchief and rubbed his eyes with it. He went to the camp office of Deputy Collector Sardar Muhammad Yaqoob, who was camped in a tent.

The Hur historians write:

> When Bachu Badshah entered the camp office of Sardar Muhammad Yaqoob, established in a tent in Sanghar, the Indian officer was surprised to see a strong man with long hair, beard, and turban. "Who are you?" Sardar Muhammad Yaqoob asked.

> "I am Bachu Badshah," was the answer, and listening to it, the deputy commissioner became so scared that he tried to hide beneath the table. "Don't get afraid of me. I am here to surrender on the orders of my spiritual leader," Bachu Badshah told him.

Some suggest that Bachu Badshah and Piru Vizir, despite being promised general amnesty, were hanged along with their comrades, publicly in the town of Johl, while others say they were hanged inside the jail at Sanghar.

According to Laiq Zardari, the first Hur rebellion lasted for twelve years but was crushed by modern weaponry and repression from the British. Thousands were arrested, villages burnt down, and the Hurs' lands and other properties were seized.

Since the days of providing support to Syed Ahmad Shaheed, Pir Pagaro and his disciples were always under surveillance by the British agencies. Pir Sibghatullah II was fourteen years of age when he ascended to the throne following the death of his father. The political conditions were volcanic at the time of his birth in 1909 and while he was growing up in the undivided subcontinent.

Anti-colonial, anti-imperial nationalist movements were starting all over the colonized world. In the Indian subcontinent, new leaders like Gandhi, Sabash Chandra Bose, and Muhammad Ali Jinnah were gaining immense popularity. The Jallianwala Bagh Massacre was still fresh in the minds of the masses, which created among the natives an upsurge of resentment against their British colonizers.

In 1929, the mother of a boy named Ibrahim Kori filed a complaint against Pir Pagaro Sibghatullah II, alleging he had kept her son under wrongful confinement at his residence, Pir Jo Goth. The woman was later killed. This prompted the colonial British authorities to conduct a raid on the residence of Pir Pagaro at Pir Jo Goth.

According to noted historian Dr. Hamida Khuhro, the servants inside Pir Pagaro's residence were acting as police informers. They kept the doors inside the house open, as instructed by the police, when police conducted the raid at the bungalow of Pir Pagaro.

Police claimed to have recovered the boy from a trunk; he was still alive. Police also claimed recovery of a huge quantity of arms and ammunition, including twelve rifles, three guns, two revolvers, 1,500 cartridges, and other explosive material. Pir Pagaro was arrested, imprisoned, and tried on charges of abduction, wrongfully confining a boy, and having his mother, Mai Mariam, murdered. The guns that were recovered from Pir Pagaro's possession were all licensed hunting weapons. In order to falsely implicate Pir Pagaro, the licenses for these firearms were cancelled prior to the arrest by the deputy collector.

With the help of Shahnawaz Bhutto and Ayub Khuhro, Barrister Muhammad Ali Jinnah was hired as defense lawyer for Pir Pagaro at a sum of 500 rupees a day. Jinnah came to defend Pir Pagaro at Sukkur. All his expenses were borne by Jamaat through Faqeer Muhammed Mahar. However, Jinnah withdrew from the case in frustration at the flagrant bias with which the trial against Pir Pagaro was being conducted. As the British were predetermined to convict Pir Pagaro, Motiram Advani, who was assisting Jinnah in preparing the defense of Pir Pagaro, also withdrew from the case.

The local magistrate at Sukkur, Udharam, after a brief lopsided trial, declared Pir Pagaro guilty and sentenced him to rigorous imprisonment for ten years. According to Nasir Aijaz's account, Jinnah filed an appeal to the Chief Court of Sindh, against the verdict of the Sukkur magistrate in Sindh's Chief Court. The Sindh Chief Court, in appeal, commuted the sentence of ten years to eight years. Not even once was Pir Pagaro allowed to be present in the court while the trial was being conducted. His lawyers were only able to consult with him in jail. It was essentially a trial held in absentia.

Pir Pagaro Syed Sibghatullah Shah was lodged in different jails outside Sindh, such as Ratnagiri Jail, Rajshahi Jail, and the Alipore and Midnapore Jails in Bengal while his trial was being conducted in Karachi. His khalifas visited Pir Pagaro in jail. Some of his faqeers and khalifas went on foot when he was in Ratnagiri Jail. Through visiting khalifas, Pir Pagaro used to write letters to his disciples and friends. The letters were smuggled out of jail by these khalifas, especially his khalifa, Mohabbat Faqeer, who disguised himself as an ordinary man and played courier between Pir Pagaro, Jamaat, and Pir Pagaro's friends.

In jail, Pir Pagaro announced a hunger strike to press his demands, which included being provided with books, being transferred to any jail in Sindh, and being provided with the food of his choice at his expense. A delegation of Sindhi-elected members of the Bombay Legislative Assembly met with the governor and asked him to release Pir Pagaro. To counter increasing anger among his 1,000,000 followers of all faiths during his jail time, the pir stopped receiving *nazrana*, or contributions, from his disciple, but he was still served income-tax notices to pay 6,000 rupees. However, he asked his disciples not to pay any taxes or buy any foreign goods until he was released.

Having served his full term, Pir Pagaro was released on November 25, 1936. A train was chartered from Calcutta to Khairpur by Hur Jamaat to take Pir Pagaro home. A tumultuous welcome by thousands of his Hurs, friends, and well-wishers was accorded him at Khairpur Mirs station.

After his release, the governor of Sindh, Sir Lancelot Graham, sent the pir a message inviting to fix the broken relations between him, his Jamaat, and the British. Pir Pagaro visited the governor with Ghulam Hussain Hidayatullah as his interpreter and donated 50,000 rupees to the war fund. Then he went to perform hajj. Many believe he met Ubaidullah Sindhi, the leader of the famous Reshmi Rumal Movement against the British, who was living in exile in Mecca. The British knew all about the activities of Pir Pagaro, and they were not happy that he was spending time in his riverine ketty in the forest with his disciples and khalifas; they had received reports that the pir was training his people.

In April 1941, Hugh Dow became the new governor of Sindh, and he served an order on Pir Pagaro, restricting his movements within the district of Karachi and banning his travel to his native village of Pir Jo Goth and his home. Pir Pagaro defied the order and left Karachi for Pir Jo Goth. Pir Pagaro also undertook a tour of Hur villages and towns that sent tremors through British administrations. Some historians believe that Pir Pagaro and his Hurs had been preparing for years to launch a guerrilla movement in Sindh, coordinating it with All India National Congress's Quit India Movement.

The governor instructed Sukkur's collector, Sydney Ridley, and the superintendent of police at Pir Jo Goth to bring Pir Pagaro back to Karachi. According to Dr. Hamida Khuhro, on their way back to Karachi, Ridley and the superintendent of police had lunch with a minister of the Khairpur state, Mr. Aijaz Ali, but the arrest of Pir Pagaro was kept secret. He was brought back to Karachi, and on October 24, 1941, he was arrested under regulation XXV (1827). He was later taken to Lahore by train, and from there, on an Indian Railway train to Seoni Jail in Central India.

Reacting immediately to the arrest of their spiritual leader, Hurs began an enormous revolt.[113] The first immediate reaction to Pir Pagaro's arrest was from Pir Pagaro's own village, Pir Jo Goth, where the protest so intensified that Deputy Commissioner Ridley ordered the imposition of a curfew in the town. Allah Bux Osto and Kachhomal, editors of the *Pir Jo Goth Gazetteer*, the newspaper started by Pir Pagaro, were among the first to be arrested after the arrest of Pir Pagaro himself. Hurs initiated a full-scale guerrilla operation using hit-and-run tactics against the British establishment. On March 14, 1942, in a major ambush in Nara, they attacked the police station and killed Police Inspector Ghulam Rasool Shah. This Hurs ambush of the police became known as the Battle of Khenwari.

---

[113] Khuhro, *Sindh Through the Centuries*.

The Sindh Assembly, consisting mostly of handpicked British informers, passed legislation named the Hur Act, also known as the Suppression of the Hur Bill, to quell and crush the Hur rebellion. In a secret session on April 10, 1942, all forty-four members of the assembly voted in favor of the bill. The prime minister of Sindh, Allah Bux Soomro, undertook a tour of the province to garner support for the bill.

In Mīrpur Khās, the prime minister, and other notables criticized the Hurs and announced they would crush the insurgence. Within hours, Seth Sitaldas, who attended the meeting and spoke against the Hurs and their spiritual leader, was gunned down. According to Dr. Hamida Khuhro:

> *Hurs were outraged against Allah Bux Soomro because of his actions against them and their pir. They derailed the Lahore Mail, near Hyderabad, on May 16, 1942.*

They attacked a compartment of the train in which Allah Bux Soomro was supposed to be traveling. He, at the last minute, had changed his travel plans. So instead of him, they found the son of Ghulam Hussain Hidayatullah, who was killed in the ambush. Another minister, Nehchaldas Vazirani, who was also traveling in the same train car, saved his life by hiding in a toilet.[114]

On May 31, 1942, the British government declared martial law on eastern Sindh, mainly the Hur areas; this act is commonly called the Hur Martial Law. Major Richardson was appointed as martial-law administrator. Hur villages were bombarded by fighter planes of the British Royal Air Force. Pir Pagaro's Ganang bungalow near Sanghar was completely destroyed by their aerial bombings.

---

[114] Khuhro, *Sindh Through the Centuries*.

It is reported that Air Marshal Asghar Khan, who later became the chief of the Air Force of Pakistan, was assigned to bomb Pir Goth and Hur villages in 1942 as a young pilot in the British Royal Air Force. He refused to obey orders and was going to be court-martialed, but the proceedings were stopped after the creation of Pakistan.

In January 1943, Pir Pagaro was secretly flown back in a plane that landed near Hyderabad at Bholari Airstrip. He was lodged at Hyderabad Central Jail, in a death cell that was fitted with bugging devices. He was arraigned on charges of waging war against the British. He wanted Muhammad Ali Jinnah to defend him, but Jinnah declined, using the excuse of prior engagements, despite being offered twice the fee he usually charged.

Pir Sibghatullah Shah, Pir Pagaro, popularly known as Soreh Badshah, the Hero King, was secretly hanged in March 1943.

The British arranged his secret burial at an undisclosed location. His execution was supervised by Magistrate Hashim Raza. It is said that a few hours before his execution, the pir was totally composed, calm, and present-minded. To prove this, he challenged the jail superintendent to play a round of chess with him, and he beat the superintendent easily. To date, some of his disciples still believe that Soreh Badshah was never hanged, as angels took his body from the gallows to the skies before his captors could hang him.

After the hanging of Pir Pagaro, his two sons, Sikandar Shah and Nadir Shah, ages fourteen and twelve, respectively, were taken into custody and exiled initially to Aligarh, India, and later to London, England. All properties owned by Pagaro, shrines, and Hurs were forfeited to the British. Hurs continued their revolt against the British colonizers, the strongest superpower of the time, and its most tyrannical, repressive measures.

About 3,000 Hurs were arrested between 1942 and 1943, and more than seventy were executed. A whole generation of Hurs was born and raised in concentration camps called *lorrha* (hedges).

Even after the departure of the British colonizers, most Hurs continued to be incarcerated in concentration camps on the soil of their motherland, for which they and their previous three generations had shed blood. The government of the newly created country did nothing to change this situation and continued enforcing the same policies that had been enacted by their previous colonial masters.

To the contrary, on the other side of the border, the first prime minister of the newly created country Jawaharlal Nehru visited the Hurs on the Indian side of the border and announced the immediate abolishment of lorrhas. This gave Hurs on the Indian side the option to live as free and equal citizens of the new country or to be repatriated to the other side of the boundary to be among the majority of their fellow Jamaat members. Most Hurs on the Indian side decided to stay in their homes on that side.

Sikandar Shah, the older son of late Soreh Badshah, visited Pakistan in 1948 to try to have his disciples released on the Pakistani side and have his gaddi restored. But it is said that the first prime minister of the country, Liaquat Ali Khan, known for his racist views and policies against indigenous Sindhis, refused to meet with Sikandar Shah. Thus, feeling dejected, Sikandar Shah went back to England.

It was not until 1952, and only after the death of Liaquat Ali Khan, that Sikandar Shah was allowed to come back to Sindh.

On his return, the seats of Pir Pagaro, their shrine, and Hur Jamaat were restored, but only after considerable pressure was exerted by his Hurs living on the Indian side of the border, as they had started gathering funds to build a new Garang bungalow and establish a Pir Jo Goth on the Indian side.

The newly formed government of Pakistan, realizing the grave security and political implications of this, finally allowed the conditional return of Pir Pagaro's sons. In a grand ceremony, Sikandar Shah was elected as Pagaro VII by the council of khalifahs. He was given the title of Pir Shah Mardan Shah. Through his efforts, his Hurs were eventually released from the concentration camps, and the Pakistani government announced general amnesty for all of them.

Pir Shah Mardan Shah spent the rest of his life trying to restore and rehabilitate the Hur Jamaat, for which he, at times, was the target of severe criticism by Sindhi nationalists because of his overly conciliatory policies toward the security establishment of Pakistan. Only history will judge how effective or otherwise his policies will prove to be for the Hur Jamaat and Sindh.

Partition, Flight, and Plight of Sindhi Hindus

At the stroke of midnight of August 15, 1947, while the world slept and India awakened to freedom, Sindhis woke up to the bitter truth of finding themselves homeless, landless, and stateless. This is the price they had to pay for freedom. They had certainly not bargained for this tryst with destiny.[115]

The Partition of India resulted in one of the largest human migrations in human history. Indigenous Sindhi Hindus were forced to leave their motherland, only to be replaced by Muslims migrating from the other side of newly created borders. Shaikh Ayaz, the great Sindhi poet, eloquently depicted this disenfranchisement of Sindhis in their homeland:

ڏيھي پرڏيھي ٿيا پرڏيھي ڏيھي
پرايا پيھي والاري ويا سنڌڙي

---

[115] Subhadra Anand, *National Integration of Sindhis* (Delhi: Vikas Publishing Pvt. Ltd., 1996), 24.

Natives have become aliens. Aliens are now owners.
Foreigners have with force occupied the whole Sindh.

The British Colonial era was a mixed bag for Sindh and Sindhis. The latter half of the nineteenth century was the era of progress for all humanity, including the Indian subcontinent and Sindh in particular. A network of railway lines, metal roads, and irrigation canals was laid throughout the region.

The construction of Sukkur Barrage irrigated hundreds of thousands of barren Sindh lands on both banks of the River Indus. An irrigation system unique in the world, it consisted of canals, tributaries, and lined channels. Sindh bloomed as if it were the Garden of Eden. But nobody knew before 1947 that this Garden of Eden was only being built for it to be burned to ashes in the aftermath of the Partition of India.

These technological advances also affected Sindh's traditional socioeconomic system, which experienced a new, rapidly rising urban middle class where none had been, as it had been mostly an agricultural-based economy. Though, compared to the rest of the Indian subcontinent, Sindh had always enjoyed the most peaceful intercommunal relationships across religious and ethnic lines.

Within twelve years of the conquest of Sindh, the entire North India was up in arms against the British as the Ghadar Movement of liberation had already erupted. Sindh was such a nice, quiet, sleepy place in the midst of the 1857 war, while the rest of North India was up in flames. The British, not under any threat of a local rebellion in Sindh, only kept a few platoons there, choosing to send most of their troops to Delhi as reinforcements.

In 1850, Sir Bartle Frere, known as "Sindh's man" among his fellow British officers, was appointed the commissioner of Sindh. He took his leave in England and then traveled to Karachi.[116] Seth Naomal Hotchand, commenting on his friend, said, "I have known intimately Englishmen and Europeans gifted with many admirable qualities, but none could equal Sir Bartle in various powers of patience, forethought, discernment, and courage, which he displayed in those days of trouble and anxiety."

Before the British conquest, Persian was the official language of the court of Sindh. Persian was also used by educated Hindus as the main language of business. In the mid-nineteenth century, the British government of India ordered that all official correspondence regarding the affairs in Sindh be written in Sindhi. At the same time, Sindh was experiencing a boom in new schools and colleges. So Bartle Frere, as commissioner of Sindh, directed that a committee be formed to develop a script for the Sindhi language. The committee formulated a Sindhi alphabet based on Arabic script. Sindhi textbooks were printed in the Sindhi-Arabic script, and then schools were opened.

Bherumal Meharchand Advani writes, "Before the British conquest, there were *mektabs* taught by *Akhunds*, or local mallah,

---

[116] Rekha Ranade, *Sir Bartle Frere and His Times* (New Delhi: Mittal Publications, 1990) 15-16.

where sons of Hindus went with sons of Muslim landlords to take a few lessons of Persian and Khudabadi Sindhi."[117]

As Sindh was the last province to come under British rule, Sindhis had lagged behind in learning the English language. According to Bherumal Meharchand Advani, "Hindus had a penchant for learning English. Qandharani was a brand of Advani [that] belong[ed] to Akali Sikhs. They were fond of joining police and army, so British officers filled up all vacancies of *mukhtiarkars* with eleven Advanis out of thirteen vacancies."[118]

The first three high schools were established in Naushahro Feroze, Hyderabad, and Shikarpur. A training college for teaching was set up in Hyderabad to educate the teachers. In 1885, Hassan Ali Effendi built the Sindh Madressah. Philanthropic Sindhi raised funds to establish Sindh College in Karachi. Hyderabad became the center of education and the nerve center of Sindhi political and cultural activities.

---

[117] Bherumal Meharchand Advani, *Sindh Je Hindu Ji Tarekh (History of Hindus in Sindh)*. Bombay: Shardha Prakashan, 1991.

[118] Advani, *Sindh Je Hindu Ji Tarekh (History of Hindus in Sindh)*.

Significant progress was also made in the education of females when, in the beginning of the twentieth century, philanthropists like Rishi Dayaram Gidumal, Noval Rai, Motiram Shoqiram, and later Sadhu Vaswani came forward to set up schools and colleges for girls and women.

With the advent of printing presses in the beginning of the twentieth century, there were a number of Sindhis who began investing in the publishing business. Publishers like Pokardas Thanwardas established their publishing houses during the 1880s in Shikarpur. Sindhi Adabi Board was set up in 1901 in Hyderabad. Karachi, Hyderabad, and Shikarpur became hubs for printing literature.

These were the times when Mirza Kalich Beg was emerging as an established writer. Motilal Jotwani brings us back to the times of the publishing boom in Sindh:

> *From among the institutional publishers, mention may be made of Sikh Youngmen's Association of Hyderabad (a reincarnation of Sikh Sabha, est. in 1868 at Karachi by Sadhu Navalrai Advani and Munshi Udharam Mirchandani), which published a monthly series of tracts on Sikhism: Sindhi Sahita Society (est. in 1914) of Jethmal Parsram and Lalchand Amardinomal, which published scores of books on various subjects by different authors, viz. Mirza Kalich Beg's Motiyun jee Dab'lee, Lilaramsingh Watanmal's novel Sundari and Lalchand Amardinomal's Shahaano Shah and Soonhaaro Sachal. And Muslim Adabi Society (est. 1931) by Muhammad Siddique*

Memon, which published historical books from the Islamic standpoint. Sindhi Adabi Board, a government institution (est. in 1940), brought a quarterly Sindhi magazine called Mehraan in 1940.

But the age of printing presses in Sindh that gave the British government worries was the release of the publication, Jot, by Parmanand Mewaram in 1900 and, especially, the newspaper, Hindvasee, brought out by Jethmal Parsram in 1917. These were the times when the Ali brothers, Shaukat Ali and Muhammad Ali, also published their famous newspaper, Comrade, from Delhi.[119]

---

[119] Motilal Wadhumal Jotwani, *The Sindhis Through the Centuries* (Aditya Prakashan, 2006) 65-70.

The Bolshevik Revolution of Russia in October 1917 and the end of World War I changed the balance of power in the world, along with the political scenario in subcontinent British India. After siding with Germany, Turkey lost the war against new Western colonial European powers. With the end of the Ottoman Empire's caliphate, the Ottoman sultan also lost control of holy places Mecca and Medina in Arabia. This sent waves of shock and anger across Muslim society, as well as in India, where Muslims constituted twenty percent of the population.

Mian Abdul Bari belonged to the Firangi Mahal in Lucknow. Historically, the Firangi Mahal was renowned and held high influence among most of the Sufi shrines of Bihar, Delhi, Lucknow, Ajmir, and Sindh. Bari, Maulana Abdul Kalam Azad, and Mian Muhammad Shafi from Lahore were at the forefront of the movement supporting restoration of Ottoman caliphate.

Mahatma Gandhi joined Azad in what became known as the Khilafat Movement, asking Muslims and Hindus of India to join in opposition to the British. He had previously participated in a noncooperation movement against British colonizers in South Africa. He wanted a boycott of the colonial rulers in India, but a nonviolent one to avoid colliding with British military power, because he wanted to deal with the British on civil issues.[120]

---

[120] Dietrich Reetz, *Hijrat: The Flight of the Faithful: A British File on the Exodus of Muslim Peasants from North India to Afghanistan in 1920* (Berlin: Klaus Schwarz Verlag, 1996) 13, 19-20.

Gandhi gave the call of *satyagraha* (passive resistance). The British government introduced the Rowlatt and Government of India Acts in 1919. Gandhi gave the call of *hartal* (strike) to Hindus and Muslims and asked that they unite in protest against the Rowlatt Act. In Amritsar, Punjab, crowds gathered in Jallianwala Bagh to protest. The British decided to suppress the protest by using full military force. Under General Dyer, British soldiers opened fire and many—including Hindus, Muslims, and Sikhs—were killed or injured as a result.

Jethmal Parsram, editor of the Sindhi newspaper *Hindvasee*, from Hyderabad, published his editorial against the Jallianwala massacre, quoting a line of verse from Shah Abdul Latif Bhittai:

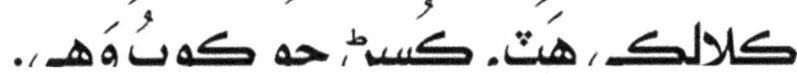

There continues the business of beheading at shop, o winemaker.

A criminal case of sedition was filed against Jethmal Parsram by the British government. Jethmal Parsram was sent to jail, tried, and convicted, receiving a one-year imprisonment and a fine of 1,000 rupees. As is often seen throughout the history of mankind, the imprisonment, trial, and later conviction of Jethmal Parsram turned out to be a pivotal moment for Sindh and Sindhi literature.

The trial judge in Jethmal Parsram's case, H. T. Sorley, was so moved by Bhittai's poetic line that he started reading and researching his poetry, which culminated in the publication of Sorley's historical book on the shah, *Shah of Bhit*, which introduced Shah Abdul Latif Bhittai to the rest of world for eternity.

The second decade of the twentieth century brought all India's national leaders to Sindh. Gandhi undertook his tour of Sindh from Karachi to Jacobabad. He met with young G. M. Syed during his train stop at Syed's native village of Sann. Syed was so impressed by Gandhi that he immediately announced joining Gandhi's movement. He also started wearing *khaadi* (locally weaved simple cotton fabric) and opened a *charkha* (weaving wheel) school at his village. He was on a campaign to boycott foreign goods. A huge portion of the funds for his party came from the Sindhi Hindus of Hyderabad and Jacobabad. Syed also attended the Khilafat conference at Larkana, where Maulana Abdul Kalam Azad, Mian Abdul Bari, and Saifuddin Kitchlu were the main speakers.

Shaikh Abdul Majeed Sindhi, a newly converted Muslim, was a rising star of Sindh politics. He started a movement for separation of Sindh from Bombay and convened the Azad Sindh Conference in September 1932. This movement was also supported by the Sindhi Hindu business community because they had experienced a great number of hardships while dealing with the bureaucracy in Bombay. Shaikh Abdul Majeed Sindhi was joined by Muhammad Ayub Khuhro and Ghulam Muhammad Bhurgri, who were then members of the Bombay provincial assembly. They jointly proposed a resolution for the separation of Sindh from Bombay's administrative and political control.

Sindh achieved freedom from Bombay on April 2, 1936. Shortly thereafter, general elections for national and provincial assemblies were held all over India, including the newly formed provincial assembly of Sindh.

Future shining stars of Sindhi politics included Abdullah Haroon, Shaikh Abdul Majeed Sindhi, G. M. Syed, Shaikh Ghulam Hussain Hidayatullah, Nehchaldas Vazirani, Roopchand Vaswani, Bhoj Singh Gurdinomal, Miran Mohammad Shah, Muhammad Ayub Khuhro, and Pir Ilahi Bux; they were among those elected to the newly formed Sindh Assembly. Each one of them would go on to play critical roles in the subsequent history of Sindh.

In a spectacular development, and as proof of the ancient values of equality, democracy, and secularism held by Sindhis since time immemorial, Shaikh Abdul Majeed Sindhi, coming from a poor socioeconomic background, was able to defeat Sir Shahnawaz Bhutto in his native town of Larkana. This was a major blow to the all-powerful Bhutto feudal clan until the rise of his son, Zulfiqar Ali Bhutto. The heads of the Bhutto household had been returning to assemblies since the first day of elections for the Bombay Council, but the election defeat of Sir Shahnawaz Bhutto at the hands of Shaikh Abdul Majeed Sindhi sent Sir Shahnawaz Bhutto into political obscurity for the rest of his life.

On March 23, 1938, Ghulam Hussain Hidayatullah was elected prime minister of Sindh, and he formed a new cabinet. But the province had been experiencing increased tensions between Hindus and Muslims since the previous elections of 1937. The government had failed to control this escalating situation, and Ghulam Hussain Hidayatullah admitted on the floor of the Sindh Legislative Assembly that there was indeed a breakdown of law and order.

> *Even now, as it is, I receive everyday a bundle of telegrams complaining that the minorities are in danger. Shoals of telegrams are being received by me every day, sir. There is no safety for the minorities.*

G. M. Syed and Allah Bux Soomro brought a no-confidence motion against the prime minister, which was supported by Hindu members, and it brought down the government of Sir Shaikh Ghulam Hussain Hidayatullah. Allah Bux Soomro, with a lead of one vote, was elected the new prime minister and formed his cabinet on March 23, 1938.

Allah Bux Soomro's election as prime minister of Sindh was opposed tooth and nail by Shaikh Abdul Majeed Sindhi, Muhammad Hashim Gazdar, and the Muslim League. On March 28, 1938, a public meeting was convened by Muhammad Ayub Khuhro, Muhammad Hashim Gazdar, and Shaikh Abdul Majeed Sindhi outside Sindh's Assembly Building. The speakers branded the prime minister and his cabinet as "stooges of Hindus."

In October 1938, a two-day provincial conference of the All-India Muslim League was held at Karachi and chaired by Muhammad Ali Jinnah and the prime ministers of Bengal and Punjab. Strongly worded resolutions were passed to accuse Allah Bux Soomro's government of establishing Hindu rule in Sindh. Another resolution condemned the Congress government in its attempts to prefer Devanagari script in the province. It is said that during his stay at Karachi, Mr. Jinnah advised Muslim members to form the Sindh Muslim League group; the Sindh legislative assembly happily obliged.

In 1938, Hindu-Muslim tensions ran high as the issue of Masjid Manzilgah arose at Sukkur. Muslims claimed it belonged to them. The mosque was built by Mir Masoom Shah, a historian and minister in Mughal court. Hindus claimed the Manzilgah was actually their holy place as it was close to their place of religious rituals, Sadh Belo. Sukkur's Sindhi Muslims persuaded the Muslim League to support their claim.

In order to eke political mileage out of the Manzilgah issue, the Muslim League threw its weight behind the Sindhi Muslims of Sukkur, and the Manzilgah Restoration Committee was formed. Sindhi Muslims held a public rally. Thereafter, August 18 would be known as Manzilgah Day. Sindh Muslim League leadership and cadres from all over Sindh reached Sukkur. Abdullah Haroon was served orders to leave Sukkur. Muhammad Ayub Khuhro was arrested. A committee was formed to organize protests for restoration of Manzilgah. In the absence of Abdullah Haroon and Muhammad Ayub Khuhro, G. M. Syed became the president of the committee.

The situation at Sukkur became tense, as at the central bazaar of Sukkur City, a young son of Pir Bharchundi was maltreated by some Hindu miscreants. In retaliation, the followers of the pir gunned down saint and Sufi singer Bhagat Kanwar Ram while he was travelling by train near Ruk Railway Station in Shikarpur.

The local Muslim League leadership put out a call to take over the Masjid Manzilgah. Throughout Sindh, there were violent protest rallies and sit-ins. The government of Allah Bux Soomro attempted to pacify the people, but police were given the power to arrest agitators without warrants.

G. M. Syed, Muhammad Ayub Khuhro, Pir Ali Muhammad Shah Rashdi, Naimatullah Qureshi, and Wajid Ali Shaikh were at the forefront of the Masjid Manzilgah movement, which turned violent. Finally, they took to the streets and gave a call to start *satyagraha* (agitation) on October 1, 1939. Thousands of volunteers took to the streets in Sukkur and other parts of Sindh. Hundreds were arrested, including the Muslim League leadership in Sindh. Police used tear gas to round up those who occupied the Masjid Manzilgah.

Masjid Manzilgah was vacated by the police. This was one of the most tragic events in an otherwise pristine history of interfaith relations in Sindh. Masjid Manzilgah and the assassinations of Bhagat Kanwar Ram and Professor Hasaram Pamnani were the three main events that disturbed the sociopolitical and communal equilibrium among Hindus and Muslims in Sindh. It was a major turn for the worse.

Allah Bux Soomro, then prime minister of Sindh, was blamed by both sides. He was accused by the Hindus of being a weak head of state for his perceived inability to control the situation, while the Muslim League accused him of siding with Hindus. A no-confidence motion was proposed against Allah Bux Soomro, but this was defeated by a margin of one vote cast by the speaker. However, Allah Bux Soomro later stepped down voluntarily.

> *In one of the greatest ironies in the history of Sindh, G. M. Syed delivered a speech on the floor of the Sindh Assembly on June 30, 1941, in which he said:*

I have also said that the words "Hindu-Muslim unity" are dangerous. As proof of truth of my contention, I will refer to the political history of our province during the last four years and show how all such efforts to bring about Hindu-Muslim unity have proved futile. The underlying reason for the failure of such efforts is to be traced to the fact that both of these nations are made with different material, which, apart from being in no way secular, are quite opposite and sharply in contrast to each other. Between these two nations are the political, cultural, economic barriers so much so if one can be characterized as North Pole, the other will be as dramatically opposite to as South Pole. It is therefore impossible to unite such antagonizing and mutually repellent materials. Any effort in that direction will result in a most artificial and temporary arrangement, which, instead of doing any good, will really do a lot of harm. According to historic traditions, the heroes of one nation are the enemies of the other. The language of the Hindu is influenced by Sanskrit, whereas the language of the Musselman is very much influenced by Arabic. In short, we are separate in everything. Our food, our matrimonial ethics, our dress, etc., are separate.[121]

In early March 1943, G. M. Syed proposed the Resolution of Pakistan in the Sindh Assembly; it was passed on March 3, 1943. While debating the resolution, Muhammad Usman Soomro,

---

[121] G. M. Syed, Sindh Assembly, 1943.

a member of Sindh Assembly, remarked that "independent doesn't mean that our Sindh province should be combined with Baluchistan, Punjab, or Pakistan, or with other provinces."[122]

However, the year 1943 brought an ugly turn in the history of Sindh and its politics. This was the year when Allah Bux Soomro, a Sindhi secular nationalist leader, was assassinated. In the words of Sara F. Ansari: "One of the biggest what-ifs of the mid-twentieth-century Sindhi history is to speculate on the course that politics in the province could have taken in the years immediately preceding independence had Soomro not been murdered in May 1943."[123]

Allah Bux Soomro, a self-made middle-class member from Shikarpur, was bestowed the title of Khan Bahadur by the British, and he was known by his peers as KB. The British revoked his title when he joined the Congress and supported All-India Congress's Quit India movement in 1942.

The Quit India movement had significant influence in Sindh as well. The British announced elections in 1945 and 1946 in Sindh. G. M. Syed parted ways with Jinnah and the Muslim League after developing differences with Muhammad Ayub Khuhro and Yusuf Abdullah Haroon.

---

[122] Muhammad Usman Soomro, Sindh Assembly 1943.

[123] Sarah F. Ansari, *Muslim Nationalist or Nationalist Muslim? Allah Bakhsh Soomro and Muslim Politics in 1930s and 1940s Sindh* (Cambridge University Press, 2018) 285-286.

Following the death of Yusuf Abdullah Haroon, G. M. Syed was made president of the All-India Muslim League in Sindh, with Syed Ghulam Haider Shah as its secretary-general. In years to come, Syed rose to become a vocal critic of Jinnah and the Muslim League. Syed also started demanding that Sindh be an autonomous state after India was partitioned.

Jethi Sipahimalani, who was elected as deputy speaker of the Sindh Assembly in the 1946 elections, expressed her concern on the floor of the assembly.

> *There is the terror of insecurity which has spread from village to village and to the cities. Even the great city of Karachi is not without fear. Only the other day in the public meeting, members of the Muslim League incited the public to shoot and kill down persons obnoxious to them. They openly hinted that if there were no revolvers obtainable, knives and daggers should be used and by any means they must be destroyed. I ask you in all fairness whether with such incitement in Sindh, can any man expect the establishment of law and order in the province. While contemplating the conditions of the province I cannot but hang my head in shame.*[124]

In areas of trade and business, education, moneylending, and industry, more stringent and discriminatory laws were introduced, only to make the lives of the Sindhi Hindus miserable.

---

[124] Jethi Sipahimalani, Sindh Assembly, 1946.

On July 9, 1947, Dr. Choithram Gidwani, president of the Indian National Congress, Sindh province, stated, "Injustices against all of us are innumerable. Our industries have been strangled. Our trade has been emasculated, the education of our children seriously jeopardized, and our joint share in government usurped."[125]

On June 3, 1947, the British government announced that they would leave India. Muslim-majority provinces of India were given the option to join the newly created confederation named Pakistan. The same day, Muhammad Ali Jinnah summoned a council of the All-India Muslim League in Delhi.

In June 1947, Karachi became the capital of the newly established country of Pakistan. Pakistan's first governor-general, Muhammad Ali Jinnah, arrived in the new capital on August 7, 1947, to lead the independence celebrations. They were also attended by the last viceroy of India, Lord Mountbatten.

Unlike Punjab, Bengal, and other provinces, there was no partition-related violence against Sindhi Hindus, though this man-made catastrophe—the Partition of India—led to 1,000,000 killed, tens of millions uprooted, and hundreds of thousands raped. This will forever remain one of the biggest upheavals ever witnessed in human history.

Ironically, though there was no mention of transfer of populations in any of the documents relating to the Partition of India, Sindh, unlike some other provinces, was never divided

---

[125] Choithram Gidwani, Indian National Congress, Sindh Province, July 9, 1947.

geographically. However, it suffered the worst consequences in its aftermath, with the transfer of populations, the influx of millions of Muslims from other areas, and the forced expulsion of millions of Sindhi Hindus from the urban areas of Sindh.

> *At the stroke of midnight, of August 15, 1947, while the world slept, and India awakened to freedom, Sindhis woke up to the bitter truth of finding themselves homeless, landless, and stateless. This is the price they had to pay for freedom. They had certainly not bargained for this tryst with destiny. In a country as Sindh where Hindus ask a Muslim potter when will the holy day of Diyari be celebrated, because it was Muslim potters who made the clay lamps used to celebrate this Hindu holy day. Social discrimination on layman level was recorded for the first time. It was Shah Panjo in Dadu District where a local landlord, Syed Nabi Shah, ordered his village folks that "Muslim cowherds shall not lead out for grazing cows, buffaloes, and goats belonging to Hindus nor shall Muslim barbers, washermen, etc., serve Hindus."*[126]

---

[126] Anand, *National Integration of Sindhis*, 25.

Violence against Sindhi Hindus started in Quetta. Then a military-garrison town, Quetta was a hub of dry-fruit trade controlled mostly by Sindhi Hindus and Sikhs. Both communities were settled in Quetta for decades before the partition. On August 20, 1947, assailants massacred around one hundred Hindus and Sikhs, including many Sindhis, and burned down their houses and properties.

According to historians, these post-Partition attackers were Muslim refugees who had emigrated from East Punjab during the partition. This violence spread from Quetta to Karachi, and then other cities of Sindh, when Muslim refugees started pouring in from North India through the Khokhropar and Wagha borders.

Scholar and historian Nandita Bhavnani brings back the nightmarish memories of partition-related violence against Sindhi Hindus and Sikhs:

> *On the heels of these attacks on Hindus, in temples and in trains across Sindh, came communal violence in Central Sindh town of Nawabshah and its adjoining areas. According to one account, a one hundred-fifty-strong armed mob attacked a Sikh colony in the middle of the night of 30 August. With the Sikhs fleeing for their lives, there were not many casualties, but several houses were looted and set on fire. These Sikhs were targeted simply*

> because Punjabi Sikhs had played a very visible role in the recent carnage in East Punjab.[127]

Although, in comparison to Punjab, violence against Sindhi Hindus and Sikhs was of lower intensity in the beginning. However, it intensified when masses of migrants disembarked the trains from North India. Trains and temples in Karachi, Nawabshah, and Sukkur were attacked, and about thirty Hindus and Sikhs were reportedly killed between August and September 1947. Such incidents accelerated forced migrations of Sindhi Hindus and Sikhs.

Subhadra Anand recalls:

> The panic button had been pressed. Hindus started fleeing after Muslim masses have turned against them, and the police were definitely siding with the Muslims and was, in fact, anti-non-Muslim. By the end of August, a large number of Sikhs started leaving Sindh. Passenger trains in Upper Sindh were attacked.[128]

Labana Sikhs from the Sukkur District were butchered while they were emigrating to India and had stopped to rest in a Karachi *gurdwara*.

---

[127] Nandita Bhavnani, *The Making of Exile: Sindhi Hindus and the Partition of India* (New Delhi: Westland and Tranquebar Press, 2014) 3, 5.

[128] Anand, *National Integration of Sindhis*, 29.

> *Newspapers of those days reported during September, four thousand non-Muslims were leaving Sindh easily from Mīrpur Khās and other stations from Sindh (via Hyderabad), and about two thousand people leaving daily from Karachi by rail, sea, and air. Special trains were being run by Jodhpur Railways. Hyderabad Railways junction witnessed a tremendous rush.*[129]

Most of the affluent Sindhi Hindus abandoned their properties and businesses, which were worth billions of rupees at that time. It is important to note, however, that there were instances of Sindhi Muslim neighbors and friends risking their lives to rescue fleeing Hindu families. Many kept the houses and properties abandoned by Hindus as their *amanat*, with the hopes the original owners would return soon after the tensions subsided. Instead, the abandoned properties were taken over by the refugees pouring into Karachi, Hyderabad, and the rest of Sindh.

Sindh was totally in the grips of hordes of occupiers and troublemakers. A report by the district magistrate at Karachi shed light on the menace:

> *The lawbreakers are mostly non-Sindhis. As soon as they find certain tenements are kept locked, they break open the lock and occupy the tenements unlawfully with all the belongings of the tenants. The protest of landlords and neighboring tenants are of*

---

[129] Anand, *National Integration of Sindhis*.

> *no avail. This has naturally created a very dangerous situation in the buildings concerned and added to the great panic that already exists in the city.*

This resulted in a modern-day Gold Rush; hundreds of criminals came to Sindh. City after city was handed over, for free, to the incoming immigrants under the guise of relief for evacuee property. From August 1947 to January 1948, Karachi and all major cities of Sindh witnessed unchecked violence against Sindhi Hindus and Sikhs who were being forced to flee by rail, sea, or road.

Muhammad Ali Jinnah visited Swaminarayan Mandir, where thousands of Sindhi Hindu families had taken refuge. He implored them not to emigrate and promised them security in their homes.

"We could trust you, but we cannot rely on officials of your government," was the reply of outgoing Hindus and Sikhs.

By far, 1947 and 1948 were the years with the largest exoduses of Sindhi Hindus, but this phenomenon continues today.

Vazira Zamindar writes, "Ayub Khuhro, the premier of Sindh, and other Sindhi leaders also attempted to retain Sindh's minorities, for they also feared a loss of cultural identity with the Hindu exodus."[130]

---

[130] Vazira Zamindar, *The Long Partition and the Making of Modern South Asia: Refugee, Boundaries, Histories* (New York: Columbia University Press, 2007) 5, 52, 58-60.

On January 6, 1948, Khuhro toured Sindh, along with Indian High Commissioner Sri Prakasa, to urge the Sindhi Hindus not to leave their homes. They did not have much success. It is said that amidst the violence and plundering of Hindus' lives and properties, the prime minister of Sindh, Muhammad Ayub Khuhro, went out into the streets, carrying a pistol, to try to protect Hindu families. But instead of being rewarded for his bravery, Mr. Khuhro's government was dismissed by Liaqat Ali Khan, himself an immigrant from India.

Violence, followed by the unchecked and unabated pouring in of immigrants, only sped up the exodus of Hindus from Sindh. Thus, Sindhis suffered one of the greatest national catastrophes of any nation in the postindustrial era. All their cities were snatched away and handed to strangers—a catastrophe that Sindh and Sindhis are still recovering from.

Disenfranchisement of Sindhis in Sindh

> *That geographically contiguous units are demarcated regions, which should be constituted with such territorial readjustments as may be necessary that the areas in which the Muslims are numerically in a majority as in the northwestern and eastern Zones of (British) India should be grouped to constitute "independent states" in which the constituent units should be autonomous and sovereign.*
>
> *~Lahore Resolution, as written and prepared by Muhammad Zafarullah Khan*

The Lahore Resolution

Also commonly known as the Pakistan Resolution, the Lahore Resolution was written by Mr. Muhammad Zafarullah Khan and presented by the prime minister of Bengal, A. K. Fazlul Huq, at a general session of the All-India Muslim League on March 23, 1940. It was formally adopted as the vision for the protection of the Muslim-majority provinces of India. It called for independent states that would be autonomous and sovereign. This was the premise on which Sindh had elected to join the newly formed country. But soon after its creation, Sindh found itself neither independent nor sovereign.

To the contrary, this was the start of the worst exploitation of Sindh's resources, outsiders' dominance and hegemony, interference from the federation, and the oppression of Sindh; to date, these conditions continue. Thus, *disenfranchisement* and *alienation* are two of the most commonly used words in the lexicon of all Sindhis, although Sindhis were at the forefront during the creation of Pakistan, as it was the Sindh Assembly, led by G. M. Syed, that passed the resolution for Pakistan as a separate homeland within India. But since August 1947, Sindhis have reaped nothing but exploitation, oppression, and state-sponsored terror of the worst kind at the hands of successive regimes. There has been no end to the great looting of Sindh's natural resources and the killings of Sindh's sons and daughters.

The indigenous Sindhis have become the minority in their own homeland. They have been driven away from urban areas. Revenues generated in Sindh have been taken away by the federation, with no reciprocity. By construction of multiple mega-dams on River Indus, Sindh's lifeline is being choked in what is probably the worst form of hydrorobbery committed anywhere in the world.

All the greatest leaders of Sindh have either been killed, jailed, or tortured. Publicly elected leaders have been removed and hanged. Mutilated bodies of young Sindhi activists have been thrown into the streets after they were tortured to death by the infamous secret services of the government.

Incarceration and house detention of Sindhi leader G. M. Syed, proponent of modern Sindhi nationalism, for most of the last three decades of his life, until he breathed his last breath while still under detention, is a symbol of how Sindhis have suffered. G. M. Syed himself had drawn the graphic details of this exploitation and oppression as:

> *However all these wonderful plans for uplifting the social and cultural soil of Sindh were shelved and vanished like a dream. Almost entire cities and towns vacated by the fleeing Hindu urban population were handed over to refugees. In small towns in the interior, they behaved like vandals, willfully digging up the floors, bringing down the roofs, unhinging doors,*

windows, and almirahs, and tearing up anything worth a paisa (penny), and sold everything in the bazaar outside; and with cash in their pockets, they veered round again towards the big cities in the province.

Almost the same thing happened with the evacuee farmlands and gardens, which were allotted to them in preference even to toilers of the soil who worked on them. New townships and posh colonies were built for them around Karachi and Hyderabad on the lands in the Kotri Barrage command area, and on the Makhi Forest lands, and a number of modern townships were raised for new settlements from the Punjab. The villages and hamlets of Sindhi people, which got interspersed among the new colonies and townships around the cities for the refugees or in the interior for the Punjabi settlers, were mostly razed to the ground and the human dwellers therein driven away as one drives away packs of animals from forest clearings. Those such villages and hamlets that were temporarily spared because of consideration of expediency could still be seen, as standing witness to the status of second-class citizenry to which the Sindhi people were reduced in their own homeland in Pakistan.[131]

Pakistan's Prime Minister Liaqat Ali Khan, who himself was an immigrant from Kernel in East Punjab, notoriously called Sindh "a donkey-driving and camel-grazing nation." Sindhis

---

[131] G. M. Syed, *Sindhudesh: A Nation in Chains* (Karachi, 1974) 85-86.

faced racial discrimination and were turned into foreigners in their own country, their lands and jobs snatched away.

Liaqat Ali Khan highly encouraged an unending series of immigration into Sindh and accommodated the new arrivals under the Department of Settlement and Rehabilitation in Sindh. A free hand was given to the gangs of immigrants to attack, loot, and kill Sindhi Hindus and occupy their properties. False claims filed by immigrants in Sindh were accepted without any scrutiny, and the property of fleeing Sindhi Hindus was given to the new immigrants at no charge. The lands of Sindhi Hindus were allotted to the urban middle-class immigrants, instead of to Sindhi peasants. Demographics of the Sindhi were falsely and dramatically doctored. Sindh's big cities, like Karachi, Hyderabad, and Sukkur, wore the look of alien cities of North India.

It is interesting to note that in Sindh, there was little to no violence against Sindhi Hindus at the time of the partition. The communal violence in Sindh started only after the large influx of immigrants who started looting, burning, and killing Sindhi Hindus, and it continued unchecked and unabated by the newly formed government.

Massive exchanges of entire sectors of the population were not mentioned in any of the resolutions for the creation of the new country. Jinnah himself continued to hold properties in Bombay and Delhi, hoping to return soon, even after the Partition of India, but ended up being a victim of the calamity of division of India. In the words of M. S. Korejo:

The partition of Punjab led to bloody riots and the two-way migration of population. When Pakistan came into being, leaders like Chaudhry Khaliquzzaman, Allama Shabbir Ahmad Usmani, I. I. Chundrigar, and others, who were to remain behind in India, were in fact the first to pack up and move to Karachi. This created in the minds of Indian Muslims fear of persecution by India and hope of a bright future in Pakistan. Thus, the Urdu-speaking leadership betrayed their own cause, their own ideology, and their own people. The history of the Indo-Muslim nation will not forgive this betrayal, which destabilized millions of Urdu-speaking Muslims, on the one hand, and choked the province on the other.[132]

Thus, Sindhis found themselves in circumstances not very different from other indigenous populations around the globe. Muhammad Ayub Khuhro, the premier of Sindh, was dismissed when he tried to intervene to stop the lawlessness of the immigrant gangs who were attacking the lives and properties of Sindhi all over the province. Liaqat Ali Khan placed a ban on native Sindhis' purchasing property in the cities of Sindh, leaving whatever was available for the incoming immigrants to claim. Anyone immigrating from India only had to file a claim alleging the worth of the property they left in India; then they were given almost the same value in property abandoned by Sindhi Hindus in Sindh.

---

[132] M. S. Korejo, *A Testament of Sindh: Ethnic and Religious Extremism, A Perspective* (Oxford University Press, 2003).

Immediately after the death of Muhammad Ali Jinnah, his sister and political heir, Fatima Jinnah, was banned by Liaqat Ali Khan's administration from any public speeches. It was only after Liaqat Ali Khan's death that she was allowed to make a radio address to the nation, but even that was heavily censored by the administration.

In 1955, she wrote a biography titled, *My Brother*. But even her book was banned from being published for thirty-two years due to censorship by the establishment who accused Fatima Jinnah of wanting to publish "anti-nationalist material." The biography was eventually published in 1987, only after several pages from the book's manuscript were forcibly extracted from the final publication.

Within the first few years of the partition, big and small cities and towns of Sindh, immovable properties, buildings, and agricultural lands, including Karachi, Hyderabad, Sukkur, Nawabshah and Mīrpur Khās, were claimed by immigrants, making the Sindhis aliens in their own homeland. It was generally observed in such cities and towns that bureaucracy showed immense sympathy and support to immigrant occupiers who claimed the Hindus' properties. Two of the most thuggish departments in governments of Sindh and at the federal level—Settlement and Rehabilitation and Evacuee Properties Trust—were carved out to facilitate fraudulent claims of refugees who wanted to take possession of the assets of indigenous Hindus; they acted very much as if they were an invading army distributing war booty to its soldiers.

Uneven settlement of refugee populations from India—mostly concentrated in Sindh, without any attempts at assimilation—created new ethnic tensions between the locals and new settlers; to date, this has only continued and gotten worse. The xenophobia of Liaqat Ali Khan et al against Sindhis was the cornerstone of the foundation for the Mohajir Qaumi Movement (MQM) in days to come.

The flight of Hindus from Sindh deprived Sindh of its extraordinary, highly educated businessmen and bureaucrats. The vacancies left by Sindhi Hindus were filled by immigrant refugees. This vacuum created by the departure of the Sindhi Hindu middle class still remains unfilled.

In a malicious and deliberate attempt to destroy Sindh and Sindhis forever, the Sindhi language—which under the British raj, had been the language for all official business, trade, and instruction in most educational institutions from elementary to the university level—was replaced with Urdu, a language not spoken by any of the indigenous populations. Urdu was declared the only national language. Criticizing the Urdu language was treated as an act of treason, and those who opposed the decision were politically persecuted and prosecuted on one pretext or the other. In an act of extreme irony, this decision was supported by Governor-General Jinnah, though he himself hardly spoke more than a few words of Urdu and carried out most of his communications in the language of his colonial masters—that is, English.

Systematically, the Sindhi language and its speakers became exiled in their own native land as they were surrounded by locusts of migrants hovering and settling in Sindh. Sindhi and Hindu names of places and businesses were replaced by those in Urdu. Over time, this xenophobia against indigenous Sindhis has only gotten worse with each wave of immigrants.

One Unit—The Darkest Years in Sindh's History

Liaqat Ali Khan was assassinated while addressing a public rally in Company Bagh (later named after him as Liaqat Bagh) Rawalpindi in October 1951. His alleged assassin, Said Akbar Khan, was captured and killed on the scene. The motive behind his assassination still remains unsolved.

The West Pakistani establishment was afraid of what was then East Pakistan and its Bengali population because of their numerical superiority. To control the smaller provinces in West Pakistan, along with Bengalis, a one-unit system was declared; this abolished the provincial status of all provinces in West Pakistan and divided the country into two administrative units, East and West Pakistan. This move later proved to be the start of the eventual breakup of the country and the creation of Bangladesh.

In an absolute contradiction to the very basis for the creation of Pakistan, the Lahore Resolution—also known as Qarardad-e-Lahore, or Pakistan Resolution—was unanimously adopted by the All-India Muslim League during its three-day general session in Lahore on March 22 through 24, 1940. The resolution clearly called for independent states, and its demarcation of regions favored the majority of Muslims in areas of autonomy and sovereignty. Punjab, Sindh, Pakhtunkhwa, Balochistan, along with Khanate of Kalat, princely states of Khairpur Mirs, and Bahawalpur, were merged into one province named West Pakistan, its capital at Lahore.

The system was known as One Unit. Its aim was to suppress the lawful-rights movement emerging in oppressed provinces, including Bengal and Sindh; thus, Bengal and Sindh suffered most. The word *Sindh* was banned from being written on any document, or even on an envelope. Instead, the words *West Pakistan* were officially approved and substituted, forcing Sindh's national poet, Shaikh Ayaz, to lament:

سنڌ ڙي تنهنجو نانۡ وتو
جڙا ڪاريهر تي پير پيو

O my beloved Sindh, mentioning your name
Has become akin to stepping on a cobra

On October 22, 1954, the One Unit system was announced by Prime Minister Mohammed Ali Bogra. According to the constitution, it was mandatory to get the approval of each provincial assembly. Abdul Sattar Pirzada was the chief minister of Sindh. Governor Ghulam Muhammad approached Pirzada to get this dirty work of One Unit done and passed by the Sindh Assembly, but Pirzada declined to toe the line of the ruling clique.

Ghulam Muhammad delegated the task of getting the bill passed by the Sindh Assembly to Muhammad Ayub Khuhro, whom he had previously disqualified under the Public Representation Order (PRODA), a selective law aimed at sidelining dissenting politicians. Khuhro was given a conditional offer; his disqualification from holding public office would be removed if he could successfully win the votes of Sindh Assembly members in support of One Unit.

So Pirzada was dismissed and replaced by Khuhro as chief minister of Sindh. Khuhro, who was infamous for being cunning and using strong-arm tactics against his opponents, coerced many Sindhi members of the assembly into agreeing to vote for the One Unit bill.

There was widespread, spontaneous grassroots unrest against One Unit. A series of protests by Sindhi intellectuals, writers, and students erupted all over the province. In contrast, most of the elected Sindhi politicians, with the exception of G. M. Syed, showed little reaction.

Instead of using the Sindh Assembly Hall at Karachi, the session of the assembly members was called at Hyderabad Darbar Hall. The One Unit bill was passed by a majority vote. Abdul Hameed Khan Jatoi, Shaikh Khurshid Hasan, and Rais Ghulam Mustafa Bhurgari were the only members who voted against the One Unit. The speaker of the Sindh Assembly, Mir Ghulam Ali Khan Talpur, was taken to Umarkot, and from Umarkot he was mounted on a camel and lodged in police lockup at Mithi because he opposed the bill. According to the October 16, 2011, issue of the English daily newspaper *The Dawn*:

> *Thus, retroactively, on October 14, 1955, One Unit came into being. Khuhro surrendered Rs320 million to the West Pakistan government while Qizilbash of Khairpur state presented five annas eight paisa — one-third of a rupee — from his treasury. The money Sindh surrendered, if calculated in the present currency, would come to Rs37,600 million. What followed the formation of One Unit is no secret. It gave birth to a number of miseries for the people of smaller provinces, until General Yahya Khan finally dismembered it in 1970.*[133]

Muhammad Ayub Khuhro and Pir Ali Muhammad Rashdi betrayed the Sindhi nation by openly defending One Unit. They helped the federal government get the One Unit bill passed by hook or crook.

Water and Lands of Sindh Under One Unit

In pre- and post-One Unit eras, the waters of River Indus and the fertile lands on both sides of the river were the center of attention for plunderers of the resources of Sindh. Along with multiple mega-dams in the northern provinces of Pakistan, two barrages were built on River Indus in Sindh—the Guddu Barrage near Kashmore and the Ghulam Muhammad Barrage at Kotri.

---

[133] "One Unit: A Dark Chapter of Our History," *The Daily Dawn,* October 16, 2011.

The affected Sindhi villagers were never resettled, and not a single acre of land was allotted to them. Instead, hundreds of thousands of acres of land were allotted to serving and retired civil and military bureaucrats who were overwhelmingly non-Sindhis. It all happened under a law called Land Grant Policy, which, with few exceptions, directly favored the civil and military bureaucrats from other provinces. This colonization of Sindh's lucrative and fertile lands continues today.

Hundreds of thousands of acres of thick forests in the Makhi area were bulldozed, cleaned, and granted to the outsiders for settlement. Forests such as Pai Forest near Sakrand, Sadhooja, and Deh Salhani are glaring examples, among many others, in which forests were razed to allot the land to military and civil bureaucrats. *Chaks* modeled after Punjabi villages were built in Sindh and were inhabited by communities of farmers and soldiers from other provinces. Officials in the corrupt Department of Revenue and Irrigation, which deals with the lands and waters of Sindh, were bribed for favorable allotments of lands and rights to the water to irrigate them.

Hundreds of thousands of acres of green agricultural lands in Upper and Central Sindh and its forests were allotted to the armed forces and its sister organizations and foundations in the name of the defense and welfare of the military. In the 1980s, Sadhooja Forest in Deh Salhani at Pano Aqil was bulldozed for the construction of a military garrison, destroying thousands of acres of lands belonging to the Sindhi people. It is an open secret that the Pano Aqil garrison is the facility in which forcibly detained Sindhi political dissidents and nationalists were lodged, tortured, and killed, their dead bodies thrown away.

Famous Sindhi nationalist and student leader of his time, Yusef Jakhrani, was among those who met their fate there.

Exploitation of Mineral Resources

Pakistan's largest oil and gas deposits are located in Sindh, yet Sindh is the poorest nation in the human development index. There are thousands of educated youths unemployed in the area, while people from other provinces are imported to work in the oil fields of Kadirpur.

According to Sheikh Abdul Rashid, a writer:

> *Though Sindh produces natural resources of billions of rupees per year, it is still far behind in human development indicators. In fact, the major gas-producing districts of Sindh are the worst in their state of human development.*[134]

He dates back the history of exploration of oil and gas as well:

> *In 1925, Burmah Oil Company had drilled the first well at Khairpur, but it did not yield any output. After the discovery of Sui (Balochistan) in 1952, Northern Sindh became the target area for hydrocarbons exploration. Pakistan Petroleum Limited*

---

[134] Sheikh Abdul Rashid, "Sindh is Rich, Why Aren't Its People?" *The Nation*, April 16, 2015.

discovered gas in Khairpur (1957), Kandhkot (1959), and Mazarani (1959). In 1957, Pakistan VOC Petroleum Project had discovered a huge gas reserve of 6.8 trillion cubic feet in Mari. The same company also drilled wells in Talhar (1957), Mirpur Bathoro (1958), Nabisar (1958), and Badin. Burmah Oil Company drilled wells in Lakhra (1958), Badro (1958-59), and Phulji-Dadu (1958). In 1961, Oil and Gas Development Corporation was established, which discovered gas at Sari (1966), Kothar (1973), and Hundi (1977).[135]

Quite contrary to Article 29 of the Petroleum Concessions Agreement (PCA), indigenous Sindhis are neglected in employment. According to agreements with the province, the oil and gas companies are mandated to spend fifty percent of their profits on local development, but this is completely ignored. Exploration of the largest coal deposits in the Thar District has renewed concerns about exploitation of Sindh in general, the Thar District in particular.

Coal deposits in Thar are the largest and richest of its kind in Pakistan, with more than 175 billion tons of lignite coal. According to a scientific survey, such a massive deposit of coal spread over 400 square miles can last 400 years. However, in the name of benefiting the rest of the country, railway lines are being laid; this will prevent access to a major quantity of this mineral resource of Sindh.

---

[135] Rashid, "Sindh is Rich, Why Aren't Its People?"

Sindh Engro Coal Mining Company (SECMC), which was created for the exploration in Thar, is operating exactly as the East India Company did when the British colonized India. The locals complain of the environmental havoc being wreaked upon their ancestral villages and lands. As a result of construction of Gorano Dam, 27,000 acres of land will be submerged, including twelve villages of indigenous Sindhis; it is also estimated that 3,000 freshwater wells will be poisoned. Plus, 15,000 acres of land will become uncultivable because of the resulting contamination of both soil and water.

Mass Influx of Immigrant Populations into Sindh

In the last century, the first influx of outside population to Sindh happened in the 1930s. After the construction of Sukkur Barrage, the British brought farmers from Punjab to clear forested areas for farming. The second-largest influx of outside population happened during the Hur movement of the 1940s, when soldiers from Punjab and Bugti tribesman from Baluchistan, who had shown unconditional loyalty to their colonial masters, were settled in Sindh to counter the movement, especially around Mukhi Forest and other areas of Sanghar.

The largest influx of outside population in Sindh was the advent of the mass migration from northern and other parts of India during the partition. According to the census held under the British in 1941, 47.6 percent of the population in Karachi consisted of Sindhi Hindus. This number has dropped now to less than one percent.

According to Vazira Zamindar, historian and scholar on the Partition of India:

> *Most of the Muslim refugees of Delhi and north India arrived in the city of Karachi. In comparison to Delhi, Karachi had been a small, sleepy port city that served the Sind hinterland, and was largely tied to Bombay and the Malabar coast for the mercantile links. However, as Sindh's provincial capital, its highly educated Sindhi Amils and other Hindu communities were an essential part of Sindhi culture and literature, and the region's proud Sufi tradition. As the city's status underwent a dramatic change, from the periphery of British India to being declared the federal Pakistani state, almost all of its entire Hindu population had left the city. According to the census of 1951, the city's population had tripled with the arrival of Muslim refugees from north India.*

The next major change in Sindh's demographics came in the form of One Unit in 1951. Numerous discriminatory and anti-Sindhi laws were introduced. The ecological systems of Indus River were destroyed with the construction of multiple dams and barrages.

In October 1958, General Ayub Khan declared martial law in the country. Sindh was the worst victim of the draconian laws implemented under martial law. In his book, *Friends, Not Masters*, Ayub later confessed that he imposed martial law in order to save the One Unit system.

G. M. Syed was elected a member of the West Pakistan Assembly. In October 1958, he tabled the bill for abolishing One Unit and received overwhelming support from the majority of the members. Ayub Khan imposed martial law to prevent this. G. M. Syed was arrested and had to live the next decade either in jail or under house arrest.

It was during Ayub Khan's times when large numbers of Pathan populations began settling in Karachi, Hyderabad, and other parts of Sindh. Gohar Ayub, son of Ayub Khan, contested the elections. His supporters resorted to violence against the Urdu-speaking population of Karachi. He led a procession to celebrate his victory in Karachi.

It is said that the deputy martial-law administrator of Sindh, General Tikka Khan, who later acquired the infamous title of the Butcher of Bengal, banned the teaching of the Sindhi language as a compulsory subject in all Sindh schools because his son had failed the subject. After the dismemberment of former East Pakistan in 1971, Zulfikar Ali Bhutto took over as the president and civilian chief martial-law administrator on December 16, 1971.

Zia-ul-Haq's era of military dictatorship lasted over a decade. He presided over the Afghan crisis, followed by the former Soviet Union's invasion of Afghanistan, during which 5,000,000 Afghan refugees poured into Pakistan. This deluge of Afghan refugees was followed by Iranian, Burmese, and Bengali immigrant populations.

Apartheid Against Sindhis

Sindhis were highly discriminated against in jobs and academic institutions throughout the cities of Sindh. Of the three elected Sindhi prime ministers who assumed their offices as heads of government, one was executed, another was assassinated during her election campaign, and the third, Muhammad Khan Junejo, was sent packing by dictator General Zia-ul-Haq.

During Zulfikar Ali Bhutto's period from 1972 to 1977, Sindhis had some opportunities to resettle in their own cities. Zulfikar Ali Bhutto introduced the system of lateral entries in government services, thus allowing a number of eligible candidates from rural areas of Sindh to compete with the rest of the country. Bhutto founded Pakistan Steel Mills with the help of the former Soviet Union and the port authority of Port Qasim, through which passed a number of educated Sindhis moving back to Karachi.

Zulfikar Ali Bhutto was overthrown in a military coup, tried on fabricated charges of ordering the murder of a political opponent, hanged in the middle of the night, and his body buried without even giving his family the opportunity to provide a proper burial. The hanging of Zulfikar Ali Bhutto sent waves of shock and anger never seen before among Sindhis. It was popularly believed that the only reason he was killed was because he was a Sindhi.

Later, his older son, Murtaza Bhutto, was shot in front of his house and left to bleed to death without any medical intervention. His other son, Shahnawaz Bhutto, died in France from suspected poisoning. And his daughter, Benazir Bhutto, was assassinated while leading a political rally in Rawalpindi in 2007. In the last century, these are the worst tragedies that any political family has suffered, hauntingly similar to the Kennedys of the US and Gandhis of India.

To suppress a reaction against the hanging of Zulfiqar Ali Bhutto, Sindh was brutally oppressed by the military. Political leaders, intellectuals, and activists were flogged, jailed, and tortured. Many were killed while in the custody of government agencies.

Nazeer Abbasi, a leftist Sindhi student leader, was arrested and tortured to death. In October 1984, buses carrying Sindhi students from Sindh University, Jamshoro campus, were stopped at a security checkpoint at a Thori railway crossing. The security forces randomly started firing at the students when they tried to resist the illegal arrest of many of their peers. This resulted in the death of five Sindhi youth and injuries to many. Those who survived were taken into custody and jailed for years.

On October 2, 1978, a Sindhi female medical student, Shireen Soomro, was allegedly gang-raped by a group of army officers in Nawabshah. Students on campuses all over Sindh resorted to protests. Two soldiers were killed in Jamshoro. In response to this, the security forces arrested, interrogated, and tortured hundreds of Sindhi students. Campuses of institutions of higher learning were shut down for over a year as they and the level of education in Sindh were systematically destroyed. Campuses and their dorms were converted into complexes resembling jails, with barbed wire, check posts, and stop-and-search operations by security agencies employing paramilitary personnel.

Sindh's villages were destroyed, and many cases of extrajudicial killings by security forces were reported; though many more went unreported, as families of victims were intimidated into not reporting such incidents. Lawlessness increased in Sindh with the breakup of jails, the most infamous being the maximum-security jail in Sukkur; it was known to house the worst offenders, those accused of the most heinous crimes. The Sukkur Jail escapees, the most dangerous criminals, were helped to find shelter in the thick forests on both banks of the River Indus, thus killing two birds with one stone. On the one hand, widespread armed robberies, kidnappings for ransom, and murders by these escapees terrorized the populace into submission. On the other hand, their presence in these same forests was used as an excuse for the deforestation of thousands of acres. And these lands were allotted to retired officers from other provinces.

Armed operations against unarmed civilians and exploitation of Sindh's resources by Zia-ul-Haq paved the way for the eruption of rural uprisings against his regime. Sindhi commoners, peasants, political activists, and leaders took to the roads to confront security personnel. Zia-ul-Haq's government and state security forces unleashed a state of terror against the common Sindhis; this further aggravated the situation in Sindh, as things took a violent turn. Hundreds were killed and thousands were imprisoned in rural Sindh. In 1983, Sindhi resistance against Zia erupted in the form of the Movement for Restoration of Democracy (MRD). Ian Talbot defined the Sindhi rural uprising this way: "This was particularly explosive in Sindh, where Sufism had always been an integral component of regional cultural identity."[136]

In the words of Sindhi scholar and sociologist, Dr. Feroz Ahmed, who had himself been active in the Sindhi-rights movement against Zia during the time:

> *Therefore in August 1983, when the eleven-party alliance, the Movement for Restoration of Democracy (MRD), gave a call for a countrywide civil disobedience movement, it turned into a prolonged mass upsurge in the interior of Sindh. It was suppressed by brutal methods. However, it succeeded in galvanizing the issues surrounding the resentment of Sindhi people.*[137]

Benazir Bhutto, daughter of executed Prime Minister Zulfiqar Ali Bhutto, returned and led MRD in 1986. Sindhi villages were shelled using helicopters, and many villagers were machine-gunned to death while participating in protests.

Intelligence agencies surveyed Sindh and decided not to let such protests be repeated. They discreetly patronized gangs of bandits in rural parts of Sindh and ethnic urban organizations like MQM in the cities of Sindh. Ethnic strife was engineered in cities; hundreds of Sindhis were killed, injured, and maimed.

---

[136] Talbot, Pakistan: *A New History*.

[137] Feroz Ahmed, *Ethnicity and Politics in Pakistan* (Oxford University Press, 1998) 61-62.

Large settlements of Sindhis in the urban centers of Karachi and Hyderabad were attacked by MQM hit squads.

In the big cities of Sindh, especially Karachi and Hyderabad, the native Sindhi inhabitants were forced to abandon their ancestral homes and old neighborhoods. They had to settle in the outskirts or build new townships. The demographics of Sindh were violently changed. This process of complete disenfranchisement started widespread resentment and a sense of deprivation among indigenous Sindhis.

Sindhi Nationalist Movement

In subcontinent South Asia, modern-day Sindhi nationalism ignited many of the nationalist and political movements that took place in the first four decades of the twentieth century. Between the movement for the separation of Sindh from Bombay and the movement for independence from the British at the end of the Second World War, Sindh was exposed to modern nationalistic ideas and influences of numerous political movements that were launched on its soil and abroad. Although Ghulam Murtaza Syed, popularly known as G. M. Syed, born and buried in the tiny, sleepy village of Sann, is thought to be the founding father of the Sindhi nationalist movement of today, the origins of the latest wave of Sindhi nationalism dates back to the early part of the twentieth century when Sindh was colonized by the British.

Sindhi nationalism draws its enormous inspiration from centuries of Sindhi literature and poetry filled with love for the motherland. It reached its zenith after the secession of the Bengalis and the creation of Bangladesh in 1971, led by G. M. Syed, who had coined a new term, *Sindhudesh*, to rhyme with the newly created country of Bangladesh, which was seen as the culmination of their successful struggle for freedom.

Sindhi Nationalist Movement Pre-Partition

The end of the First World War marked the beginning of anti-British Colonial movements in India, which had a direct influence on Sindh as well. In 1920, Gandhi called for civil disobedience, and that movement was received very well in Sindh. In 1925, it was Shaikh Abdul Majeed Sindhi who demanded the separation of Sindh from Bombay. Later, that demand was echoed by the Indian National Congress and All-India Muslim League. Sindh's Freedom from Bombay conferences were organized in Karachi. Shaikh Abdul Majeed Sindhi, Muhammad Ayub Khuhro, Pir Ali Muhammad Rashdi, Abdullah Haroon, and Jethmal Parsram participated.

Jethmal Parsram wrote an editorial after the massacre in Jallianwala Bagh and quoted Bhittai:

اِڳِيان اَڏِن وَتِ، پوِيَن سِرِ سنڀاها؛
ڪات نہ پوين قبولَ مِ، مَچُنَّ پائين گَهتِ؛
مِتا مُهايَنِ جا، پِيا نہ ڏِسِين پَتَ؟
ڪلالڪي هَتِ، ڪَسُنُ جو ڪوپُ وَهِي.

The ones in front willingly lay their heads on the butcher's block
Those behind anxiously await their turn
See the heads of lovers, Piled on the ground
The trade of slaughtering goes on In the tavern of the master

A case of sedition was filed against him by the colonial British government, and he was convicted and fined. The separation of Sindh from Bombay on April 1, 1936, proved to be the catalyst for many future political movements in Sindh.

> *I do hereby confess before my nation, intellectuals, and fighters of new generations that, because of having less political awareness and scarcity of experience, I was stuck in quagmire of All-India politics. Instead of demanding Sindh as a completely independent country, we asked for the fully autonomous province within India, while the fact was that the way British had enslaved our independent country, we should have launched a movement for its freedom.*[138]

---

[138] G. M. Syed, *Sindhudesh: A Nation in Chains*. Karachi: 1974.

With Jamshed Nasarwanji and Mir Mohammed Baloch, G. M. Syed founded Sindh Hari Committee for the rights of Sindhi *hari* (peasants). He also tabled several bills in the Sindh Legislative Assembly for the welfare of Sindhi peasants. Hyder Bux Jatoi, who was then the deputy collector, later succeeded G. M. Syed as president of the Sindh Hari Committee. Hyder Bux Jatoi equated the hari rights to those of Sindh at large.

The leaders of the peasants and rights movement, writers, and student and Indian nationalism activists from congress shaped the future of the Sindhi nationalist movement. Two booklets proved to be handbooks for the war cry for Sindhi rights and Sindhi nationalism. The first booklet, *Faryad-e-Sindh*, written by an anonymous source, portrayed the plight of Sindhis against the inflow of outsiders against the backdrop of the construction of the Sukkur Barrage. The second, another Sindhi masterpiece in political literature, was famously titled *Save Sindh, Save the Continent: From Feudal Lords, Capitalists and Their Communalisms*, authored by Muhammad Ibrahim Joyo in 1947. Its foreword was written by G. M. Syed. As it is obvious from the title and sub-title of the book, Joyo Sahib graphically depicted the slavery-like life of peasants, the oppression, and the exploitation by feudal lords and capitalists. He rejected the communalism that was rife in Sindh at that time under the guise of Hindu-Muslim tensions.

Long before the actual movement, Muhammad Ibrahim Joyo had been a proponent of progressive thought in Sindhi nationalist ideology. He went to Bombay for further education and became immensely influenced by the writings of M. N. Roy, a lifelong Socialist ideologue. In his booklet, Joyo Sahib rejected the division of India and called instead for an autonomous and independent Sindh.

Dutch scholar Oskar Verkaaik analyzed Muhammad Ibrahim Joyo and his political masterpiece as follows:

> In short, in Joyo's analysis the notion of class struggle, Islamic revivalism, and early Sindhi nationalism come together in an optimistic belief in "the river of Progress," in which the Sindhi Muslim peasants constitute the progressive potential, struggling against the reactionary forces of landlords, traditional religious specialists, and recent Punjabi immigrants. Recognizing the class and national differences between Muslims, he also criticizes Muslim nationalism, saying that "[t]o talk of Muslim nationalism would be as meaningless and self-contradictory as to talk of world-nationalism, for Islam represents universalism, and can be embraced by any one of the hundred and one nations of the world."[139]

Sindhi Nationalist Movement Post-Partition

Before and after the Partition of India in 1947, communal tensions, riots, and violence were followed by forced exiles and emigrations of Sindhi Hindus. Those who emigrated from Sindh to India included Sindhi writers, poets, intellectuals,

---

[139] Oskar Verkaaik, "Reforming Mysticism: Sindhi Separatist Intellectuals in Pakistan," *International Review of Social History: Popular Intellectuals and Social Movements: Framing Protest in Asia, Africa, and Latin America*, Vol. 49 Supplement 12 (Cambridge University Press, 2004) 79-86.

and publishers. The flight of Sindhi Hindus, who consisted of an overwhelming majority of the urban middle class, caused a severe blow to Sindhi literature and politics. Writers like Hashoo Kewalramani, Keerat Babani, Gobind Punjabi, Gobind Malhi, Mohan Punjabi, A. J. Uttam, Jethmal Parsram, Gulab Bhavnani Ayasahi Vidyarthi, and many others left for India. But some, like Poho Mal and Sobho Gianchandani, refused to leave their native Sindh and lived there until their last breath.

A new generation of Sindhi literary and political minds poured into post-Partition Karachi. By then, the sleepy village of Mai Kolachi had been flooded with immigrants and had become the capital of the newly formed country of Pakistan. But for the native Sindh, it seemed like a foreign city, causing the legendary Sindhi poet Shaikh Ayaz to lament for what he described as "Heartbreaking Karachi."

روشني جا گيت ڳائيندڙ ڪراچي، دل ڏڪائيندڙ ڪراچي

Karachi, Singing Songs of light
The Heartbreaking Karachi

A group of Sindhi students living in Metharam Hostel started a grassroots movement by pasting stickers around town with the slogan "Write Sindhi, Read Sindhi, Speak Sindhi." In 1952, G. M. Syed started a newspaper named *Naeen Sindh* (*New Sindh*) with Sobho Gianchandani as its editor. Other newspapers that were vocal on the atrocities against Sindh were dailies like *Qurbani*, *Khadim-e-Watan*, and *Al-Waheed*. These newspapers continued until One Unit was abolished.

In 1955, the provincial status of Sindh was made part of a newly created province of West Pakistan. G. M. Syed was sent to jail and later placed under house arrest. He was arrested at Karachi, taken to Hyderabad Jail for one night, and then later delivered to his native village, Sann, where he was to remain under detention for three months. Abdul Ghaffar Khan, Abdul Samad Khan Achakzai, and peasant leader Hyder Bux Jatoi were also arrested.

G. M. Syed was elected to the West Pakistan Assembly in 1956, where he left no stone unturned in his efforts to abolish One Unit. In the West Pakistan Assembly, he was the strongest voice for Sindhis and against the havoc One Unit was wreaking in what he called "economic, cultural, and ethnic losses to Sindh." During West Pakistan Assembly sessions, Syed raised the issues about the rights of Sindhis, such as lands given away to military and civil bureaucrats, plight of Sindhi peasants, and job discrimination against educated Sindhis. He forged an alliance with the ruling Republican Party to do away with One Unit.

Finally, when G. M. Syed was about to succeed in bringing to the floor of the assembly a unanimous resolution for the abolishment of One Unit, to counter this, General Ayub Khan declared the nation under martial law on October 10, 1958. After the imposition of martial law, G. M. Syed was immediately sent to jail with other leaders. He spent the next ten years—from October 10, 1958, to April 11, 1968—in jail. After his release, he once again became active on the cultural platform as he organized Bazm-e-Soofia-e Sindh and started addressing gatherings at traditional Sufi and Sindhi festivals at the shrines of Sindhi Sufis and saints. Shaikh Ayaz and Rasool Bux Palijo also delivered speeches at these gatherings.

Dubbing these actions as seditious, Ayub Khan's government placed G. M. Syed under house arrest again within a year of his prior release. He was again served detention orders to be confined to his house in Sann, while Zulfikar Ali Bhutto, who at the time was a minister in the cabinet of Ayub Khan, was an advocate of One Unit. According to G. M. Syed, "On one occasion of Urs [anniversary] of Shah Abdul Latif Bhittai, Zulfiqar Ali Bhutto claimed that had Shah Latif been alive today, he would have supported the concept of One Unit."[140]

Hyder Bux Jatoi, Qazi Faiz Muhammad, Ghulam Muhammad Laghari, and others formed Sindhi Awami Mahaz, which was composed of peasant-rights activists, known as hari workers, and groups of Sindhi students, writers, poets, and intellectuals. In 1953, Sindhi Adabi Sangat (Sindhi Literary Organization) was formed by a group of writers in Karachi, and it emerged as a representative for Sindhi writers.

Sindhi Awami Mahaz, with Shaikh Abdul Majeed Sindhi as its president and Qazi Faiz Mohammed as its secretary-general, became active in the anti-One Unit movement. Nuruddin Sarki, Shaikh Ayaz, Fateh Malik, Tanveer Abbasi, Abdul Karim Gadai, Muhammad Usman Diplai, Ghulam Mohammed Grami, Sobho Gianchandani, Poho Mal, and Rashid Bhatti rose to prominence as writers, intellectuals, and human-rights activists. Hyder Bux

---

[140] G. M. Syed, *Sindhudesh: A Nation in Chains.* Karachi: 1974.

Jatoi coined the war cry of the movement—"Jeay Sindh"—which is the title of one of his poems. Still today, this is the most powerful slogan of the Sindhi nation and its nationalist movement; it will likely remain so for quite some time.

Hyder Bux Jatoi wrote several books and pamphlets against One Unit and the subjugation of Sindhis by the dictatorship; he was jailed on multiple occasions for it. The people of Sindh, out of their love for him, started calling him Baba-e-Sindh (Father of Sindh). Hyder Bux Jatoi's hari-movement slogan, Hari Haqdar (Peasant Is the Holder of Rights), was another widely used war cry for the rights movements of the era.

The beginning of the 1960s witnessed the renaissance of the Sindhi nationalist struggle in poetry and prose. Peoples' patience was running out, and there was growing unrest all over the country against the dictatorship of Ayub Khan. Sindh was at the forefront of this unrest. Progressive leftist student and labor movements against Ayub Khan emerged.

G. M. Syed, who had been the leading force behind the formation of the anti-One Unit front in the 1950s, revived this in the 1960s, again successfully drawing support from likeminded leaders and parties from other provinces, including Sheikh Mujibur Rahman and his Awami League from former East Pakistan; Mengal, Marri, Bizenjo, and Akbar Bugti from Baluchistan; and Khan Abdul Ghaffar Khan, Bacha Khan, from Pakhtunkhwa. He launched a wider movement against One Unit this time.

Sindhi writers, intellectuals, poets, and journalists were also part of the anti-One Unit movement. There were about fifty Sindhi newspapers and periodicals, including Hamid Sindhi's *Rooh Rehan*, under which Sindhi rights activists and educated youths, scholars, poets, and intellectuals congregated in the name of its yearly Jashn Rooh Rehan. Jashn Rooh Rehan became a pivotal annual gathering of cultural literary activities. Shaikh Ayaz was given the title of Sindh Jo Awaz, or Voice of Sindh. Shaikh Ayaz became the star attraction at these gatherings. His revolutionary poetry sent bolts of patriotic energy throughout the Sindh youth. Any nationalist or political gathering without recitation of his poetry is considered incomplete.

Feeling threatened by this uprising of the populace, the regime of the dictator Ayub Khan enacted the Pakistan Press and Publication Ordinance, with which the government acquired the authority to ban all publications. Soon after, citing the notorious censorship law, it banned the Sindhi monthly *Rooh Rehan*.

At one Jashn Rooh Rehan, Shaikh Ayaz was banned from entering Hyderabad City to recite his poetry. Sindhi students, writers, and other people accorded him a rousing welcome and saw him off at Kotri Railway Station, where he recited his revolutionary nationalist poetry.

Another draconian law to try to crush the voice of the people opposing dictatorial rule and the state's oppression was the Defense of Pakistan Rule (DPR). Over the decades, hundreds of political activists, nationalist leaders, poets, and writers, including G. M. Syed, Hyder Bux Jatoi, Shaikh Ayaz, Qazi Faiz Muhammad, Yousuf Laghari, Jam Saqi, Rashid Bhatti, Rasool Bux Palijo, Fazil Rahu, and Ibrahim Munshi, were jailed under the notorious DPR.

During the 1965 India-Pakistan War, Shaikh Ayaz and Sobho Gianchandani were detained in Sukkur Jail as suspected enemy agents and remained there until the war was over. Ayaz was detained because of the poem that he wrote and dedicated to his friend, Indian Sindhi poet Narayan Shyam, in which he says he will not fight against his fellow Sindhi and brother poet.

هي سنگرام
سامهون آ نارائڻ شيام!
هن جا منهنجا
قول ب ساڳيا
ٻول ب ساڳيا
هو ڪوٽا جو ڪاڪ ڏٺي، پر
منهنجا رنگ رتو_رتول ب ساڳيا
ڏيٺ ب ساڳيو
ڍول ب ساڳيو
هانءُ ب ساڳيو
هول ب ساڳيا
هن تي ڪيئن بندوق کڻان مان!
هن کي گولي ڪيئن هڻان مان!
ڪيئن هڻان مان!
ڪيئن هڻان مان!!
ڪيئن، هڻان مان...

We are at war
Facing me is Narain Shyam His and mine
Quotes are the same So are our words
He is the king of Poetry The colors of our blood
and our expressions, are the same
Our sand dunes are the same
Our beloved ones are the same
Our souls are the same. Our fears
are the same. How can I raise a gun against him?
How can I shoot a bullet at him?
How Can I, How Can I, How can I…

March 4th—The D-Day of the Sindhi Nationalist Movement

Sindhi students brought the Sindhi nationalist movement to the masses and gave it new blood. They began by giving their own blood on the streets when police and state apparatuses way-laid their busloads on March 4, 1967. This laid the foundation for mass Sindhi nationalist students' movements from the new campuses of Sindh University Jamshoro.

It all started when the martial-law authorities of Ayub Khan began interfering in the affairs of the university's medical and engineering campuses. Masroor Hasan Khan, then commissioner in the administration of the Hyderabad division, acting as agent of the dictatorial government of Ayub Khan, tried to dislodge the vice chancellor, Hassan Ali Abdul Rehman.

The students resisted the shenanigans of Commissioner Masroor and his administration's interference into the university's affairs. Commissioner Masroor's actions raised the suspicion that he wanted to clip students' budding politics as the University of Sindh was becoming a center of Sindhi awareness of national rights.

Earlier, the university was visited by martial-law authorities, but they faced protests against their plans to eliminate Sindhi subjects from MA examinations. Zulfiqar Ali Bhutto, while he was an advocate of the One Unit system, had previously visited the university, only to face tough questions against One Unit by Sindhi students. On sensing that the vice chancellor was being harassed, and may be removed, Sindhi students marched against Commissioner Masroor at old and new campuses.

On March 4, 1967, a big convoy of busloads of students led by Yousuf Laghari, Masood Noorani, and others was on their way to Hyderabad City when they were waylaid by heavy contingents of police. The protesting students were trying to reach the commissioner's office to register their protest against the administration's interference in university affairs and harassment of the vice chancellor, but they were surrounded by police from five districts and were forced off the buses. They were beaten, tear-gassed, charged with batons, and arrested in bulk. About 200 students were initially arrested, and later dozens of leaders and their supporters were jailed. Many of those arrested were injured.

The whole of Sindh rose against these barbaric police crackdowns on the students of Sindh University. However, the arrests and manhunts for the rest of the student activists and leaders continued. Police arrested many of the students' leaders, including Jam Saqi, the next day, March 5, in Hyderabad City.

Students of Sindh University, especially those in jail, received enormous sympathy and support from Sindhis across the province. Sindhi lawyers Rasool Bux Palijo, Muhammad Memon, and Qazi Azam filed bail papers for them. Affluent Sindhi people posted the bails, and Sindhi judges like Bakht Ali Jakhrani granted them. Within days of the March 4 incident, there were protest rallies, public meetings, and boycotts throughout Sindh against the police action and arrests.

The slogans and disenchantment were not directed only at Commissioner Masroor Hasan. This had grown into a full-fledged movement against the atrocities suffered by the Sindhi nation as a whole, and specifically against Ayub Khan, his dictatorship, and One Unit. Zulfikar Ali Bhutto, who had by then parted ways with the dictator Ayub, issued a statement against the police brutality suffered by the Sindhi students.

G. M. Syed himself was placed under detention, yet again, on charges that he had met with the leaders of the March 4 movement to destabilize the country and had been inciting the unrest in Sindh's universities.

But the students' movement initiated by Sindhi students at the University of Sindh turned into a popular backstory for the Sindhi nationalist movement. Students at Sindh University, then organized as the Hyderabad Student Federation, invited Zulfikar Ali Bhutto to the campus and hosted a reception in his honor in December 1967. This reception in honor of the former foreign minister was held on the grounds of a local school, Jama Arabia, in Hyderabad.

Sindhi students convened a caucus of students from all over Sindh. This centralized the movement that up to this point had been divided into small, local district organizations like the Jacobabad Students' Federation, Nawab Shah Students' Federation, and Hyderabad Students' Federation. This first convention of Sindhi student activists from all over Sindh was held at the Indus Hotel Hyderabad, and for the first time, the protesters were organized under one name—Sindh Nationalist Students' Federation—with Jam Saqi and Mir Thebo as president and secretary-general, respectively. Shah Muhammad Shah, who then represented Nawabshah Students' Federation, became joint secretary of the newly formed Sindh Nationalist Students' Federation. This student organization announced its struggle against One Unit and Ayub Khan.

There was another student organization, Sindhi Cultural Students' Organization (SSCO), led by Yousuf Talpur and Masood Noorani. Together, these student organizations ran a campaign to get all public signs on official buildings and on streets displayed in the Sindhi language. During Shah Abdul Bhittai's gathering, Mir Thebo and other students were arrested for distributing badges that read, "Sindhi language: National language." They were convicted by military courts and sent to Karachi Central Jail.

Irrespective of political and organizational affiliations, Sindhi students went on hunger strikes at the old campus of Sindh University to press their demands that electoral lists of voters be printed in the Sindhi language. This time, the protesting students were joined by their female counterparts, including Akhtar Baloch, Riaz Memon, and Naseem Thebo. They were also joined by senior politician Rasool Bux Palijo, peasant leader Qazi Faiz Muhammed, and Sindh's celebrated singer, Zarina Baloch, popularly known as Jiji (The Mother). Women's participation was a turning point of bravery in the history of the Sindhi Nationalist Movement.

One night, police violently attacked the camp of peaceful hunger strikers; Qazi Faiz Muhammad was injured. All male and female hunger strikers were arrested. Zarina Baloch and her daughter, Akhtar Baloch, were sent to Sukkur Jail; while incarcerated, Akhtar Baloch wrote her jail notes, which were later published under the title *Qedyani ji Diary*, which translates to *The Diary of a Female Prisoner*. This is yet another masterpiece of Sindhi nonfiction. The book has been translated into many languages, including in English, as *Narrative of a Prisoner*.

Day-to-day protests against One Unit continued. Sindhi students, writers, and intellectuals declared a Break One Unit week in Sindh. During this week, Sheikh Mujibur Rahman toured Sindh. Succumbing to the populace's protests and the civil disobedience by students, workers, and political parties at every level, Ayub Khan resigned and handed over the country's reins to another military dictator—his second-in-command, General Yahya Khan.

Detentions of Sindhi nationalists and the jailed hunger strikers continued. In 1969, Yahya Khan declared an adult-franchise general election for the first time in the history of the country to be held in December 1970. He announced the release of political prisoners, including the hunger strikers and G. M. Syed, and the date for the abolition of One Unit. That year, youths and students close to G. M. Syed formed Jeay Sindh Nojawan Mahaz; its leaders include Iqbal Tareen, Shah Muhammad, Abdul Hai Palijo, and others.

In 1969, Sheikh Mujibur Rahman accompanied his comrades Professor Muzaffar Ahmed and Tajuddin Ahmed on a tour of what was then West Pakistan. In Karachi, G. M. Syed hosted a reception in the sheik's honor. In July 1970, Yahya Khan abolished One Unit and made Balochistan the fourth province in West Pakistan. During British Rule, current-day Balochistan consisted of four princely states—Makran, Kharan, Lasbela, and Kalat—along with the districts of Quetta, Pishin, Harnai, Sibi, and Thal-Chotiali. In this realignment, these states and districts were merged into the single province of Balochistan.

This announcement was celebrated all over Sindh; Sindhi newspapers published special supplements about it. Hyder Bux Jatoi, who had dedicated his life to fighting for the rights of Sindh, including the breaking up of One Unit, died in May1970, but only after hearing that One Unit would be abolished. His funeral in Hyderabad was attended by a large number of Sindhis, including nationalist leaders and workers, political leaders, intellectuals, and his comrades from all over the country. Among those who came from outside Sindh were Nawab Akbar Bugti, Ataullah Mengal, and Sher Muhammad, whose alias was General Sherov.

Sindhi Nationalist Movement Post-One Unit

G. M. Syed announced his candidacy under the new Jeay Sindh Muttahida Mahaz party. The government allowed the candidates of all political parties to discuss their manifestos on national television. G. M. Syed forcefully argued for the welfare of Sindh with irrefutable facts and figures. However, Syed lost the elections to a local tribal chief, Malik Sikandar, in December 1970.

In the 1970 elections, Zulfikar Ali Bhutto's PPP (Pakistan People's Party) emerged victorious in two provinces, Sindh and Punjab. The National Awami Party, led by Khan Abdul Wali Khan, along with a right-wing party, Jamiat Ulema-e-Islam, won majority seats in the North-West Frontier Province (NWFP) and Balochistan. Sheikh Mujibur Rahman ran his campaign on a nationalist manifesto based on his Awami League's famous "six points." These points included the demand for maximum provincial autonomy, leaving only three areas under the federation's rule: foreign affairs, defense, and currency. Rahman's Awami League swept elections across former East Pakistan and emerged as a single victorious party.

The ruling junta of the time, which was overwhelmingly dominated by individuals from the western wing of the country, perceived this as a threat to the country's integrity and national security. Sheikh Mujibur Rahman and his party were not invited to form the government, despite winning by a clear majority. Bhutto opposed summoning a national assembly session at Dhaka. However, leading a delegation of his party, Bhutto went to Dhaka in a failed attempt to open negotiations with Sheikh Mujibur Rahman. This resulted in military operations and the genocide of 3,000,000 Bengalis, and ultimately led to war between India and Pakistan, the third war between the two nations in three decades.

This war ended with one of the greatest military defeats in the history of modern warfare, the surrender of approximately 90,000 soldiers. The end of the war also resulted in the breakup of Pakistan and the creation of a new independent country named Bangladesh, which consisted of what was previously the eastern province of Pakistan. This humiliating defeat forced the top brass of the Pakistani Army to finally relinquish their control of the reins of the remaining country. Zulfiqar Ali Bhutto assumed the office of president and, ironically, that of civilian chief martial-law administrator.

Sindhi nationalists, writers, and poets supported the Bangladesh movements. Many opposed and protested against the genocide of Bengalis. Sindh's national poet, Shaikh Ayaz, and Rashid Bhatti were jailed for condemning the military operation in Bangladesh. G. M. Syed was placed under house arrest. Sindhi students, writers, and teachers were arrested from Jamshoro campuses. Vice Chancellor Sayad Ghulam Mustafa Shah was placed under house arrest. Professors and teachers, including Ghulam Ali Allana, Arjun Lal, student leaders Yusef Jakhrani, and LMC student Nandlal Varyani, were jailed as security risks.

The real motive behind these state atrocities against Sindhi youths and intelligentsia was to terrorize them, as the University of Sindh and other campuses at Jamshoro were considered to be strongholds of the Sindhi nationalist movement, similar to Dhaka University, which had been the main hub of Bengali nationalism. At Dhaka University, Pakistani security forces killed a number of Bengali professors, students, and intellectuals overnight and buried them in mass graves. Hostels inhabited by Bengali Hindu students and teachers were razed overnight in March 1971. Instead of being deterred, writers continued to create a good portion of Sindhi literature and poetry in support of the Bangladesh liberation movement.

Sindhi poet and journalist Anwar Pirzado, then a pilot in the East Pakistani Air Force, wrote a letter to a friend and teacher at Sindh University. In it, Pirzado described the atrocities being committed against Bengalis. The letter was intercepted and Pirzado was arrested, court-martialed, convicted, and jailed for seven years.

Zulfikar Ali Bhutto's government released political prisoners, poets, and intellectuals arrested by the previous regime, including Shaikh Ayaz, Rashid Bhatti, Anwar Pirzado, and G. M. Syed. G. M. Syed renamed his Sindh Muttahida Mahaz; it became Jeay Sindh Mahaz.

In 1972, a large rally was organized in Hyderabad to commemorate March 4, 1967, the day of the violence against Sindhi students. Baluch leader Attaullah Mengal also participated in this function. Jeay Sindh Mahaz observed the fourth of March all over Sindh. Shaikh Ayaz recited his poetry in a public meeting in Sukkur.

Mir Rasool Bux Talpur was appointed as governor, and Mumtaz Ali Bhutto was elected as chief minister of Sindh. Bhutto's ruling Pakistan People's Party (PPP) created the official narrative of Sindhi nationalism and formed its own students' branch, Sindh People's Students Federation (SPSF).

In December 1970, Jeay Sindh Nojawan Mahaz and a splinter group of Jam Saqi's Sindh Nationalist Student Federation (SNSF) merged to form the Jeay Sindh Students' Federation (JSSF). Jeay Sindh Students' Federation became a main resource for G. M. Syed to mobilize Sindhi youths and muster their support. Iqbal Tareen, a famous student leader and orator of his time, was the founding president of JSSF.

Its first convention was held in Nawabshah, during which Shah Muhammad Shah was elected as president and Madad Ali Sindhi as secretary-general. The emblem of a red flag with a black hatchet is credited to Iqbal Tareen and Madad Ali Sindhi. G. M. Syed's birthday was celebrated publicly for the first time and attended by many of his followers, family, and friends. This later became a grand annual political festival of Sindhi nationalists; it was held at Sann on January 17 of each year. Even when Syed was incarcerated, especially while he was confined to his home under house arrest, his followers flocked to Sann to join him in a tradition that continues today.

The summer of 1972 in Sindh was a season of discontent, as Sindhis witnessed ethnic violence after Sindh's Chief Minister Mumtaz Ali Bhutto tabled the bill called the Sindhi Language Act of 1972; it proposed that Sindhi be the mandatory and official language of the Sindh province. Urdu-speaking members of the Sindh Assembly sat on the opposition's benches; they included Zahoorul Hassan Bhopali, Shah Faridul Haq, G. A. Madni, Usman Kennedy, Nawab Muzaffar Khan, and others who had overreacted to the bill. This caused the Urdu populace of Sindh to take to the streets against Sindhis. The next day's issue of the Urdu newspaper, *Jang*, carried a highly inflammatory headline by Rais Amrohvi:

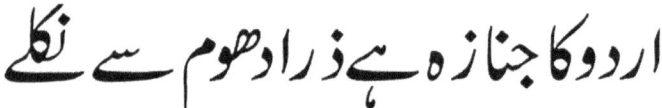

This is the funeral of Urdu language. Let us carry it with pomp and circumstance.

This ethnic tensions in Sindh on fire again, as armed groups of new immigrants started rioting and attacking Sindhis living in the cities of Karachi, Hyderabad, Mīrpur Khās, Tando Allahyar, Sukkur, and almost every big city and town of Sindh. The government imposed curfews in Karachi and Hyderabad. Both Sindhi- and Urdu-speaking populations suffered deaths and injuries, though most of the casualties were predominantly Sindhis. At Hyderabad Polytechnic College, a Sindhi instructor, Abdul Razzaq Soomro, was slain by men claiming to be champions of the Mohajir cause. Rashid Jadgal was killed in Karachi, and two youths were killed in Tando Jam. Zulfiqar

Ali Bhutto summoned a meeting of Sindhi- and Urdu-speaking intellectuals and leaders at the president's house in Rawalpindi. Shaikh Ayaz and Qazi Faiz Muhammad were among those who presented the case of Sindhis and Sindhi language before President Zulfikar Ali Bhutto.

Amidst the ethnic riots, Bhutto rushed to Karachi. He drove to Burns Road, a predominantly Urdu-speaking neighborhood, and delivered an emotional speech wherein he told his audience he never had any problem with Urdu, as his sister had married into an Urdu-speaking family. Concluding his address, he apologized to the Urdu-speaking audience. He also announced the withdrawal of the implementation of the Sindhi Language Bill by presidential decree, which led G. M. Syed to start a ground tour of Sindh. He was joined by a large caravan of Sindhi writers, poets, singers, youths, and his comrades, such as legendary Sindhi singer Allan Fakir, Ali Baba, Hafeez Qureshi, Abdul Wahid Arisar, Shah Muhamad Shah, Saif Banvi, Iqbal Jatoi, and many others.

Syed was to address a public meeting on the premises of Muslim College Hostel when a bomb exploded. Syed remained unharmed; however, Dost Mohammad Piracha, a great friend of Sindhi nationalism and president of Punjabi, Adabi Sangat, was killed on the spot, and student activist Umar Shoro was maimed for life; one of his legs was permanently damaged. Syed, despite surviving and suffering a heart attack, continued his journey to warn the Sindhi people to wake up and see the atrocities to which they were being subjected.

Warrants for the arrest of Syed and his comrade, Hafeez Qureshi, were served under the notorious Defense of Pakistan Rules while he was in Sukkur. Syed was initially taken to his house in Karachi, and then to his native village of Sann, where he remained under house arrest again for most of Bhutto's rule.

In 1973, the newly elected constitutional assembly of the remaining Pakistan was finally able to give the country a constitution, but a quarter of a century after its inception and only after more than half the country had already seceded from the original Pakistan. Although this was achieved under the leadership of Zulfikar Ali Bhutto, many intellectuals and political leaders in Sindh felt that the new constitution failed to protect the rights envisioned in the original Pakistan resolution of 1940. The new constitution included many authoritarian articles and gave the federal government brutal powers not previously enjoyed by it. Merely to speak of autonomy for the provinces was considered a crime punishable with up to seven years of imprisonment.

On April 28, 1973, at the annual convocation of the University of Sindh, Vice Chancellor Ghulam Mustafa Shah announced the awarding of an honorary doctorate in law to law minister Abdul Hafeez Pirzada, the primary author of the new constitution. Jeay Sindh Students' Federation announced the launch of their Naoon Aeen Na Khapay (New Constitution is Not Accepted) protest and warned the vice chancellor not to let Abdul Hafeez Pirzada enter the university premises because he was believed to be instrumental in the formulation of this anti-Sindhi constitution.

However, the vice chancellor refused to rescind his invitation to Pirzada who, accompanied by Chief Minister of Sindh Mumtaz Ali Bhutto and Governor Begum Ra'ana Liaquat Ali Khan, attended the convocation to receive his award and honorary degree. His presence started an uproar among the JSSF supporters and activists, but the administration decided to push ahead with the convocation proceedings amid the commotion, which culminated in an altercation between the students and organizers.

According to many eyewitnesses, it was Mr. Pirzada who first hurled profanities at the student leaders, especially Ismail Wasan, a prominent student leader of JSSF. This escalated the situation even further and resulted in Wasan slapping Pirzada. The police were let loose on the students, including Wasan, who was brutally beaten, as were other JSSF activists and students. Wasan was immediately arrested and taken away by the police.

Immediately afterward, police conducted midnight raids and arrested JSSF youths and supporters all over Sindh. Student leaders were expelled from the university, and the university was closed down for many months. G. M. Syed was put under house arrest again, where he remained until Bhutto was overthrown by military dictator General Zia in July 1977.

Sindhudesh Movement

After the creation of Bangladesh, as a result of atrocities committed by the Pakistani security forces against Bengalis, most of the smaller ethnicities in the remaining country realized that their future was bleak. For the first time, G. M. Syed openly demanded the right of self-determination for Sindhis. Prior to this, he had always fought for a sovereign state of Sindh within the framework of Pakistan, as had originally been promised in the Pakistan Resolution of 1940.

In 1973, at his birthday celebration in his native village of Sann, Syed outlined his vision for restoration of the autonomous status Sindh enjoyed before the British conquest. He shared his dream of a new and free Sindh with her ancient name, Sindhudesh, to be counted among the rest of the free nations of the world as a proud member of the United Nations. In 1975, he published *Sindhudesh Cho Ain Chha Laye* (*Sindhudesh: Why and What For*), now translated into English as *Sindhudesh: A Nation in Chains*. In his book, he cited many examples of independent Western nations who were smaller in size and population than Sindh, but who stood tall among the community of the world's free nations.

Keerat Babani, the veteran Sindhi writer and freedom-fighting nationalist, acted as ambassador between the Sindhis who had migrated to India and the Sindhis still living in Sindh. Syed was the first leader in the country to adopt public, as well as diplomatic, advocacy as tools to achieve his national goals. The national liberation of Bangladesh was the model on which Syed based his ideas. After the separation of Bengal, Syed openly declared autonomy for Sindh as his eventual goal.

As a consequence, after the creation of Pakistan, he had to spend most of life incarcerated. Yet he remained steadfast in his convictions and never caved in or wavered. The last time he was placed under house arrest was immediately after he addressed those attending his birthday celebration in Nishtar Park Karachi on January 17, 1992. In a written speech, he reiterated his determination that Sindh be free. He was placed under house arrest on January 18,1992, under the Nawaz Sharif government, and remained so under Benazir Bhutto's government and until Syed's last breath on April 25, 1995. The Bible, *Bhagavad Gita*, Torah, Quran, and *Shah Jo Risalo* were carried by mourners in his funeral procession. He was buried in his native village of Sann in the motherland of Sindh; Sann is still thought to be the center of gravity for Sindhi nationalists.

His politics were unique. Instead of street power, public gatherings, long speeches, or cheap popularity, he chose to spread his message by educating the masses through his writings. He was one of two contemporary Sindhi politicians who spread their messages through their books, the other being Rasool Bux Palijo. Syed was a firm believer of nonviolence in all circumstances. Though a lifelong, staunch, unwavering Sindhi nationalist, he never showed any signs of being a fascist. He was a true Sufi who believed in love for all of God's creations, though his love for his motherland overarched his love for anything else.

Syed spoke of formulating a group of spiritual nations rather than becoming part of the capitalist and communist bloc. He also talked of restructuring the United Nations, which had failed to end oppression and genocide of smaller and weaker member nations. He talked of nonviolence as the only weapon to achieve goals. On his concept of Sindhudesh, Syed wrote:

The people of Bangladesh have won freedom not without paying the cost of it. Nearly ten million of their people had to leave their homeland and live as fugitives facing untold hardships and innumerable sufferings. Two hundred thousand of their good and gentle women folk had to suffer disgrace at the hand of the brutal enemy. Three million of their sons had to sacrifice their lives and give their blood at the altar of freedom. With us here in Sindh, as we have already noted here, our elite, the Zamindar, the Kamoras (bureaucrats), the pir, the mullah, and the petty trader are content with playing agents to the alien and collecting their preferred share in exploitation. Here, too, the burden to lead the struggle lies on the shoulder of the awakened workers of Jeay Sindh movement and on its courageous students' continence.[141]

Syed's followers borrowed Bangla slogans from the Bangladesh freedom movement, literally translating them from Bangla to Sindhi. For example:

Tuhinjo Desh, muhinjo Desh, Sindhudesh
Your Country, My Country, the Country of Sindh

Umar Desh, tumah Desh, Bangladesh
Your Country, My Country, the Country of Bengal

---

[141] G. M. Syed, *Sindh Ja Soorma (Heroes of Sindh)*. Karachi: Naeen Sindh Publications, 1974.

Tuhinjo Rahbar, muhinjo Rahbar, G. M. Syed G. M. Syed
Your Leader, My Leader, G. M. Syed, G. M. Syed

Umar Neeta, tumah Neeta, Sheikh Mujib Shaikh Mujib
Your Leader, My Leader, Sheikh Mujib, Sheikh Mujib

These catchy phrases cost Mr. Syed his freedom. Generations of workers and leaders in his Jeay Sindh movement had to suffer jail time, lashings, forced disappearances, torture, exile, and even death. Unfortunately, these practices by the state may have varied in their intensity, but continued unabated, even when there were Sindhis at the helm of affairs, including the Bhuttos. With the declaration of martial law by Zia-ul-Haq, oppression against Sindhi nationalists intensified. Although Syed was released from his house detention at the time, it proved to be a brief freedom. He was arrested again when he undertook his tour of Sindh in 1984.

The 1980s were a decade of reemergence for the Sindhi nationalist movement in the face of oppression by the martial-law authorities. Sindhi people rose up against the martial-law rule and supported of the Movement for the Restoration of Democracy, but they were brutally repressed. Sindhi nationalists drew massive support, village to village and town to town.

On October 17, 1984, security personnel at a Thori railway crossing halted busloads of Jeay Sindh students and their leaders and opened indiscriminate fire. At least five were machine-gunned to death, including Amanul-lah Vistaro, Mitho Buledi, Anwar Abbasi, Zikriya Memon, and Abdul Malik Khushk. Dodo Maheri, Abdul Wahid Areesar, Allah Bachayo

Marnas, and Naz Sanai are the names of a few of the Sindhi-nationalism activists who were sentenced to be lashed; there were many more.

Oppression and violence against the Sindhi people on a daily basis rallied the masses, as they felt that they were being victimized and targeted because they were Sindhis. From the end of the 1980s through the mid-1990s, Sindh witnessed its worst period of ethnic violence, gun fights, and target killings; 6,000 people were slain in Karachi and Hyderabad.

The death of G. M. Syed proved to be the beginning of the end of this latest wave of Sindhi nationalism, which had started in the early twentieth century. His party fragmented into multiple factions. Some of his followers were coerced into leaving politics due to extreme persecution by the authorities, including arrests, abductions, torture, and more. Others were bribed to change their loyalties. Some died under mysterious circumstances, a prime example being the death of Bashir Khan Qureshi, considered by many the true political heir of Syed.

Over the last few decades, most nationalist politicians have given up their Sindhi nationalism and tried to merge into the electoral politics of Pakistan, but have not had significant success against Zulfiqar Ali Bhutto's Pakistan People's Party. The top goal of Bhutto's neosocialist agenda was nationalization of most major sectors of the society. To fulfill this, his government nationalized major industries and educational institutions. Ironically, this policy was later reversed by his own daughter a few decades later when she became the prime minister of the country. An unintended crown jewel of his nationalization scheme was the nationalization of Sindhi nationalism, which has not yet been reversed. But in the words of one of the greatest nationalist Sindhi poets of the recent past, Juman Darbadar:

وتي هر جنم وربو مٺا مهراڻ ۾ ملبو
ختم اونداه ٿي ويندي چنڊءَ چانڊاڻ ۾ ملبو
پنهنجي جا جنگ آ جاري سا ٿيندي نيٺ سوياري
مري ويندا مڙيئي ماري سچيءَ سرهاڻ ۾ ملبو

We will be born again and again, to meet on the banks of Indus
This darkness will vanish, we will reunite under the bright moonlight
Our eternal battle that is on, will end in our victory
Our tormenters will all perish, we will meet in rapture

The Rise and Fall of Bhuttos

Sindhis have had a strange and unexplainable infatuation with the Bhuttos for the last half a century. Bhuttos were not a household name among Sindhis until Zulfikar Ali Bhutto (ZAB) entered politics and shot to popularity in Pakistan and abroad. A popular, dynamic, and theatrical leader, ZAB turned his clan into one of the most well-known political dynasties of recent times. In the words of one of the most prolific contemporary Sindhi writers, Hasan Mujtaba, "He lived like a Roman emperor, and died like a player in a Greek tragedy."

Supremely arrogant, with a sense of entitlement when it came to ruling the masses, this dynasty's rise to prominence in Sindh can be traced back to the early nineteenth century when the British awarded large tracts of lands to Dodo Khan Bhutto after Charles Napier conquered Sindh. Dodo Khan Bhutto was the son of Pir Bux Bhutto, whose roots go back to old Rājputana. The head of the clan was Sahato Khan, who converted to Islam during the rule of Mughal Emperor Aurangzeb. Sahato Khan was said to be a courtesan in the Mughal court.

Originally, the Bhuttos were of Arain origins, from the Rohtak and Hisar areas of the present-day Haryana state in India. Arains are a community of vegetable growers who came to Sindh in the beginning of the eighteenth century to escape the drought and famine in Rajasthan. Biographers such as Stanley Wolpert see Bhutto's ancestor, Pir Bux Khan, as having locked into disputes with Abras, who were close to the Kalhora rulers. Pir Bux Bhutto showed his loyalties to Talpur ameers when they brought about the end of the Kalhora rule in Sindh.[142]

After the conquest of Sindh by the British, the Bhuttos aligned with the new masters. In return, they acquired immense influence in British corridors of power and were granted large estates in Larkana, Sukkur, and Jacobabad. Brooke Allen, journalist and author of *Benazir Bhutto: Favored Daughter*, depicts the Bhuttos' immense affluence and power.

> *Dodo Khan consolidated the immense family holdings in Sindh, while Bhuttos from other branches of this large extended family received titles from the queen-empress and land from the Raj administration. At the height of the family's power, Bhutto land in Sindh stretched nearly eighty miles—a demesne that dwarfed comparable aristocratic holdings in Europe.*[143]

---

[142] Vaqar Ahmed, "Bhutto: Man and Myth," *Newsline*, April 2019.

[143] Brooke Allen, *Benazir Bhutto: Favored Daughter*, ICONS Series. (New York: New Harvest Houghton Mifflin Harcourt, 2016).

It is said that, at the peak of their holdings, the Bhutto estate was so widely spread that "if a man rode his horse to survey Bhutto's[sic] lands, starting at breaking of dawn, he could not reach the farthest end, even by sunset." According to the local folklore, the Bhutto clan did temporarily break up with their British patrons when Ghulam Murtaza Bhutto, young son of Khuda Bakhsh Bhutto, the chief of the clan at the time, had an affair with the mistress of the local British colonel. On finding Murtaza Bhutto with his young mistress, the British colonel became outraged and hit Murtaza Bhutto with his horse whip. The young, athletically built Murtaza Bhutto turned the tables on the old colonel and thrashed him with the same whip. To avoid public humiliation and scandal, the British deputy collector kept quiet until he could find the most opportune time to take his revenge. Two years later, the British officer had the opportunity to settle his scores.

Colonel Mayhew, working with his local crony, Inspector Sher Mohammad Shah, falsely implicated Murtaza in an assassination attempt on Colonel Mayhew, who masterminded the entire thing. Ghulam Murtaza Bhutto was tried for murder in a Larkana court. Though Murtaza was acquitted by an English judge, it cost him a lot of money and time. Ghulam Murtaza Bhutto, fearing further persecution by the British deputy collector, escaped to Afghanistan. Back home, his estate and all his valuables were confiscated. One of his bungalows was burned down. His wife and young son had to run barefoot for miles to save their lives.

A few years later, his father, Khuda Bux Bhutto, was killed while visiting his land at Jacobabad. Mir Ghulam Murtaza returned, initially disguised as a Sikh trader. Later, he requested a pardon from the British authorities. It was granted, and his estates were restored. Shahnawaz Bhutto, son of Ghulam Murtaza and father of Zulfikar Ali Bhutto, experienced both heights of affluence and extremes of poverty while growing up as his father went through these tribulations.

Bhutto's biographers believe that Murtaza acquired a lot of wisdom from the experiences. In the words of Stanley Wolpert, "He was careful to seize any advantage for his family's fast-rising fortune, and never forgot his loyalty, almost as great as that premier loyalty to the Bhutto family, to his region and its people."[144]

Sir Shahnawaz Bhutto was a great mentor for his brilliant, ambitious son and indirectly for his granddaughter, Benazir Bhutto. Shahnawaz was a traditional but enlightened Sindhi Muslim feudal. He received his initial education at Mullah Mektab, a local religious seminary, and later transferred to the newly established Sindh Madrasa School in Karachi, and then to Saint Patrick's School, also in Karachi. He was both a highly conservative traditional Muslim and a fully anglicized feudal lord.

In 1920, the British held elections for the Bombay Imperial Legislative Council. Shahnawaz won a seat representing Sindh. He also became president of the District Board Larkana and chairman of Sindh Cooperative Society. He was part of a twenty-member team from Sindh sent to the Imperial Round

---

[144] Stanley Wolpert, *Zulfi Bhutto of Pakistan: His Life and Times* (Oxford University Press, 1993) 8-14.

Table conference in London in 1930, where he was said to have raised the call for separation of Sindh from Bombay. In 1930, Shahnawaz Bhutto was knighted by the viceroy of India, Lord Irwin, ever after to be referred to as Sir Bhutto.

He was also famous for his flamboyance. It is said that while attending a cultural event in Hyderabad, he fell in love with one of the performers, Lakhi Bai. She later became his second wife, Lady Khursheed Bhutto. They had three children: one son, Zulfiqar; and two daughters, Benazir and Munawar.

In 1934, he founded Sindh People's Party, which included among its prominent members G. M. Syed and Abdullah Haroon. Sindh was separated from Bombay and made a province in British India in April 1936. In 1937, it was announced that elections would be held in the newly restored province of Sindh. Shahnawaz Bhutto formed another party named Sindh United Party, which suffered a humiliating defeat in the elections and could not win any seats. He himself lost to Shaikh Abdul Majeed Sindhi, a person from an extremely humble socioeconomic background, who was a recent convert to Islam and working as a *munshi*, or cashier, at a local law office.

This is a classic example of Sindhi political acumen and secularism; one of the biggest feudal lords of Sindh lost to a person who had just converted to the religion of the majority of the voters and who also had run in the election despite having absolutely no economic means. This again proves that Sindh has always been centuries ahead of the rest of the region when it comes to political awareness.

The electoral defeat of Shahnawaz Bhutto at the hands of Shaikh Abdul Majeed Sindhi practically ended his political career and was a major setback for the whole Bhutto feudal clan until Zulfikar Ali Bhutto's meteoric rise in the Pakistani political landscape of the 1960s.

In early 1947, Shahnawaz Bhutto was appointed as *deewan* (prime minister) of the princely state of Junagadh, where he remained attached to the court until September 1947. After the Partition of India and abolition of the princely state, he moved back to Pakistan, where he concentrated on the development and growth of his lands. He was a close friend of Iskandar Mirza, then defense minister and later president of Pakistan. Through that connection, Bhutto was able to get his thirty-year-old son appointed as a minister in the federal government of Pakistan in 1958.

Martial law was declared in Pakistan on October 7, 1958, by President Iskandar Mirza, who then appointed General Muhammad Ayub Khan as the chief martial-law administrator and Aziz Ahmed as secretary-general and deputy-chief martial-law administrator. However, three weeks later, General Ayub Khan, who had been openly questioning the authority of the government before the imposition of martial law, deposed Iskandar Mirza on October 27, 1958, and assumed the presidency that practically formalized the militarization of the political system in Pakistan.

Young and highly ambitious, Zulfiqar decided to shift his loyalties to his new master, General Ayub Khan, at the cost of his previous benefactor, Iskandar Mirza. Bhutto became a trusted ally of and advisor to Ayub Khan, rising in influence and power despite his youth and relative inexperience. Bhutto aided his president in negotiating the Indus Water Treaty in India in 1960 and the next year negotiated an oil exploration agreement with the Soviet Union, which acceded to provide economic and technical aid to Pakistan.

In 1962, as territorial disputes increased between India and China, Beijing planned to stage an invasion in the northern territories of India. Premier Zhou Enlai and Mao invited Pakistan to join the raid to wrest the states of Jammu and Kashmir from India. Bhutto advocated for the plan, but Ayub opposed the plan; he was afraid of retaliation by Indian troops. Instead, Ayub proposed a joint defense union with India.

Bhutto was shocked by the proposal and felt Ayub Khan was unlettered in international affairs. Bhutto was conscious that, despite Pakistan's anti-communist Western alliances, China had refrained from criticizing Pakistan. In 1962, the US assured Pakistan that the Kashmir issues would be resolved according to the wishes of Pakistanis and the Kashmiris. Therefore, Ayub did not participate in the Chinese's plans. Bhutto criticized the US for providing military aid to India during and after the 1962 Sino-Indian War, which was seen as an abrogation of Pakistan's alliance with the United States.

Meanwhile, Ayub Khan, heeding Bhutto's counsel, launched Operation Gibraltar in a bid to liberate Kashmir. It ended in a fiasco, and the Indian Armed Forces launched a successful counterattack on West Pakistan. This war was an aftermath of brief skirmishes that took place between March and August

1965 on the international boundaries in the Rann of Kutch, Jammu, Kashmir, and Punjab.

Bhutto joined Ayub in Uzbekistan to negotiate a peace treaty with Indian Prime Minister Lal Bahadur Shastri. Ayub and Shastri agreed to exchange prisoners of war and withdraw their respective forces to prewar boundaries. This agreement was deeply unpopular in Pakistan, and it caused major political unrest against Ayub's regime. Bhutto's criticism of the final agreement caused a major rift between him and Ayub. Initially denying the rumors of dissension, Bhutto resigned in June 1966 and expressed strong opposition to Ayub's regime. Bhutto's jingoistic slogan, "We will be fighting for one thousand years with India," made him popular in Punjab and the northern areas of Pakistan close to the Indian border, territories from which most of Pakistan's military came.

In 1967, speaking to a gathering of Sindhi students in Hyderabad, despite pressure from his large Sindhi audience, Bhutto refused to oppose One Unit, stating that he did not wish to upset Punjab by demanding the abolishment of One Unit. "I cannot barter the interests of Punjab," he said, although he had previously written a scholarly article in a Dhaka-based newspaper against One Unit. In his article, Bhutto had asked for equal division of power among the provinces and federal government. He had also acknowledged discrimination against his native province of Sindh.

In November 1967, he formed his own Pakistan People's Party in Lahore with a socialist manifesto and the popular slogan of

"*Roti, kapda aur makaan*" ("Bread, clothing, and housing for all"), borrowed from the famous poem by poet Habib Jalib:

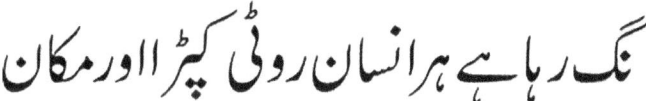

Food, clothing, and a house are the demands of every human being

Zulfikar Ali Bhutto (ZAB), like his father, was also a highly educated, Westernized feudal lord who at the same time was deeply connected to his identity as a Muslim. He popularized his unique brand of Socialist ideology and called it Islamic Socialism. This was the era of leftist movements by students and laborers all over the world, led by the anti-Vietnam War movements on university campuses in America and Europe.

Back home in Pakistan and Sindh, labor, student, and prodemocratic forces were gathering against the dictatorship of Ayub Khan like storms on the horizon of Pakistani politics. It was a period of anarchy and chaos in Pakistan. Sindh was shackled in One Unit. And there was growing disenchantment with the status quo all over the country, especially in Bengal and Sindh.

Bhutto, with his charming personality, flaming oratory, and fresh ideas, influenced and attracted large segments of those in Pakistani politics and society. He quickly became the hero of the western province of Pakistan. Leftists, socialists, laborers, peasants, students, writers, and journalists joined the PPP. He politically launched himself at the Dow Medical College annual convention of the National Student Federation. He was joined by J. A. Rahim, Meraj Muhammad Khan, Dr. Mubashir Hassan, and Shaikh Rashid, all prominent progressives from Punjab. From Sindh, he was joined by his cousin Mumtaz Ali Bhutto; the Talpur brothers, Mir Rasool Bux and Mir Ali Ahmad Talpur; veteran peasant-rights activist and comrade Mir Muhammad Talpur; freedom-loving religious leader Maulana Abdul Haq Rabbani; and a large number of Sindhi nationalists.

Bhutto took a train journey from Rawalpindi to Lahore. He was greeted by hundreds of thousands on his route. Feeling threatened by his rapidly increasing popularity, the Ayub Khan regime arrested him, his comrades, and his talented cousin Mumtaz Bhutto. They were locked in Sahiwal Jail, where Shaikh Ayaz was already serving his jail time.

Bhutto shot to popularity among the people of Sindh and the rest of West Pakistan. There were demonstrations by students and laborers on a daily basis; this forced Ayub Khan to release Bhutto. He later resigned and handed over the reins of the country to another military general, Yahya Khan, his second-in-command, instead of to a civilian leader.

Bhutto convened his first party convention in Hala, Sindh; it was known as the Hala Convention. One of Sindh's most important pirs, Makhdoom Muhammad Zaman Talibul Moula, who was made the party's senior vice chairman, hosted the convention. Bhutto's old comrades objected to the inflow of feudal lords in the party but were reprimanded by Bhutto.

He truly was an extraordinary man with extraordinary qualities. He was known for having an exceptional memory; he could remember the names of anyone he only met once in his lifetime. He was a dreamer with an uncanny capacity to get the masses to believe in his dreams of a great future for all. Coming from one of the richest feudal families of Pakistan, he could easily connect with other feudal elites. But at the same time, he sincerely empathized with the oppressed masses and genuinely felt their pain.

While delivering an emotionally charged speech at the United Nations Security Council, Bhutto famously tore a copy of a resolution tabled by Poland for a ceasefire between India and Pakistan and then walked out of the Security Council. Being humiliated by this crushing defeat, the top brass of the army were forced to finally hand control of the rest of the country back to the civilians after almost two decades of military rule that culminated in the dismemberment of the country. Bhutto—as the leader of Pakistan People's Party, which had won the highest number of seats in the country—was sworn in on December 16, 1971, as the new president and first civilian chief martial-law administrator of what remained of Pakistan. "This is a new Pakistan. My Pakistan," he said in his nationally televised address. One of the first things he did was call all his potential challengers and threaten them to be careful, as he was the president.

Bhutto's most prominent challenger was Pir Pagaro, the most powerful pir in Sindh, who, just a few years earlier, had helped Bhutto reach the corridors of power during Iskandar Mirza's and Ayub Khan's eras. Within the first few months of assuming the roles of president and chief martial-law administrator, Zulfikar Ali Bhutto went after any dissenting voice raised against his government. His government dealt severely with his own party members of parliament, and labor leader Mukhtar Rana was the first to criticize Bhutto's actions as civilian chief martial-law administrator. Mukhtar Rana was jailed and brutally tortured. He was forced to go into exile in London, never returned home, and died there.

Bhutto's government presented a provisional constitution in April 1972, wherein the rights of provinces and minorities were grossly restricted. At the time, the country was still under martial law, and Zulfikar Ali Bhutto was acting as a civilian martial-law administrator.

About the brutal beginning of Bhutto's era, Ayaz Gul, then a promising young Sindhi poet, sarcastically wrote a verse:

مرکز يل مضبوط کيو صوبن جو قتلام کيو
جهانگيئڙن جو خون وهائي
عام يلي اسلام کيو
(اياز گل)

Make the center strong, Commit genocide of the provinces
Shed blood of the indigenous people
To try to spread Islam

Bhutto's government arrested young Sindhi leftist leader, Jam Saqi, to make him serve the conviction pronounced on him, by a military court during Yahya Khan's dictatorship, for organizing a protest rally and writing pamphlets against military operations in Bengal. He was sent to Multan Jail to serve his term. Speaking on the floor of the national assembly, Bhutto proudly credited his government's arrest of Jam as the "progress it made within its first months."

The PPP government infamously used an old draconian law from the British Colonial era. Previously called the Defense of India Rules, it was promulgated under the new name, Defense of Pakistan Rules (DPR). It was especially used against Sindhi nationalist and political opponents. Bhutto's own party dissidents, colleagues, writers, poets, journalists, and editors were also frequent targets of DPR if they were perceived as a threat to his rule.

In Sindh, Bhutto's government banned about forty books, magazines, and other publications. Those proscribed publications included literary journals, including the monthly *Sohni*, along with the nationalist publications *Agte Qadam*, *Pegham*, and *Tehreek*. Even monthly *Sojhro*, a women's magazine, was banned. Most of these books remain banned today.

Anyone critical of Bhutto's regime was arrested, including Tariq Ashraf, editor of the monthly *Sohni*, and legendary Sindhi poet Ibrahim Munshi. Ibrahim Munshi's son died during his imprisonment, but Munshi was not allowed to attend his young son's funeral. At the same time that some of the most renowned Sindhi literary personalities were being persecuted, Bhutto's government introduced other Sindhi artists, singers, musicians, and Sufi singers from outside of Sindh, especially to the west, Southeast Asia, and America, to replace them.

Bhutto fired about 1,300 high-ranking civil bureaucrats, technocrats, and judges from all over the country, including senior Sindhi civil servants and judges. Most of them were never proven to be involved in any corrupt practices, but they were dismissed because they were felt to be disloyal to the regime, and thus severely weakening civil bureaucracy. This created an imbalance between the civil and military factions and allowed the military to again reassert its unchecked control of the country. This state of imbalance eventually proved to be the main cause of Bhutto's downfall. To strengthen his grip on power, Bhutto came down hard on his political opponents. He continued G. M. Syed's detention under house arrest, and most of the Sindhi nationalists remained jailed throughout his tenure. The nationalist leaders and workers who went into hiding, their families, including women and elderly family members, were arrested and locked up.

Bhutto established his gestapo-like federal police called Federal Security Force. Local superintendents of police, notorious for torture and extrajudicial killings, were tasked with dealing with the government's opponents and dissidents. A brilliant lecturer at the engineering college Jamshoro, Ashok Kumar, was the first Sindhi victim of an enforced disappearance in 1973. He was arrested by the police and never seen again.

When Muhammad Khan Junejo was home secretary, Jam Sadiq Ali had the task of dealing with Bhutto's opponents in Sindh. Six of Pir Pagaro's Hurs, including Khalifa Amin Faqeer, were arrested in Sanghar and Khairpur Mirs. They were granted bail by Sessions Judge Owais Murtaza, but the judge himself was arrested in his own chambers under the infamous

DPR. The six Hurs were rearrested, taken out of police lockup in the middle of the night, and shot to death. Their extrajudicial murders were reported as having occurred in a shoot-out with police. Bhutto, through his police and other state agencies, harassed and hounded other government functionaries and private citizens whom he suspected of being loyal to Pir Pagaro.

After a successful conference of the Organization of Islamic Countries (OIC), Bhutto openly declared Pakistan's intention to build a nuclear bomb, later named the "Islamic bomb" by the Western media. This was being done with the blessing and financial support of Saudi King Shah Faisal, along with the Shah of Iran and Colonel Gaddafi of Libya. This was the pinnacle of Bhutto's ascension to power, both domestically and internationally.

But it did not last long, and things started to turn sour for Bhutto after the assassination of Shah Faisal of Saudi Arabia. King Fahd, who took over after Shah Faisal, was much more pro-United States and unwilling to continue his patronage of Bhutto's pan-Islamic policies.

At the same time, the Shah of Iran was dethroned, and Gaddafi was facing threats from the West. The OIC was beginning to crumble, while the Soviet Union was trying to increase its influence in Afghanistan with the eventual goal of reaching the warm shores of the Persian Gulf through Pakistan. Suddenly, Pakistan became the epicenter of international geopolitics, and it was not in the interest of anti-Soviet forces to have a left-leaning leader in Pakistan; what suited them much more was a military dictator who would enforce their policies.

Bhutto, feeling the noose getting tighter, announced early general elections in March 1977. There were reports of pre- and post-poll rigging on a large scale from all over the country. In Bhutto's hometown of Larkana, his opponent, Jamaat-e-Islami's Jan Mohammad Abbasi, was abducted by police on his way to file nomination papers for his election's candidacy. He was released only after the time to file paperwork for his candidacy had expired. There was a widespread outcry in and outside the country against the rigging. This was the beginning of the end of Bhutto and his regime.

An alliance of nine mostly right-wing political parties, called the Pakistan National Alliance (PNA), was formed with Pir Pagaro as its head. The PNA started a series of protests all over the country; they took a violent turn as Bhutto's government attempted to suppress the movement. Eventually, there were gun battles between police and agitated activists and PNA members, and scores of people were killed and injured. Pir Pagaro himself was placed under detention in his hotel room at the Intercontinental Hotel in Rawalpindi. This resulted in a violent reaction in Sanghar and the rest of the Hur belt in Sindh.

From March through April, fueled and financed by international agencies, the country was in a violent crisis. A curfew was imposed in many cities and towns. Martial law was declared in cities such as Rawalpindi, Quetta, Faisalabad, Multan, Karachi, and Hyderabad. Bhutto announced reelections, but the agitated opposition rejected the offer. They demanded the resignation of Bhutto and his government en bloc. Air Marshal Asghar Khan, another opposition leader who took a role in Bhutto's release during Ayub Khan's last days, demanded that the army intervene. Negotiations between Bhutto and PNA leaders reopened but failed.

Bhutto came to Karachi and summoned Sindhi political prisoners to the chief minister's house to confer with him. Bhutto asked the Sindhi political prisoners to support him against the PNA movement, but he could not win them over, as it was too late to make peace with the Sindhi nationalists. The political prisoners who were brought from jails to confer with Bhutto included Shah Mohammad Shah, Abdul Wahid Arisar, and Nazeer Abbasi.

Between the nights of July 4 and July 5, troops led by General Faiz Ali Chishti stormed the prime minister's house and official residences of Bhutto's ministers at Islamabad. Bhutto, his ministers, colleagues, and leaders of the opposition of PNA were arrested. General Zia-ul-Haq, then chief of the Pakistani troops, whom Bhutto had promoted to the top slot in the army by leapfrogging generals senior to him, declared himself the chief martial-law administrator.

Bhutto was later released. He took a train from Rawalpindi to Lahore and was received with a warm welcome at every train stop by multitudes of his supporters. This panicked General Zia and his closest allies, and Bhutto was arrested again, this time on charges of ordering the murder of his friend-turned-foe, Ahmad Raza Kasuri's father, Nawab Muhammad Ahmed Khan Kasuri.

A judge of the Lahore High Court, Justice K. M. Samdani, ordered the release of Bhutto on bail. But his freedom proved brief as he was rearrested in September 1977. He was kept in Kot Lakhpat Jail in Lahore, and later in Rawalpindi. He was tried on murder charges, convicted of being a coconspirator in the murder of his opponent, and given a death sentence. From its outset, the Bhutto trial was seen by many jurists as being a sham, inconsistent with international humanitarian law, in violation of due process, and against the standards for dispensing justice. The murder case against Bhutto was referred to the Lahore High Court, a provincial appellate court, instead of the district court. Generally, murder cases are tried by district judges in India and Pakistan. Bhutto was not given that opportunity. The presiding judge, Maulvi Mushtaq, was biased against Bhutto and repeatedly ridiculed him while hearing the case. Judge Mushtaq even questioned Bhutto's being Muslim. In an open mockery of judicial standards, neutral judges were removed from the bench. There are lingering questions, even today, as to how Bhutto was executed.

One school of thought is that he was never really hanged and was actually tortured to death because his body was buried by the authorities without allowing his family and friends see it. His supporters and many independent observers called Bhutto's execution a judicial murder. His dead body was transported in a military C-130 cargo aircraft to the airport in Jacobabad and then was flown by helicopter to Bhutto's village of Garhi Khuda Bakhsh.

Before the landing of the helicopter containing Bhutto's coffin, security agencies clamped a curfew on the entire village and sealed exit and entry points of the village. No one was allowed to attend Bhutto's funeral prayers except a local mosque's imam, Bhutto's land manager, and a few local peasants. The martial-law administration buried the most popular prime minister in the country's history under the shadows of their guns without giving his family the opportunity to say goodbye to him or to provide him with a proper burial.

Sindh sank into deep shock and anger after Bhutto's death. It is the opinion of the overwhelming majority of Sindhis across all political allegiances that the only reason Bhutto was hanged was because he was a Sindhi. He would never have been hanged had he come from any other province of Pakistan. "After Bhutto's hanging, Pakistan will be a foreign place for Sindhis forever," wrote Sindhi leader and intellectual Rasool Bux Palijo in his monthly *Tehreek*. A statement that holds true even today and is often repeated every time Zulfiqar Ali Bhutto's name is mentioned in front of a Sindhi in Pakistan.

A wave of silent but extreme rage and anger spread throughout Sindh, the likes of which had never been seen before. Bhutto's closest allies and the top leaders of his party were bribed with foreign funds, which were now pouring into the country, to start a jihad against the Soviet Union. Those who refused to be bought were jailed, tortured, lashed, or permanently silenced by the ruling junta. Bhutto's daughter, Benazir Bhutto, and wife, Nusrat Bhutto, were placed in detention, first at Sahala near Islamabad, and later both at their residence in Karachi and the Al-Murtaza house in Larkana. Benazir was also imprisoned in Sukkur Jail in the intensive heat of summer.

"My sons will not be my sons if they do not drink the blood of those who dare to shed my blood if I am assassinated," Zulfikar Ali Bhutto wrote in his jail notes. However, both of his sons, Mir Murtaza Bhutto and Shahnawaz Bhutto, opted for exile in Afghanistan during their father's trial. They formed a radical organization, al-Zulfikar, to clandestinely carry on militant activities in Pakistan.

While on death row, Bhutto appointed his wife, Nusrat Bhutto, as acting chairperson of his political party, the Pakistan People's Party (PPP). Nusrat and Benazir managed the affairs of PPP while both incarcerated and under house arrest. Both Bhutto women remained in and out of jails until 1990.

In March 1980, the Movement for Restoration of Democracy (MRD)—comprised of parties opposed to Zia-ul-Haq, including PPP—was formed. Begum Nusrat Bhutto was elected as its chairperson.

Within days of the formation of MRD, a passenger aircraft of Pakistan International Airlines (PIA) bound for Karachi from Peshawar was hijacked. The hijackers claimed that they belonged to the Bhutto brothers' al-Zulfikar organization. Their demands were for all political prisoners in the country to be released, for martial law to be lifted, and for elections to be announced. The hijacked airplane was taken to Kabul, where Mir Murtaza Bhutto, Bhutto's eldest son, visited the hijackers on the plane.

Zia-ul-Haq did not waste any time in accusing MRD, the Bhutto women, and the Bhutto brothers of the hijacking. The MRD and prodemocratic groups claimed that Zia-ul-Haq conspired to orchestrate the hijacking in order to crush the Movement for the Restoration of Democracy.

The hijackers forced the pilot to fly the plane to Damascus, where they demanded the release of fifty-three political prisoners in exchange for the plane's passengers. Jail authorities and Zia-ul-Haq's agencies stormed into Pakistani jails and collected and coercively bound the political prisoners to fly them to Damascus to meet the hijackers' demands in return for freeing the hostages, which included two Americans.

Jam Saqi and his comrades, who were also on the list, adamantly refused to go to Damascus. "Zia needs to be sent. Not us," Jam Saqi told jail authorities.

Among those Sindhi nationalist student leaders who were sent to Damascus were Qadir Bux Jatoi, Ali Haider Shah, and Sindhi nationalist leader Shah Mohammad Shah.

In 1981, Zia-ul-Haq's regime finally released Benazir Bhutto from house arrest and allowed her to travel to London, England. Though this, on the surface, was done for medical reasons—while incarcerated, she had become partially deaf after suffering an ear infection—the actual reason for her release is believed to be the political pressure applied in Washington by her friend, US Senator Peter Galbraith. Galbraith demanded a meeting with her in Pakistan at her family house at 70 Clifton, where she was being kept under house arrest. Begum Nusrat Bhutto was also allowed to go to France for her cancer treatment.

Benazir's days of exile in London were recounted by one of her biographers, Brooke Allen, in her book, *Benazir Bhutto: Favored Daughter*, as follows:

> *In London, Benazir rented a flat at the Barbican Estate, and there, in relative safety, finally began to*

regain not only her health but also her once ebullient personality. She also visited the United States and met a number of lawmakers in Washington, including Senators Stephen Solarz and Claiborne Pell.[145]

In 1984, Benazir Bhutto's younger brother, Shahnawaz, died under mysterious circumstances while vacationing with his family at Cannes in the south of France. Many believe he was poisoned, while others believe he committed suicide by poison. It is said that both the Bhutto brothers, in their times of exile, always carried a lethal dose of poison. This was reportedly provided to them by the Syrian Intelligence Agency in case they were ever captured by Pakistani intelligence agencies, as they preferred to die from self-administered poison than be tortured and humiliated. Some suggest Shahnawaz was poisoned by the Pakistani intelligence agencies; they believe his Afghani wife, who was on their payroll, was ordered to do it.

Devastated, Benazir Bhutto brought home the coffin of her younger brother to bury him at Garhi Khuda Bakhsh, Larkana. Thousands of people and supporters greeted her and the coffin at Mohenjo-Daro Airport. This went a long way to restoring her confidence in her father's followers. She regained her self-confidence and determination.

Seeing this public display of support from the masses, the martial-law authorities put her under house arrest again at her Karachi residence. When people came to offer their condolences

---

[145] Allen, *Benazir Bhutto: Favored Daughter.*

on her brother's death, Zia-ul-Haq accused her of meeting with groups of terrorists. Eventually, she was released, only to be forcibly put on a plane back to London. But under increasing international pressure, Zia-ul-Haq was forced to allow her to return in December 1986. She was received by an exuberant mass of humanity estimated to be 1,000,000 people in Lahore, Punjab, though attendees came from all over the country, especially Sindh. Their slogan was:

Benazir has come. She has brought revolution.

Benazir herself recalled the historic event in her autobiography, *Daughter of Destiny*.

> *There are moments of life which are not possible to describe. My return to Lahore was one of them. The sea of humanity was lining the roads, jammed on the balconies and roofs, wedged on trees and lamp posts, walking alongside the truck and stretching back across the fields, was more like an ocean. The eight-mile drive from the airport to Minar-e-Pakistan in Iqbal Park usually takes fifteen minutes. On the unbelievable day of April 10, 1986, it took us ten hours. The figure of one million people at the airport*

> *grew to two million, then three million by the time we reached the Minar-e-Pakistan.*[146]

Benazir Bhutto undertook a tour of the whole country, and everywhere she went, multitudes accorded her a rousing welcome. She was said to have become obsessed with her popularity and the way people received her. The revolutionary poet Habib Jalib wrote a poem in her honor; it was titled *Eik Nihati Larki* ("The Weaponless Girl").

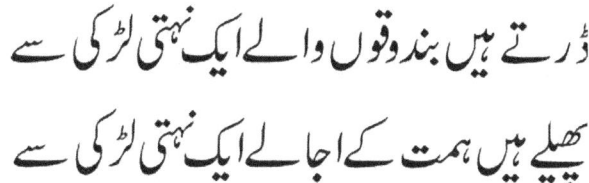

Those with guns are afraid of a weaponless girl
Light of courage has been spread by a weaponless girl

Her craving for popular support was nothing new to those close to her. According to her biographer, Brooke Allen:

> *It might be more correct to say that she became addicted to adulation, and if so, this return to Pakistan was a key moment in the process. Benazir loved it all: she played the crowd masterfully and drew inspiration and sustenance from its palpable love.*[147]

---

[146] Benazir Bhutto, *Daughter of the East.* (New United Kingdom: Hamish Hamilton, 1989).

[147] Allen, *Benazir Bhutto: Favored Daughter.*

In August 1986, the second round of the MRD movement was launched. Benazir announced she was to lead a rally in Faisalabad. Zia-ul-Haq's secret services and police were posted in every nook and cranny of Sindh and its borders. Covering herself in a burqa, Benazir tried to take the Khyber Mail Express train from Mirpur Mathelo, Sindh, but was arrested. She was brought back to Karachi and placed under house arrest at her residence. By now, her political fortunes were turning for the better due to the changing international political situation. The Soviet Union had been badly defeated in Afghanistan and was beginning to crumble at its core. Thus, Pakistan's dictator, Zia-ul-Haq, and his regime's services were no longer required by the Soviet Union.

On August 17, 1988, Zia-ul-Haq died in a plane crash. Members of his junta, including chief of the Inter-Services Intelligence (ISI), General Akhtar Abdul Rahman, and US ambassador to Pakistan, Arnold Raphel, were also among those who died in the crash. Reportedly, a bomb planted in a box of mangoes exploded while the plane was in flight.

Zia-ul-Haq was succeeded by General Mirza Aslam Beg as chief of the army. Ghulam Ishaq Khan, then chairman of the senate, took over as president of the country. Benazir commented on Zia-ul-Haq's death, "This averted the death that was lurking upon many of us."

Elections were held in October 1988. Bhutto's party won the maximum number of seats. Bhutto was sworn in as the country's first woman prime minister, but only after many compromises. She accepted conditional power by getting Ghulam Ishaq Khan elected president by her party, and she appointed Yaqub Ali Khan as foreign minister. Her term lasted less than two years. On August 6, 1990, President Ghulam Ishaq Khan forced her to step down after charging her with mismanagement and corruption. This was a direct result of her operations against Mohajir Qaumi Movement, which literally means "Immigrant Nationalist Movement." She had ordered a crackdown by the Sindh Provincial Police after MQM gathered a large store of weaponry in the historical fortress called Pucca Qila in Hyderabad. The MQM used this fortress as the command and control center for their terrorist activities against indigenous Sindhis and other ethnic populations. This move by Benazir Bhutto was especially disliked by Chief of Army Staff Mirza Aslam Beg of the Pakistani Army, as he himself was an immigrant.

Her disgruntled party leader, Jam Sadiq Ali, was made caretaker chief minister in Sindh. He had previously been a top disciple of Pir Pagaro, but then he turned against the pir after joining Zulfiqar Ali Bhutto. He switched his loyalties once more and turned on Benazir Bhutto. Ghulam Mustafa Jatoi was appointed caretaker prime minister of Pakistan. He was previously one of Zulfiqar Ali Bhutto's closest confidants and had served as both a federal and chief minister of Sindh with ZAB, but was forced out of the top leadership of Pakistan People's Party by Benazir Bhutto. A secret elections cell, led by General Rafaqat, was formed in Islamabad, a massive rigging of the election was organized, and Benazir Bhutto lost the elections. Nawaz Sharif, a young, emerging politician from Lahore, won the elections in a landslide; he was asked to form the federal government in Islamabad while Jam continued as Sindh chief minister.

A massive witch hunt of political opponents and Sindhi nationalists continued under Jam in Sindh. Jam and MQM were partners in the governing of Sindh with the blessings of the establishment. Jam Sadiq also hobnobbed with some Sindhi nationalist groups who were anti-PPP in their ideologies.

Jam Sadiq Ali died from cancer and was succeeded by Muzaffar Hussain Shah. Military operations were announced in June 1992 in Sindh. Many Sindhis were tortured and died in extrajudicial killings by security agencies.

In 1993, a power struggle ensued between President Ghulam Ishaq Khan and Prime Minister Nawaz Sharif. This led to another round of elections in the country. Benazir Bhutto won the elections again and became prime minister for a second time. The second term of Benazir Bhutto's government proved disastrous for Sindh, Sindhis, and her own estranged family members. First, she had Murtaza Bhutto arrested on his return from exile. She later kicked her mother, Nusrat Bhutto, out of the PPP because Nusrat Bhutto had sided with her son instead of with her daughter, Benazir. Hundreds of Sindhis were killed by MQM terror squads in Karachi, Hyderabad, and Sukkur, which led her interior minister, Naseerullah Babar, to initiate operations against MQM in the cities of Sindh. Finally, her second government was dismissed immediately after the killing of her own brother, Mir Murtaza Bhutto, and his party comrades in a shoot-out on September 20, 1996, in front of the Bhutto family home in Karachi. Ostensibly, the police party was led by an officer loyal to Benazir's husband, Asif Ali Zardari. And Murtaza Bhutto was refused any medical care while he bled to death for a few hours after being shot.

Mir Murtaza Bhutto's daughter, Fatima Bhutto, and his party accused Benazir, her husband, and the government of the murder of Mir Murtaza Bhutto. The theory became popular that Mir Murtaza Bhutto was murdered on the instructions of Benazir's husband to gain control of the family fortunes and the Pakistan People's Party. This was confirmed years later, in the minds of many, when Zardari ascended to absolute power and gained total control of the PPP. He became not only the chairman of PPP, but also the president of Pakistan after the assassination of Benazir Bhutto.

However, the most commonly held belief is that Murtaza Bhutto was assassinated by the intelligence agencies because they never pardoned him for his clandestine activities with the al-Zulfikar organization, including plane hijacking and killing of an ex-army captain. Benazir's estranged uncle, Mumtaz Bhutto, was another of ZAB's closest allies; he was appointed caretaker chief minister of Sindh, with the main focus of eradicating Benazir's political influence in Sindh, especially in her hometown of Larkana.

In the 1997 elections, Nawaz Sharif returned as prime minister for a second time. His rule was popularly called the Second *Takht* Lahore (Second Throne of Lahore), the first being that of Ranjit Singh in the first half of the nineteenth century. Bhutto went into self-exile in 1998 and remained there until Dictator Pervez Musharraf and former ISI Chief General Ashfaq Parvez Kayani negotiated and made a deal with her, reportedly through mediation conducted by the US and UK governments. Musharraf was losing control due to a popular lawyer's movement against him in 2007.

Cases against Benazir Bhutto; her spouse, Asif Ali Zardari; and party colleagues were withdrawn. Elections were scheduled for 2008, and Benazir declared her return from self-exile. Musharraf wanted her to return after the elections. Benazir returned on October 18, 2007. On arrival in Karachi, she was reportedly received by more than 1,000,000 followers; however, her reception procession was attacked by a suicide bomber. Benazir narrowly survived this assassination attempt, but 150 of her party workers were killed.

On December 27, 2007, there was a second suicide attack on Benazir Bhutto at Liaqat Park in Rawalpindi. Benazir Bhutto and many of her party loyalists were killed in the attack. Later, her mother, Begum Nusrat Bhutto, suffering from Alzheimer's disease, died in Dubai. After Benazir's death, her husband, Asif Ali Zardari, took over the reins based on a handwritten, previously unknown will attributed to Benazir Bhutto. Her son, Bilawal Zardari, was renamed Bilawal Bhutto Zardari and added as co-chairperson and new face of the PPP. In the words of Benazir's friend and biographer, Bhatia:

The Bhutto drama will continue for another one hundred years, though most people believe that Benazir's death was the end of the Bhutto family legacy, and a sad saga of one the best known political families of the world, in the recent history.[148]

---

[148] Shyam Bhatia, *Goodbye Shahzadi: A Political Biography of Benazir Bhutto* (Lotus Roli Books, 2008).

1942
1958
1969
1977
1999

Sindh Under Martial Law

*All other countries have militaries.
But in Pakistan, the military has a country.*
~Anonymous

Pakistan has remained under direct martial law for forty out of its seventy-six years of existence, and indirect martial law for the rest of the time. Direct martial laws may come and go for the rest of the country, but there has never been an end to martial law for Sindhis. Pakistan, like most third-world countries on the current world map, is a country born of expediency after the collapse of the European colonial era of the nineteenth and twentieth centuries. Weakened after the Second World War, these colonial masters could not hold on to their colonies and abandoned them in haste, leaving a mess all over the map. In doing this, no nation was worse than the British.

The newly formed country of Pakistan, faced with the fear of imminently being overrun by its nemesis five times its size, decided to put defense at the top of its priorities. Pakistan quickly became one of the most powerful military powers in the world and one of the select nuclear powers. But the cost of allowing its armed forces to use expediency as justification for acquiring omnipotence, unfortunately, was the severely stunted natural growth of the country. After seven decades of existence, Pakistan is still experimenting with different forms of governance. It still is a country, but it has not evolved into a true state in which each arm works in harmony, caring and protecting its citizens as if they were its children. The Sindhi people's poet Ibrahim Munshi once said:

"اهو ميجر اهو ڪرنل اهو جرنل جگر کائي
رهي آ سنڌ ويچاري مثل فوٽبال مرکز م
(ابراهيم منشي)

The same major, the colonel, the general eat our liver
And the poor Sindh is as always kicked as a football.

On October 10, 1958, Pakistan's president, Iskandar Mirza, abrogating the constitution, declared martial law throughout the country. He was a bureaucrat turned president who acted as if he were a puppet with strings being pulled by Pakistan's young but powerful military under the command of their ambitious, Sandhurst-trained Chief of Army Staff General Muhammad Ayub Khan. Only seventeen days later, On October 27, Ayub Khan led a coup against Iskandar Mirza and proclaimed himself the president and chief martial-law administrator of Pakistan. He forced the resignation of Iskandar Mirza and sent him into exile.

Hyder Bux Jatoi, the great Sindhi peasant leader, wrote the following verse upon imposition of martial law in the country by Ayub Khan:

مارشل لا ملڪ جو دستور ٿيو
هڪ سپاهي گهر جو مالڪ مور ٿيو

سڀ زبانون بند ٿيو اعلان ٿيو
آدمي انسان مان حيوان ٿيو
(حيدر بخش جتوئي)

Martial law has become the rule of the country
A soldier has become owner and hero of the country
No one dare move their tongue, is the promulgation
The people have been herded as animals

It was the first martial law of Pakistan, but it was the third martial law in the lives and memories of Sindhis. The first martial law was imposed in Hur areas during the first Hur rebellion from 1893 to 1898. According to journalist and historian on the Hur movement Nasir Aijaz, "The first martial law was imposed in some parts of the Jaisalmer area of India, Thar, and Parker Districts, Makhi area of Sanghar, and Nara Seders area of Khairpur Mirs, where the disciples of Pir Pagaro, Mahar, Mangrios, Rajars, and other communities used to live."[149]

The British imposed the second martial law in vast areas of Sindh on June 1, 1942, with Major Richardson as

---

[149] Aijaz, *Hur: The Freedom Fighter*, 148-151.

martial-law administrator. British archaeologist H. T. Lambrick was appointed as advisor to the martial-law administrator. The British used brutal force against the Hur rebellion, which lasted through 1943, until the execution of Pir Pagaro. They used the Royal Air Force to bombard Hur villages and killed about 200 Hur men, women, and children. Men were arrested and tortured, while Hur women, children, and elderly were placed in concentration camps surrounded by hedges called *lorrhas*. Generations of Hurs were born and grew up inside those lorrhas. About 1,600 square miles stretching from Sukkur to Nawabshah, Khairpur Mirs, and part of the Hyderabad District fell within the second marital law called the Hur Martial Law.

Shabbir Hussain Shah, an eyewitness to the atrocities perpetrated on the Hur population by the British martial-law authorities, writes in his memoirs:

> *The atrocities committed on Hurs by British seem to have no parallel. In spite of aerial bombardment, indiscriminate arrests, shooting every suspect to death, the alliance and discipline displayed during their encounter with death by Hurs was what turned the British mad. Martial law was imposed, and to make it effective, the Chief Martial Law Administrator, Major General Richardson, ordered chopping of all the trees for miles along the railway track.*[150]

---

[150] Shah Nafisa and Mujtaba Hasan, "The Raider of the Past," *Newsline*, February 1995.

Hur Martial Law was lifted quietly on March 3, 1943. But the Hurs continued to be detained in concentration camps long after that, even past 1947, under the government of the newly formed country of Pakistan.

H. T. Lambrick was a special commissioner against Hur activities in Sindh; he covered the Larkana, Khairpur, and Sanghar Districts. A special oppressive and discriminatory law called the Hur Suppression Act was passed by the Sindh Assembly. After creation of Pakistan, senior military officials of the British military during Hur Martial Law were issued posts in the senior command of the newly formed country. Most of these officers and soldiers had fully participated in atrocities against the Hurs in order to crush the Hur uprising against the British occupiers.

Catastrophes of Martial Law

After Ayub Khan declared himself chief martial-law administrator in October 1958, he appointed General Abdul Hamid

Tikka Khan as martial-law administrator of zone C, which included Sindh. To gauge the Sindhis' feelings about martial law, he took a tour of the Hyderabad District. While interacting with members of the public at Tando Allahyar, General Tikka Khan asked a senior citizen how he viewed martial law.

The old man responded, "My age is about ninety-five years. I saw the great plague; I saw First World War; I saw Second World War; I saw the catastrophe of the Partition of India. Those all were the catastrophes. Catastrophes come and are bound to go away. So will this martial law."

Martial law under Ayub Khan proved to indeed be a catastrophe for Sindh. The main purpose of imposing martial law throughout the country was to preempt the abolishment of the One Unit system, as G. M. Syed had successfully acquired the consensus of all members of the opposition in the West Pakistan Assembly to end the One Unit system. After martial law was declared, Sindhi, Pashtun, Bengali, and Baluch leaders, including G. M. Syed, Bacha Khan Abdul Ghaffar Khan, Ghaus Bakhsh Bizenjo, Akbar Bugti, and Sheikh Mujibur Rahman, were placed under arrest. During One Unit, Ayub Khan strengthened the grip of the military. He allotted himself, his family, his friends, and some civil and military higher-ups thousands of acres of Sindh's fertile agricultural land—from Thatta, Badin, to Kashmore on both banks of the River Indus—which was irrigated by the newly constructed Ghulam Muhammad and Guddu barrages.

Hundreds of Sindhi peasants and indigenous communities who rose against the taking away of their ancestral lands were jailed for years. These Sindhi peasants were framed for murders, robberies, and thefts. A campaign of punitive actions was started against Sindhi officers working in the civil bureaucracy. The vice chancellor of Sindh University, Hassanally Abdul Rahman, was relieved of his post. This triggered unrest among Sindhi students, which later evolved into the Sindhi Youth Nationalist Movement.

Throughout Pakistan, and Sindh in particular, Ayub Khan's regime came down hard on students and labor protests. Sindhi students were tortured in police lockups. It was Ayub Khan's regime that turned political victimization into a fine art. Military, police, and intelligence officials were trained in the latest techniques of torture, extrajudicial killings, and disappearances of political opponents.

Sindhi leaders like G. M. Syed, Hyder Bux Jatoi, and Qazi Faiz Muhammad; peasant leaders Ghulam Muhammad Laghari and Ghulam Haider Laghari; student leaders such as Jam Saqi, Yousuf Laghari, Mir Thebo, Mehr Hussain Shah, Shafiq Siddiqui, Masood Noorani, and Yousuf Talpur; writers and poets like Shaikh Ayaz and Rashid Bhatti; and many others were jailed for long terms. Military courts convicted many of these Sindhi leaders and Sindhi rights activists, and they were left to languish in jails in far-flung areas like Machh, Mianwali, Peshawar, Sahiwal, and Multan. Their books were banned.

Ayub Khan's name became synonymous with the word *aamriat* (*dictatorship*). That is why the martial-law rule of Ayub Khan was popularly called Ayubi Aamriat. His governor of the former West Pakistan, Nawab Amir Mohammad of Kalabagh, was a mirror image of Ayub Khan when it came to a state of terror. Besides Sindhis, Ayub Khan mistreated Baluch nationalist leaders and activists. In his government, a second massive military operation was launched in Baluchistan. Baluch rebel leader Nauroz Khan was deceivingly made to surrender from the hills with his nephews and comrades. He was given a solemn assurance that they would be granted amnesty and not arrested if they returned peacefully. But when Nauroz Khan and his colleagues returned, they were detained and tortured at Kulli Camp Quetta and other torture centers. Later, they were tried in Sukkur and Hyderabad jails and were hanged. Sindhi Talpur women received the corpses of Nauroz Khan and his young comrades and donned their *chadors* in Sindhi and Baluchi tradition. Thus, the relationship between Baluchis and Sindhis during trying times was historically established and developed further in the future.

Akbar Bugti was initially given the death sentence but was later pardoned. *Bangla Bandhoo* (the Father of the Bengali Nation), Sheikh Mujibur Rahman, was placed under arrest and tried for high treason at Agartala in former East Pakistan.

In 1965, Ayub Khan decided to lift martial law and hold elections, but through a basic-democracies (BD) system introduced by him. The BD system was a network-type presidential system in which elected members at the union-council level elected their own representatives; in turn, those elected representatives elected the president of the country.

Fatima Jinnah came out of her self-imposed political retirement and decided to head the Pakistan Muslim League and contest Ayub Khan's presidential elections. She was backed by a consortium of political parties, intelligentsia, students, and labor unions who opposed Ayub Khan. Despite massive political rigging, Jinnah was able to win the vote in two of the largest cities, Karachi and Dhaka.

All political parties, left and right, gathered around Fatima Jinnah as a democratic force in the country. Sindhi leaders Shaikh Abdul Majeed Sindhi and Qazi Faiz Muhammad also supported Fatima Jinnah. This was the decade in which Pakistan's first and largest opposition party, National Awami Party (NAP), was founded. NAP was comprised of nationalists and progressives from all provinces of Pakistan.

G. M. Syed, Rasool Bux Palijo, and Hafeez Qureshi, prominent Sindhi nationalist leaders, also joined the National Awami Party. NAP's demands included maximum autonomy for the provinces and restoration of indigenous languages—like Sindhi, Pashto, Baluchi, Punjabi, and Bengali—as national languages. Although NAP's leadership was mainly from Pakhtunkhwa, with people like Khan Abdul Wali Khan, Arbab Sikandar Khan Khalil, and Ajmal Khattak as its central leaders, it also had representation from other provinces, including Ghaus Bakhsh Bizenjo, Khair Bakhsh Marri, and Attaullah Mengal from Baluchistan, and Suhrawardy and Abdul Hamid Bhashani from Bengal. NAP joined the united front called Democratic Action Committee (DAC) against the dictatorship of Ayub Khan and demanded the holding of elections and restoration of democracy.

Time magazine, while reporting on the 1965 election campaign, wrote that Jinnah faced attacks on her modesty and patriotism by Muhammad Ayub Khan and his allies—a tactic that, to this day, continues to be used against any political figure who does not toe the line of the establishment.

Although Ayub Khan introduced land reforms through martial-law orders, he enjoyed the support and hospitality of the important, large feudal lords such as Mahars, Chandio, and Bhuttos, whom he awarded enormous influence and *charagahs* (hunting fields), lakes, and favors. Ayub Khan visited them during hunting seasons.

Ayub Khan moved the capital of the country from the city of Karachi to Rawalpindi, close to his village, Rehana, near Abbottabad. In turn, his successor, Yahya Khan, moved the capital to Islamabad.

In September 1965, war between India and Pakistan broke out. Sindhi Hindus were harassed and hounded by state security agencies. The Ayub Khan regime banned books written by G. M. Syed and Shaikh Ayaz. A large number of Hindus, including leftist leader Sobho Gianchandani, were incarcerated. Under the DPR, during the war, the Ayub Khan regime also jailed Sindh's national poet, Shaikh Ayaz for merely reciting his poetry. They had attempted to silence Shaikh Ayaz by offering him a lucrative position, but Ayaz declined. Instead, he wrote his famous verse:

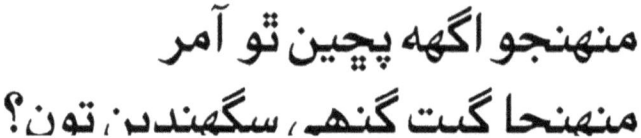

O' Dictator, you are asking my price
Can you even count by poems

In 1968, an uprising of the populace erupted against Ayub Khan; it was led by students and labor organizations, prodemocratic parties, Zulfiqar Ali Bhutto, and his PPP. By then, the PPP had gained immense popularity among the masses. The movement forced Ayub Khan to resign from his presidency. His military and quasimilitary rule came to an end. However, he handed the reins of the country to his second-in-command, Commander-in-Chief Agha Muhammad Yahya Khan, in 1969.

Yahya Khan—The Martial Law of Paradoxes

On March 25, 1969, Yahya Khan took over, imposed martial law, and proclaimed himself the new president of the country, Ayub Khan's successor. Ethnically, Yahya Khan was a Persian-speaking Pathan. He graduated from the Colonel Cambridge School in Dehradun, India, and was from the Tenth Baluch Regiment of the Pakistani Army. This self-appointed president, in a radio address to the people, promised to hold elections on a one-person, one-vote adult-franchise basis and to abolish One Unit. The end of One Unit was announced on July 1, 1970, and general elections were held in December that same year.

Yahya Khan ran the country through a coterie of people who formed his junta, namely General Umar, General Abdul Hamid, and General M. M. Pirzada. General Umar was given the task of handling Sindhi nationalist and student movements in Sindh. After abolishing One Unit, Yahya Khan appointed retired General Rakhman Gul as governor of the Sindh province and martial-law administrator of zone C.

The Quota System, which had originally been introduced by the colonial rulers in undivided India to protect the interests of minorities, was continued by Liaqat Ali Khan after the Partition to ensure opportunities for the newly arrived immigrants from India. After the abolition of One Unit, this system was further reformed as an affirmative-action program to provide direly needed opportunities for youths from rural areas of the province. To date, it remains the main bone of contention for the Urdu-speaking population of Sindh.

During Yahya Khan's regime, military courts were set up in Sindh to summarily try and convict a large number of Sindhi nationalists, student leaders, and activists. Among those who were convicted were Jam Saqi, Mir Thebo, Qazi Faiz Muhammad, Hyder Bux Jatoi, Ghulam Muhammad Laghari, and female student activists Akhtar Baloch and Riaz Memon.

Mir Thebo and others were arrested when they distributed buttons inscribed with the demand that Sindhi be the official language of Sindh. To press the demand that electoral lists be printed in the Sindhi language, Sindhi students led by Lala Qadir went on hunger strikes at the old campus of Sindh University; female students Riaz Memon, Akhtar Baluch, and Nasim Thebo participated. In their solidarity, Hyder Bux Jatoi and Zulfikar Ali Bhutto visited the sit-in camp of the hunger strikers. Qazi Faiz Muhammad and Ghulam Muhammad Laghari actually joined the hunger strike outside the old campus.

At midnight one evening, police stormed onto the campus and charged male hunger strikers with their batons; many were injured. They arrested male and female students, and all were convicted and sent to various jails around the country. Qazi Faiz Muhammad continued his hunger strike even in Hyderabad Central Jail. Later, the Yahya Khan regime accepted their demands, and the hunger strikers were released.

There was another batch of Sindhi students, writers, poets, and intellectuals arrested in a case famously known as the Pamphlet Case. A pamphlet was secretly written in protest of military operations against the people of Bangladesh. After it was printed and distributed, arrests were made, including those of Rashid Bhatti, Zahid Makhdoom, Fateh Abid Lashari, Lateef Mahar, Ghamshyam, and Narayandas from Jacobabad. Poet Anwar Pirzado, who was a pilot in the Pakistan Air Force, was arrested, court-martialed, and convicted.

It is reported that under Yahya Khan, with Tikka Khan as martial-law administrator of the former East Pakistan, 3,000,000 Bengali civilians were killed, and 200,000 women were raped; 100,000,000 people of former East Pakistan were forced to flee their native Sonar Bangla and take shelter as refugees in West Bengal and other parts of India and neighboring countries.

Tikka Khan earned the notoriety of being called the Butcher of Bengal. Later, he also earned the name the Butcher of Baluchistan. India intervened, and war broke out between India and Pakistan. The Bangladesh Liberation War ended up with a surrender of the Pakistani armed forces, their 90,000 soldiers and officers taken as POWs by India.

A new, independent country, Bangladesh, emerged on the world map. Rashid Ashraf, a progressive Urdu poet, defined the post-Bangladesh scenario in his own words:

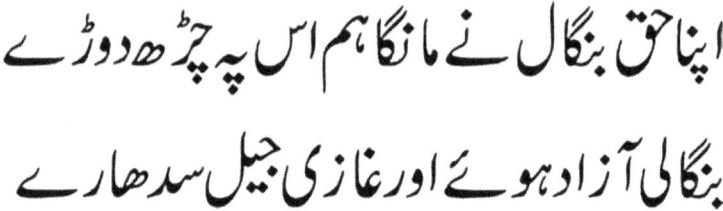

We launched an attack when Bengal demanded her rights
Bengalis got liberated and the ghazi soldiers went to the prison

After their humiliating defeat at the hands of the Indians, the military rulers had no option but to hand over the reins of power to Bhutto as successor and civilian chief martial-law administrator. Later, Bhutto, succumbing to pressure from countrywide protests against Yahya Khan and the breakup of the country, placed Yahya Khan under house arrest.

A probe into military actions in East Bengal (now Bangladesh) was conducted by Chief Justice Hamoodur Rahman. It was called the Hamoodur Rahman Commission, and ultimately it held several military generals and officers responsible for the 1971 debacle and recommended punishments for them. The Hamoodur Rahman Commission was never made public, nor was any action taken against those responsible for the East Pakistan debacle. Instead, some of the culprits were elevated to higher positions. A prime example is Colonel Aslam Beg, who was later promoted to the rank of general and chief of staff of the army, and Jehanzeb Arbab, who was made governor and martial-law administrator of Sindh during the Zia regime.

The military overthrew and executed Bhutto after using him to bring the 90,000 POWs back from Indian prisons. Under the Simla Agreement—a deal signed between Bhutto and Prime Minister of India Indira Gandhi in Simla—the Pakistani territory conquered by the Indian army during the 1970 war, including that of Thar, was reclaimed. The military needed a break to reinforce themselves.

Most intellectuals from the Sindh, Baluchistan, and Pakhtunkhwa provinces of Pakistan believe that Bhutto was serving the interests of Punjab and the military, and they killed him after he did their dirty work.

Zia and His Martial Law—Model Dictator of Asia and Mother of All Martial Laws

During the night between July 4 and July 5, 1977, Zia led a third military coup in Pakistan and imposed the country's third martial law less than six years after the second one. It was the most ruthless of them all, especially for Sindh, as this martial law primarily affected Sindhis and their households because it was aimed directly at them. Zia's military rule under martial law lasted over a decade; it was the longest in Pakistan's history and proved to be a great catastrophe for Sindhis.

Zia overthrew Bhutto, the Sindhi prime minister, tried him for the murder of a political opponent, hanged him, and sent his corpse in a C-130 cargo aircraft from Islamabad. However, Zia was the choice of Bhutto himself. Ironically, it is said that what attracted Bhutto the most was Zia's subservience and docility. Bhutto was deceived into believing that Zia would not challenge his authority as the chief of the army. Bhutto, being acutely aware of the past history of martial law in the country, fully realized that the only threat to his rule would come from the army and its chief. Thus, thinking Zia docile and loyal, Bhutto promoted Zia to chief of the army, superseding eight other generals who had more seniority than Zia and were more deserving.

Zia's rule is considered the worst period in modern history for Sindh and Sindhis, more horrific than even the worst atrocities perpetrated by the British colonizers. During Zia's martial law, many villages and cities of Sindh were forced to receive and bury dead bodies of Sindhi youth who were tortured, maimed, and killed by the authorities. It seems that after hanging Bhutto, Zia and his top brass developed a personal grudge against all Sindhis. In turn, the Sindhis demonstrated their unparalleled disgust for Zia.

Initially, Zia claimed that his intentions were apolitical and that he only wanted to restore order and hand the power over to whichever political party won the election. He also promised to stay neutral. He made it clear the army had no political intentions, and they would return to their barracks after holding "fair, free, and impartial elections within ninety days." A promise he took to his grave, although it can be said that he never really received a grave, as his body was never fully recovered from the wreckage of the plane in which he crashed.

In the words of V. T. Joshi, a former Indian journalist, author, and expert on Indian and Pakistani politics:

> *The figure of ninety is the magic number in the public affairs of Pakistan. It was a much-dreaded number, which had led to caustic comments and became a public joke during Zia- u-Haq's martial law regime, because their constitutional obligation of holding elections within ninety days whenever the contingency arose was successfully breached on one excuse or another by stretching it effectively to nine years.*[151]

The main obstacle and greatest threat to Zia and his dictatorship was Zulfikar Ali Bhutto. Bhutto was arrested in September 1977, tried on charges of ordering the murder of Nawab Muhammad Ahmed Kasuri, father of his one-time party colleague turned foe, Ahmad Raza Kasuri. Zia not only showed interest in the trial of Bhutto, but also purged personnel in the judiciary to make sure the correct judges were on the bench when Bhutto was tried. As Tariq Ali wrote:

> *It was not simply that Bhutto might win any democratic electoral contest. What frightened the corps commanders was that Bhutto alive represented permanent potential alternative to military rule.*[152]

Zia appointed Jahanzeb Arbab as governor and martial-law administrator of Sindh. PPP top-tier leadership caved in and never came out to save the life of their leader. Despite all

---

[151] V. T. Joshi, *Pakistan: Zia to Benazir* (New Delhi: Konark Publishers, 1995).

[152] Tariq Ali, *Can Pakistan Survive?* (London: Penguin Books, 1983) 10.

clemency appeals from world leaders, Bhutto was executed on April 4, 1979. People from all over Pakistan demonstrated in the streets, trying to save Bhutto's life. Nine men self-immolated in live protests.

Bhutto women were either jailed or placed under house arrest. Bhutto's trusted servant, Noor Muhammad Mughal, was found dead under mysterious circumstances. Reportedly, Noor Muhammad Mughal was arrested by the military, and an attempt was made to coerce him into being a state witness against Bhutto, but he refused to do so. He was tortured, killed, and tossed near the mausoleum of Jinnah.

The Zia regime closed university campuses in Sindh for over a year on the pretext of quelling student unrest after a Sindhi female student was allegedly raped by an army major. A military recruit was killed in the ensuing student protest on October 2, 1978. A special military court imposed the death sentence on student leaders Ali Haider Shah and Qadir Bux Jatoi in what was famously known as the Shireen Soomro Case.

During Zia's 1977 martial law, a large number of Sindhi politicians, political activists, writers, intellectuals, and even common people were jailed for years. Many of them were whipped and served long jail terms. Some of them were taken from jails, interrogated, and tortured to death.

In 1978, Zia postponed the elections, claiming that elections were un-Islamic and inappropriate for a country founded in the name of Islam. Instead, he demanded *Islamization* in all spheres of life in Pakistan. With new geopolitical changes in the region, especially the Iranian Revolution and the toppling of the Daoud Khan government by a Communist regime in Afghanistan, Zia's importance increased. As described by Ian Talbot, an authority on South Asia, "Redrawing of the map of West Asia greatly benefited Zia. He was transformed overnight from an international pariah to America's frontline ally in the fight against Communism."[153]

To counter the growing Communist influence in Afghanistan, the Pakistani Army, with the support of other anti-Communist world powers, started supporting jihadist forces in Afghanistan to topple the newly installed Communist government. The Soviet Union decided to send their military forces to Afghanistan to quash the unrest. This turned Zia and his regime into the new darlings of the West, as they saw him as the last hurdle to the Soviet Union and its advances towards the Persian Gulf. This provided his dictatorship a new lease on life and further emboldened Zia and his regime. They unleashed a new wave of mass arrests, especially in Sindh. Young Sindhi men were abducted by government agencies and taken to notorious torture centers, including Lahore Fort, Kulli Camp Quetta, and cantonments in Hyderabad and Karachi.

Hangings of political activists began. Bhutto supporters Ayaz Samon and Nasir Baloch were hanged on charges of conspiracy to hijack a PIA aircraft. Nazer Abbasi, a Sindhi leftist student leader and president of Sindh National Students' Federation, was arrested and tortured to death by military intelligence

---

[153] Ian Talbot, *Pakistan: A New History* (Oxford University Press, 2015) 260-262.

agencies. These agencies were also suspected of having poisoned Benazir's younger brother, Shahnawaz Bhutto, in South France.

A famous trial against Sindhi leftist leaders was held by a special military court at Karachi. Those tried were Jam Saqi, Sohail Sangi, Shabir Shar, Amar Lal, Badar Abro, Professor Jamal Naqvi, and Ahmed Kamal Warsi. Other Sindhi leftist student leaders Imdad Chandio, Muhammad Khan Solangi, and Sher Muhammad Mangrio were convicted and sentenced to seven years and fifteen lashes merely for writing and distributing a pamphlet against the dictatorship of Zia. Ghanshyam Prakash, another student leader, was abducted by the intelligence agencies, tortured, jailed for long terms, and forced to disappear. He was declared a prisoner of conscience by Amnesty International during Zia's regime.

The populace's resentment of Zia and his army increased, especially in Sindh, and reached the point of no return. So did the brutalities of the Zia regime. A 1982 report by Amnesty International fully documented human-rights violations under Zia and his regime, including tortures, jailings, disappearances, and floggings of political activists, including women. But the so-called civilized world continued its unwavering support for Zia's regime in the name of their national interests.

In Sindh, Rasool Bux Palijo's Sindhi Awami Tehreek, especially its women's branch, Sindhiani Tehreek, rose to prominence as the major participant in the movement. Members of Awami Tehreek were at the forefront of the movement in Hyderabad, Badin, and Thatta. Their leaders, Rasool Bux Palijo and Fazil Rahu, had been in jail since 1978. Now, their members, including women and children, were arrested and imprisoned in large numbers. The works of Sindhi poets like Akash Ansari, Hassan Dars, Haleem Baghi, Mazhar Laghari, Anwar Pirzado, and Manzoor Solangi, and of short-story writers like Fakir Muhammad Lashari, Badar Abro, and Munir Ahmed Manik greatly contributed to the anti-Zia movement.

At the height of MRD uprising, Zia adamantly decided to take a tour of Sindh. In Sukkur, he foolishly gave the statement in the press that the "people of Sindh had wanted martial law for more than five years." It was not true. Unannounced curfews were enforced wherever Zia went in Sindh. Before his visit to Dadu—the stronghold of MRD movement and an area Sindhis referred to as "the Vietnam of Sindh"—another curfew was imposed. Despite that, crowds of protesters appeared out of nowhere when Zia's helicopter landed at a local stadium.

In August 1983, facing massive unrest in the country, especially Sindh, in the form of the MRD movement, Zia announced a cosmetic change in his plans. He promised to lift martial law in December 1984 and hold elections the year after.

Before the elections, Zia held a referendum to get himself elected as president for five more years. Elections were held in 1985, but political parties were banned from participating. Candidates could only participate as long as they were not affiliated with any political party. MRD and PPP boycotted the elections.

Zia's handpicked Muslim League won the elections, though these elections were declared unfair by most international observers. In an attempt to appease the people of Sindh, Muhammad Khan

Junejo, a Pir Pagaro loyalist, was chosen to become the new prime minister of the country. According to Lawrence Ziring, an authority on Pakistan:

> *In choosing Junejo to be his prime minister, Zia sought to neutralize his more vocal opposition in the troubled Sindh province. He also had expectations of drawing PPP defectors to the Junejo fold. Junejo therefore became the instrument whereby martial law would be lifted.*[154]

But a Sindhi prime minister, in spite of being handpicked, cost Zia dearly. He repealed an infamous press and publication ordinance. He released political prisoners, including Rasool Bux Palijo, Fazil Rahu, and Jam Saqi detainees. He allowed controlled but limited political activities throughout the country.

The times were changing in the region as the former Soviet Union and the United States were entering into a dialogue to resolve the Afghan crisis. That dialogue, with Pakistan as one of the stakeholders, resulted in the Geneva Accord. Muhammad Khan Junejo sidelined Zia throughout the process on Afghanistan. Junejo convened an all-parties conference, inviting politicians like Benazir Bhutto and Rasool Bux Palijo. Junejo kept Zia completely out of the conference and its proceedings. He ordered a probe when catastrophe occurred at Ojhri Camp near Islamabad, where the largest arms, ammunition, and storage depot of

---

[154] Lawrence Ziring, *Pakistan in the Twentieth Century: A Political History* (Oxford University Press, 1998) 281-284.

Pakistani Army's missiles were blown up. Missiles flew all over Rawalpindi. About one hundred people were killed and more than 1,000 injured in the incident.

Feeling threatened by these actions, Zia dismissed his handpicked prime minister on August 17, 1988, while Junejo was on an official visit to China. On that same day, while on his way back from watching a demonstration of the newly acquired M1 Abrams tanks from the US, Zia died in a mysterious air crash near Bahawalpur. He was accompanied by the US ambassador to Pakistan, Arnold Raphel, military attaché Brigadier General Herbert Wassom, ISI Chief General Akhtar Abdul Rahman, and the top brass of the Pakistani Army. This case remains unsolved.

As a punishment for their leadership in the MRD movement, the establishment unleashed the worst form of state terrorism on Sindhis. Gangs of bandits were organized in rural areas and ethnic terrorist organizations established in urban centers of Sindh. Both would kidnap, torture, kill, and maim Sindhis. The hapless targets at the hands of gang kidnappings for ransom in rural areas and at the hands of ethnic terrorists in urban areas were indigenous Sindhis. Within a radius of one hundred square miles of the Pano Aqil military garrison, Sindhi Hindus were forced to emigrate after being hounded by the gangs of outlaws.

About 500 Sindhis lost their lives during both periods of Benazir Bhutto's government, including her own brother, Murtaza Bhutto. During both terms, her government was ousted on corruption charges because she had Sindhi representation. For the first time, in August 1990, she was dismissed because her government ordered the launching of an operation against MQM at Pacco Qillo, Hyderabad, the stronghold of MQM.

MQM observed three days of mourning when Zia died. A larger-than-life portrait of Zia was hung at the entrance of Pacco Qillo, Hyderabad, after Benazir was dismissed at the behest of General Mirza Aslam Beg for ordering the Pacco Qillo operation. In the words of Adeel Khan, an expert on the Pakistani political landscape, especially its ethnic and nationalist aspects:

> *The Zia years had led to the entrenchment of the army's Inter-Services Intelligence into almost every sector of the state and society. So powerful was the ISI that it not only created the main opposition party, the IJI, and endured that the people's party.*[155]

---

[155] Adeel Khan, *Politics of Identity: Ethnic Nationalism and the State in Pakistan* (Sage Publications Pvt. Ltd., 2005) 128-129.

To polarize the historically pluralistic Sufi society of Sindh, religious extremism was introduced. All kinds of jihadist organizations were incorporated and directly patronized by the state. These seeds of religious extremism, sowed by Zia's regime, later proved to be disastrous, not only for Sindh, but for the whole world. Zia will always be remembered as the dictator who introduced the Kalashnikovs (AK-47 assault rifles) and the heroin that infested the country, especially Sindh, with unending ethnic and religious violence and crimes.

The relationship between military regimes and quasi-governmental ruling was best defined by a report from Freedom House on Pakistan:

> *Pakistan's military and security agencies have managed to retain power and influence over the country's government even during civilian rule. This is best exemplified by the ten years of democracy, 1988 to 1999, when successive weak and corrupt civilian governments alternated in power while the military and its security arm, Inter-Services Intelligence (ISI), set Pakistan's ideological and international agenda.*[156]

Pervez Musharraf—Pinochet of Pakistan

The ironic tragedy of Pakistan was that it entered the twenty-first century, a new millennium, with yet another military

---

[156] Report from the Freedom House on Pakistan.

dictator, General Pervez Musharraf. This time, neither Punjabi or Pathan, nor a religious zealot like Zia, but a dictator pretending to be a liberal, an Urdu-speaking immigrant fond of whisky and Pekingese dogs. The uniformed dictator Pervez Musharraf, without declaring himself the chief martial-law administrator, appointed himself the chief executive of the country. The headline in the *New York Times* the next day was, "A Dangerous Coup in Pakistan." In its editorial, the *New York Times* wrote:

> *The military coup in Pakistan is cause for alarm in South Asia and the rest of the world. A nation newly armed with nuclear weapons, and with a volatile history of wars and internal upheavals, has been seized by generals who may be inclined to favor a more confrontational approach with India. Suddenly, after fitful steps toward India-Pakistan rapprochement, the subcontinent is once again one of the most dangerous places on earth. Gen. Pervez Musharraf, the army chief of staff who "dismissed" Prime Minister Nawaz Sharif, acted only after Mr. Sharif tried to oust him earlier in the day. But the United States and other nations must demand that the generals ensure Mr. Sharif's safety, restore him to power and respect Pakistani liberties.*[157]

Unannounced, Musharraf imposed martial law and declared a state of emergency. The constitution was partially abrogated, and judges were forced to take new oaths of office under his

---

[157] Opinion, "Dangerous Coup in Pakistan," *New York Times*, October 13, 1999.

Provisional Constitutional Order (PCO). Those who declined to do so were sent packing. The country's chief justice, Saeeduzzaman Siddiqui, was prevented at gunpoint in his residence, from going to court until the swearing-in ceremony of judges under Musharraf's new PCO was over.

The prime minister, his ministers, and other officials were either jailed or remained missing. Nawaz Sharif was jailed on charges of hijacking a passenger plane that was carrying Musharraf on the eve of the coup he had planned with his corps commanders on the ground. By the end of the first year of his regime, the arrest and torture of Sindhi nationalist activists, including Akash Mallah, Mansoor Marri, and Bashir Qureshi, the chairman of Jeay Sindh Qaumi Mahaz, was reported by Human Rights Watch. Newspapers and periodicals like *International Herald Tribune* and *The Economist* wrote editorials on the HRW report about human-rights violations under Musharraf. In Sindh, Musharraf's government banned all political activities because they were concerned about the successful peaceful street protest by Jeay Sindh Qaumi Mahaz.

While in detention, Akash Mallah, a Jeay Sindh activist, and others were severely tortured by government agencies, as reported by Human Rights Watch. Musharraf publicly called Sindhi people "lazy and inefficient," and those who criticized the Kalabagh Dam "blackmailers." His stubbornness on the proposed construction of the controversial Kalabagh Dam project drew a wide range of Sindhi protests at home and by the Sindhi diaspora in Europe and the US. *The Economist* called Musharraf a "useless dictator."

In another twist of fate, in 2001, Musharraf, like most previous military dictators of Pakistan, again overnight became a darling of the West after the tragic events of September 11, 2001. It was again in the interest of the West to have a brutal dictator do their dirty work. Like all his predecessors, Musharaf very willingly became the most compliant servant of the West in their newly declared war on terror.

But under the cover of his double role in the war on terror, Musharraf went berserk, settling his own scores against his political opponents. Sindhis were his favorite targets. Similar to dictators in South Central America during the Cold War era, the Musharraf regime started "disappearing" members and leaders of Sindhi nationalist parties. First among them in Sindh was Samiullah Kalhoro. The number of forced disappearances in the country increased exponentially during Musharraf's regime. Many were detained at unknown places and forced to remain incommunicado. They were tortured, and their dead bodies were found with torture marks and bullet wounds.

Safdar Sarki, another Sindhi nationalist leader of his own Jeay Sindh Tehreek, an American citizen, was abducted by Pakistani intelligence agencies while visiting Sindh in February 2006. He was tortured and remained missing for twenty-two months until 2008.

Musharraf successfully played a double game with the US, the European Union, and the rest of the international community, minting money in the name of the war on terror. He presented himself as a champion of the war on terror while strengthening the jihadists at home. He forged an alliance with religious extremists and right-wing parties called Muttahida Majlis-e-Amal (MMA), also known as Mullah Military Alliance by some in the country. Musharraf, acting more like a tribal war lord than a professional army officer, pretty much ran the army as his personal militia, abusing money and resources he acquired in the name of fighting the war on terror. With the same weapons and equipment provided to him by the US and allies to hunt down bin Laden and Al-Qaeda operatives, he hunted down secular anti-jihadi, Sindhi, and Baluchi nationalists.

In March 2005, an army captain from Musharraf's parent regiment of commandos, the Special Services Group (SSG), who were responsible for the security of a gas field at Sui

(Baluchistan), was accused of rape of a Sindhi female doctor, Shazia Khalid, posted in Sui. Musharraf came to the rescue of the culprit rapist, Captain Hammad, even before a judicial probe could investigate the rape case. Musharraf ordered the closing of the inquiry. Instead, unannounced, Dr. Shazia Khalid was taken into military custody. She was placed with her husband in isolation in a "safe" house near Hab (Baluchistan) and was intimidated into going into exile.

The incident with Dr. Shazia Khalid caused angers to flare among Sindhis and Baluchis and led to a standoff between the Bugti tribesmen and the Pakistan security agencies. The martial-law administrator used this Baluchi resentment as an excuse to launch another military operation in Baluchistan. Akbar Bugti took to the mountains and was eventually killed by the security agencies, reportedly on the direct orders of Musharraf.

After Akbar Bugti, Musharraf was also accused of being an accomplice in the assassination of former Sindhi prime minister and Sindhi leader of international repute, Benazir Bhutto. The first martial law, known as Hur Martial Law, saw the execution of Pir Pagaro, *Soreh Badshah* (Hero King). The second martial law under Ayub and Yahya Khan resulted in the death of one of the greatest Sindhi women known to history and the mother of the nation, Mohtarma Fatima Jinnah, and the oppression and genocide of Bengalis, which led to the disintegration of the country. Her death is subject to controversy, as some reports have alleged that she died of unnatural causes. Her family members demanded an inquiry; however, the government blocked their request.

The third martial law of Zia culminated in the death of the savior of Pakistan, Zulfikar Ali Bhutto, the man who had given the country its only constitution and its nuclear capability, the only thing that has given the country the power to ward off enemies six times larger than itself. During this martial law, thousands of Sindhis were massacred after the MRD movement. During the fourth martial law under Musharraf, Sindhi leader Benazir Bhutto and the great Baluchi leader Akbar Bugti were killed.

Such is the tragic history of martial law in Sindh. The worst part is that, in actuality, martial law never ends for Sindh and Sindhis. Sometimes it is overt, but it is always lying below the surface. One cannot ignore the painful fact that all of this could and should have been averted had other pillars of the state, especially the judiciary, honored their sworn duties. Unfortunately, instead of upholding the constitution, the judiciary always played the role of facilitator during every martial law and all other violations associated with them. The checkered judicial history of the country is filled with examples of how the judiciary has failed to honor their own oaths—from justification of the dismissal of the original constituent assembly of the country in the Federation of Pakistan v. Maulvi Tamizuddin Khan case in 1955, to the legalization of each martial law in the country, to the hanging of the popularly elected prime minister in the history of the country, to withholding the ruling on every important case until invisible powers had cleared them.

Emergence of Sindhi Diaspora

The word *diaspora* originally referred to the global migration of Jewish people across the globe. Its origin traces back to the third century BCE and the Greek word *diaspeirein,* which is a combination of the words *dia,* meaning across, and *speirein,* meaning sowing or scattering. The term has evolved and is now used to define people settled far from their ancestral homelands. According to Stéphane Dufoix, "It has become the global word that fits the global world."[158]

It represents people of all ethnicities and nationalities who abandon their own motherlands and settle in distant countries. In the words of scholar A. L. McLeod:

> *A number of ethnic and racial groups, living in alien lands, cherish fond memories of their motherland, recall their near and dear ones, friends and family and associations, and are lost in nostalgia and sense of up rootlessness. This sense of alienation is caused by*

---

[158] Stéphane Dufoix.

> awkward situations in which they are placed by their "transplantation."

Robin Cohen, in his book *Global Diasporas: An Introduction*, presented four categories of diaspora:

1. Labor
2. Victim
3. Cultural
4. Homeland

These terms were coined in the 1960s and 1970s and were used when referring to Jews, Africans, Armenians, and Palestinians. Presenting a clinical and insightful view of these diasporas, Cohen also talked about the Jewish Experience and the broadening by William Safran of the term *diaspora* to include "expatriates, expellees, political refugees, alien residents, immigrants, ethnic, and racial minorities."[159]

Melluhas in Mesopotamia—Indus Villages in Mesopotamia

Trade connected Mesopotamia and the Sindhi people called Melluhas. Melluhas may have been the descendants of the Mohanos of the Indus. Melluhas were the first people who navigated the waters of the Indus to explore trade centers

---

[159] Robin Cohen, *Global Diasporas: An Introduction* (Routledge, 2022).

throughout the world and sell their goods; some of the Melluhas eventually settled in those distant lands.

In 1932, archaeologist C. A. Gadd found the sites of several Melluha villages in the ruins of ancient Mesopotamia. Seals similar to those of Indus and weights found from the archaeological sites confirmed that traders from Indus Valley had settled in Samarra, Babylon, and ancient Mesopotamia in the third millennium BCE. Ancient texts found in Mesopotamia offer evidence of a relationship between the people of Sindhu and Mesopotamia.

According to Naeem Tahir, a renowned researcher on Melluhas of the Indus Valley:

> *Mesopotamia lacked raw material in its environs and imported metal and minerals among several other items. Evidence of the Indus Mesopotamia contact is mostly established during Sargonid period in Mesopotamia, and in the mature Melluha Period in the Indus. Moreover, these contacts were mainly through sea route, as objects found in Mesopotamia and also in Iranian sites were also found in the Persian Gulf region. It was on the basis of these finds, at least in a first stage, that the Indus Valley Civilization was dated to the Middle Bronze Age. Since then, two generations of archaeologists and philologists have attempted to investigate the problem of the Indian communities that settled in Mesopotamia in the second half of the third millennium BCE, as the identification of the land of Melluha with the coastal*

areas controlled by the Indus Civilization is almost universally accepted. The textual evidence dealing with individuals qualified as "men" or "sons" of Melluha or called with the ethnonym Melluha living in Mesopotamia and of a "Melluha village" established at Lagash (and presumably at other major cities as well) inexplicably points to the existence of enclaves settled by Indian immigrants.[160]

Sargon texts from the twenty-third century BCE mention "people and the boat of Melluha" or "the bird of Melluha," proving the inhabitants of the Indus used to travel and settle in distant places long before the Greeks coined the term *diaspora*. In her book *Trading Encounters: From the Euphrates to the Indus in the Bronze Age*, Shereen Ratnagar has drawn the trade routes

---

[160] Naeem Tahir, *Melluhas of the Indus Valley, 8000 BCE-500 BCE* (Pakistan National Council of the Arts, 2008).

of the traders between the Euphrates and the Indus Valley as pilgrimages by the Sindhis.

> *It could have been fed by routes what it is now Haryana in the east, or from the upper Punjab to the northeast, or from Multan in the southwest but equally important could have been the route debouching from the Sulaiman Range onto the Dera Ismail Khan, which sees the winter movements of the pastorals and their flocks, also having developed in later centuries into caravan stage where traders deposited their baggage and families before proceeding further towards India, at which point the Indus can be crossed. The commercial and religious importance of Multan in medieval as break- of-bulk center for goods from Afghanistan, and center of pilgrimage for Sindhis is probably relevant to the Bronze Age geography.*
>
> *Whether traveling over land or by sea, the trip would have been well over a thousand miles. There is no evidence from the Indus Valley excavation that suggests the presence of Mesopotamians. However, there are hints from the digs in the Ur, a major city state on Euphrates, that some Indus Valley merchants and artisans (bead makers) may have established communities in Mesopotamia.*[161]

---

[161] Shereen Ratnagar, Ed., *Trading Encounters: From the Euphrates to the Indus in the Bronze Age* (Oxford University Press, 2004).

According to, Stephen S. Gosch, "Ten attendants buried at Ur with Queen Puabi in 2500 BCE were women from the Indus Valley, perhaps sent to Puabi as a diplomatic agreement. DNA analysis of the remains of the attendants, who were interred wearing Indus-style carnelian beads, could confirm this view."[162]

Sindhis Come to Rome

By the dawn of the first century CE, Sindhi traders explored Europe, Java, Sumatra, and China. During the same period, Sindhi merchants had access to the markets of Rome by selling a garment called *sindon*. And there was a Sindhi proverb about those Sindhi traders who went to Rome and their modesty:

"توٹي وڃي روم ته به ڊوڊو ۽ ٿوم لکيو لوح قلم م"

They had same bread and garlic written in their destiny, no matter they have gone to Rome.

An anonymous Sindhi verse describes Sindhi merchants going to Java:

سودي خاطر سنبهي جيڪي ويا جاوا
ڪري وٺج واپار سي سگهو ٿيا ساوا
اڻ ميو ڏن اتان سو جو ڪمائين
پاڻ ته ڪائين پر تن جا پويان به ڪائين

---

[162] Stephen S. Gosch and Peter N. Stearns, *Pre-Modern Travel in World History* (Routledge, 2007) 12-13.

Those who went to Java for business
They became immediately wealthy
Earned un-estimated wealth from Java
Not did only they spend themselves but
Their descendants became wealthy too

According to Bherumal Meharchand Advani's historic account, Sindhis went to Java during the times of Raja of Gujarat Kasam Chitra in 1603 and handed his son, Bhirovuji Sajiwal, six ships loaded with 5,000 men who were artisans, farmers, soldiers, and clerks. They all settled in Java. Prince Sajiwal sent for another 2,000 artisans from Gujarat to build temples in Java. Gujarat was a part of Sindh then, and many Sindhi Hindu traders went there to set up their businesses.

Sindhworkis, Merchants of Sindh

Sindhworkis are known all over the world for their penchant for business; it is commonly said that "make gold out of the dust." They are a branch of Bhaiband Sindhi Hindus who came to prominence during the Kalhora rule in Sindh. This was at the same time that East India Company was establishing roots in Sindh. It had obtained a license to build a factory in Thatta. Sindhworkis got access to the newly established international ports in Karachi and Bombay as soon as Sindh was annexed into the Bombay Presidency after the British conquest. Sindhi Hindu traders became the civil contractors who provided necessary supplies to the British army and their civilian bureaucracy as the British were trying to expand their colonial rule to the Far East.

Sindhi traders started setting up business offices across the globe in places like China, Japan, and Sumatra. These were called *kōṭhīs*. The Watumull family was the first to set up their business in Honolulu. According to the account of Bherumal Meharchand Advani, the earliest Sindhuvarki firms based in Southeast Asia were M/S Pohoomull and Brothers, Dhanamal Chellaram, and Wasiamal Assomull in Java. Many Sindhis married Java girls and settled there. Pohoomull and Brothers even reached South America. Sindhis went to set up their businesses in the Falklands. A few of them even made it to Canada, though Indians were not allowed to settle and do business in Canada in those days.

Before the Second World War, the Sindhi diaspora was estimated to be generating an annual income of approximately 25,000,000 rupees. When transportation and communication were disrupted during the war, Sindhis expanded their trade to India. They set up their *kōṭhīs* in Calcutta, Madras, and Ahmedabad. Bherumal Meharchand Advani writes that, by 1918, Sindhworks Merchant Association was formed with Mukhi Shri Harkishindas as its founding president.

Eminent Sindhi writer Popati Hiranandani depicted the lives and times of Sindhuvarkis in her way:

> *A Sindhuvarki hears about the gold of South Africa, diamonds of Belgium and Israel, gems of Ceylon, and the electronics of Japan, when a child. As he grows, he sits at his father's shop for an hour or two after school. Visits his uncles in Lagos and spends his holidays with his grandmother in Canary Islands. As*

soon as he is seventeen or eighteen, whether he has
finished his studies or not (for degrees are of little use
to him), he joins his father or brother in business, and
by the time he is thirty, he starts on his own.

She flashed back to the pre-Partition lives in India of the Sindhworkis, whom she calls Sindhuvarkis:

Before Partition, the Sindhuvarkis used to leave their families behind in Hyderabad, Sindh. They adorned their womenfolk with pearls and diamonds, silks and brocades, and built bungalows. They owned gardens and orchards such as the well-known Dhoolandas Jo Baug or Moolchand Garden on the banks of the Phuleli Canal in Hyderabad. They brought huge sums of money to their native land, established schools and colleges, hospitals and dharamshalas and donated generously to all charitable institutions. After Partition, the Sindhvarkis continued to be the same philanthropists. They built the modern Jaslok Hospital and the Jai Hind College with large contributions of money by the Sindhuvarkis.[163]

Sindhis are basically a nation of traders and merchants. In Shah Bhittai's times, Sindhi traders went to distant countries and continents for months and even years at a time. Some had to leave their newlywed brides.

---

[163] Popati Hiranandani, *Sindhis: The Scattered Treasure* (Malaah Publications, 1980) 24-27.

،وَتِجَارِي جِي مَاءِ، وَتِجَارو نَہ پَلِيين
.آيو بَارَ هين مَاهَہ، پَٹّ، ثُو سَفَرِ سَنبَهي

As he laments in the words of newly bride of a sailor:
"Oh, mother of the sailor, it is being married to your son is hard
He has just returned after twelve months, and is now getting ready to leave again"

H. T. Sorley, biographer and the first English interpreter, a scholar of Shah Latif, also documented the economic activities in the times of Shah Latif's Sindh. He wrote in his biography of Shah Latif titled, *Shah Abdul Latif of Bhit*, "Sindh exports her own chintzes and calicos after satisfying the demands of the local market. It exports indigo, coarse cotton cloth (barton), silk manufactured goods, and salt and pepper."[164]

---

[164] H. T. Sorley, *Shah Abdul Latif of Bhit: His Poetry, Life and Times* (Oxford University Press, 1967).

In the words of Popati Hiranandani:

> *Wives of Sindhuvarkis worshipped water, praying for the safe return of their beloved husbands from their long voyages, in the same way as wives of Rajput warriors used to worship the horse, imploring it to bring their husbands back alive and safe from the battlefield.*[165]

In "Sur Srirag," Shah Latif asks the boatman to keep his oars and sails ready and the boat polished and shining. He advises him to stay awake and on watch if he wants to escape the pirates. If the tradesman is careless, his steamer will drift towards the eddy, but if he is alert and awake, he can sail safely through storms and rough waters.

After 1947, the majority of Sindhi Hindu merchants migrated to India. They had to start again from scratch, as they were forced to leave most of their belongings back home. Landing in refugee camps, not only did they rebuild their devastated lives, but they also contributed to their new country. Dada T. L. Vaswani and his nephew J. P. Vaswani built many schools, clinics, and community centers. Sindhi Hindus have since become some of the biggest philanthropists in India.

According to Bherumal Advani, some of the Sindhworki merchants funded the independence movement of Sabash Chandler Bose. Even in Panama, the Sindhi business diaspora financed the presidential elections. Gibraltar, Chile, Liberia, and

---

[165] Hiranandani, *Sindhis: The Scattered Treasure.*

Sierra Leone are the other fountainheads where Sindhi capital floats. A Sindhi trader is born with a business background, grows in an atmosphere of business, and inherits the tradition and DNA of business as the years go by. Through their trade and travel from Sindhi, they have spread their contacts to all parts of the world.

Centuries ago, the people of Babylon called Sindh *suavaasa*. The word *su* means "the good one," and the word *vaasa* means "dress material." Even now, textile is one of the main businesses of Sindhi tradesmen. Whether it is in Singapore or Hong Kong, Indonesia or Japan, many Sindhis, the Sindhuvarkis, are textile dealers.

Wealthy Sindhis who migrated to India in 1947 moved to the Far East, including Singapore and Hong Kong, in the 1960s. These emigrants turned into a diaspora in the accurate sense of the term. According to one estimate by Markovits, the Sindhi diaspora numbers today between 120,000 and 140,000 Sindhis living all over the globe, outside of Sindh and India. They comprise highly trained professionals and are exclusively traders; most were born outside India and Pakistan.

Markovits states there are 50,000 Sindhis in the United States and 10,000 in Canada. This does not include the parts of the Sindhi diaspora settled in Russia, Central Asia, UAE, and other Gulf states. This also does not count Sindhis who emigrated after the creation of Pakistan and settled in the USA, UK, UAE, Saudi Arabia, and the rest of the Middle East. According to another rough estimate, the majority of Sindhis from Pakistan, including 30,000 Sindhis, settled in the United States.[166] The first generation of Sindhi-diaspora diplomats and their household members, World Bank officials, physicians, and engineers came and settled in the United States from Sindh in the early 1960s. This diaspora developed through intermarriages, emigration of next of kin, and exchange students.

The decades of the 1960s and 1970s brought the oil boom in Gulf countries. In the mid-1970s, the government of Zulfiqar Ali Bhutto exported labor to the newly affluent, oil-rich states. Large chunks of the Baluchi and Sindhi populations went to work and live in the Gulf and Saudi Arabia.

Sindhi businessmen were among the greatest contributors to the development of modern Dubai. They came to Dubai when it was a shallow creek. The fall of Zulfikar Ali Bhutto and imposition of martial law under Zia-ul-Haq in 1977 opened new chapters of political persecution against his political opponents, changing the pattern of immigration and the composition of the Sindhi diaspora from economic refugees to political exiles. This emigration of persecuted Sindhi political activists and community members from Pakistan seeking refuge overseas in places like the USA, Canada, and the European Union continues today. Since the 1990s, there has been a considerable increase in the number of economic refugees.

---

[166] Claude Markovits, *The Global World of Indian Merchants, 1750-1947: Traders of Sind from Bukhara to Panama* (Cambridge University Press, 2000) 279-285.

Sindhi Diaspora Organizations

Since the 1980s, the Sindhi diasporas living all over the globe have formed a number of organizations. Saeed Rind, who has extensively researched and written on the diaspora of Sindhi Hindus, writes:

> *In 1989, Indian Sindhi organizations of major cities of USA formed an umbrella organization called Alliance of Global Sindhi Association. They started organizing annual International Sindhi Sammelan, or conference, in the USA. Around twenty-five to thirty Indian Sindhi groups participate in those sammelans. The first such International Sindhi Sammelan was held in 1994 in New Jersey, USA. Since 2005, this International Sindhi Sammelan went global and so far it has been organized in Mumbai, London, Jakarta, Singapore, Indore (India), Ahmedabad (India), and the 21st Sammelan held in 2014 in Kuala Lumpur, Malaysia.*[167]

Similarly, the Sindhi Association of North America (SANA) was created in 1983, mostly by Sindhi immigrants from Pakistan. The first generation of SANA founders and many of its officers and members devotedly spent their time and energy on starting a Sindhi-diaspora movement in solidarity with the MRD movement in India.

---

[167] Saeed Rind, "Rise of Sindhi Diaspora in USA: A Comparative Study of SANA, WSC and WSI" (Islamabad: National Institute of Pakistani Studies, 2017) 46, 49, 54.

SANA also published a newsletter called *Sangat* to apprise the community and its members and fellow Americans of the human-rights situation in Sindh. They invited prominent leaders, writers, journalists, intellectuals, poets, artists, and human-rights activists from Sindh to be guest speakers at their annual conventions, which are held in different cities of North America.

SANA has had very active participation by Sindhi women. They have a women's-affairs division, which mandates that its vice chairperson must be female. Women have also contested and won other important positions in SANA's Executive Council (EC). SANA selects its executive leadership through open elections every two years. Its annual conventions have become the most important gathering of Sindhi in the world. These events are attended by Sindhi men, women, and children from North America and Sindhi guests from all over the world. In the past, I have had the honor of being elected treasurer, general secretary, and president.

SANA set up the Feroz Ahmed Memorial Educational Fund (FAME), which sponsors a scholarship fund that provides financial help to needy students all over Sindh. In 1988, in the United Kingdom, Dr. G. M. Bhurgari founded a Sindhi diaspora nationalist organization called World Sindhi Congress (WSC), which consisted of Sindhi nationalists, many of whom were Sindhi political exiles living in Europe and North America. Its first president was Dr. Munawar Halepoto.

Dr. Munawar Halepoto, an elder brother of mine, is considered the true pioneer of Sindhi diaspora activism for Sindh. He raised his voice for Sindh and Sindhis at the international level.

Despite being a naturalized British citizen, he was abducted and tortured by the security agencies during one of his visits to his native village of Tando Allahyar, Sindh.

WSC's main objective is the right of self-determination for Sindhis. They hold their annual conference on various themes relevant to the issues confronting Sindh. They are registered as a not-for-profit organization in London and the USA. They have run several campaigns for restoration of the rights of Sindh, for the end of the persecution of Sindhi Hindus, for the tracing of missing persons, and for the resolution of water issues. They have represented Sindh in UNHRC Geneva and elsewhere.

In 1997, Munawar Laghari (also known as Sufi Laghari) formed the not-for-profit World Sindhi Institute (WSI). Its mission statement states it will work for the promotion of the Sindhi culture and the preservation of the human rights of the Sindhi within the present geographic ambit of Pakistan. WSI successfully ran international campaigns and hosted conferences to apprise the international community of the issues confronting Sindh and Sindhis as a question of their survival. To augment these activities, WSI published its monthly newsletter, *Sindh Watch*.

Saeed Rind, in his research paper on Sindhi-diaspora organizations, sums up his take on WSI:

> *Among Sindhi advocacy groups, the WSI was known for its financial strength and lobbying power among UN agencies, human rights organizations, and INGOs. In 1997, the WSI launched quarterly Sindh Watch to report their activities in UN and other*

INGOs. One of the important contributions of WSI in the field of Sufi literature was their compilation of a series of musical albums containing all of the poetry of famous Sindhi Sufi poet Shah Abdul Latif Bhittai. Bhittai's Shah Jo Risalo, the book on collection of his poetry, is compiled in CDs in the voice of famous local singers. Moreover, the WSI gave Khair-un-Nissa Jaffery an award for writings on Sindhi women's rights. It held its annual international conference on issues confronted by Sindh and Pakistan at large, e.g., the theme of the Fifth Annual International Conference 2004 was "Military Rule in Pakistan: Challenges to Democracy, Human Rights, and Peace in Sindh."

The WSI had a huge budget as compared to the other Sindhi groups, which was about $100,000 per year back in 2005. Therefore, the worst criticism of WSI came from their counterparts in the SANA and the WSC on their financial matters. The WSI was blamed for being funded by the Bharatiya Janata Party (BJP), whose top leadership of L. K. Advani and Ram Jethmalani in India both had ancestral connections with Sindh. However, critics were not able to substantiate their blame with any proof. They would only question where this money came from and why they did not get similar donations though they had been working for a much longer time with better dedication (they claim).[168]

---

[168] Rind, "Rise of Sindhi Diaspora in USA: A Comparative Study of SANA, WSC and WSI."

In 2014, after parting ways with WSI, Sufi Laghari formed another organization, Sindhi Foundation. It was registered as a not-for-profit organization with a new mission and zeal for the old cause of the betterment of Sindhis and their cultural and human rights on a global scale. Its first goal was building bridges between various communities, including the American public. Sindhi Foundation also went into the United Nations' Human Rights Council in Geneva and Capitol Hill in Washington to present evidence of missing persons in Sindh and forced conversions of young Sindhi women.

The US consulate in Karachi launched its website in the Sindhi language, and funds for starting a Sindhi service language from Voice of America have been allocated by the appropriations committee of congress. Work is in progress. In Washington, a Sindhi Americans Political Action Committee (SAPAC) was formed by me with the help of Sufi Laghari. SAPAC lobbies on the Hill for Sindh. With the tireless efforts of SAPAC and Sindhi Foundation, a bipartisan caucus has also been formed; it is comprised of lawmakers chaired by Congressman Brad Sherman (D-CA). SAPAC also publishes a newsletter called *Sindh Guardian*.

Congressman Sherman, whose grandfather lived in Sindh, has emerged as the most powerful advocate for Sindh and Sindhis not only in Washington, DC, but internationally. His highly outspoken support for Sindh and Sindhis has resulted in rescuing the lives of many young Sindhi activists who otherwise would surely have been tortured to death by the government agencies.

He has done more for Sindh and Sindhis in one's lifetime than most of those born in Sindh will have done, even if they got to live ten lives.

~Maqbool Halepota, President SAPAC

Future of Sindhis

تقدیر کے کا قاضی کا یہ فتویٰ ہے ازل سے

ہے جُرمِ ضعیفی کی سزا مرگِ مفاجات!

*It is the eternal decree of the ultimate judge of destiny
That the punishment, for the crime of being weak, is extinction*

~Allama Iqbal

As Vaswani once said:

> We are passing through strange times. We do not have our own state, country, or homeland. We are scattered community. And there is one thing that helps us to retain our identity and it is our language. And if there is one thing that help us to know each other, it is our language.[169]

---

[169] T. L. Vaswani, *India in Chains* (University of Michigan Library, 1921).

Countries come and go, but civilizations are forever. The valley of the great Indus River has always had a civilization of its own. Many dynasties and rulers have come and gone, and will continue to do so, but the river and its civilization will continue to survive. But for the Indus Valley Civilization and all its inhabitants—not only humans, but thousands of marine, land, and avian species—to survive, the river has to continue to flow unabated. Unfortunately, over the last century, River Indus has been slowly choked to death by unchecked construction of dams and barrages, and uncontrolled population growth.

The estimated population of West Pakistan at the time of Partition of India in 1947 is said to have been around 20,000,000, and it is currently close to 200,000,000. Thus, the population of the area fed by the River Indus has grown ten times over the last seven decades. To put things in perspective, the land area of Pakistan is one-third larger than the state of Texas, whereas its population is one-third of the whole United States. The population density of Pakistan is almost eight times that of the US, and Pakistan boasts the fastest population growth rate in the world.

Unless this trend is reversed on an emergent basis, in the near future, it is bound to result in one of the greatest ecological disasters to hit the planet. This will be disastrous for the human beings dependent on River Indus, and it already has created one of the greatest ecological disasters with the extinction of thousands of marine species, along with flora and fauna dependent on the river. This includes the largest mangrove forests on the planet, which is dependent on the delta of the river. Some of the marine species facing extinction include the blind Indus River dolphin and *palla* fish, both unique to River Indus.

For the last few decades, the mighty River Indus does not even flow to its delta in the Indian Ocean for most of the months of the year. In sharp contrast to its glorious past, its bed looks like a desert, sand flying all over, for more than one hundred miles of its path. With very little to no water flowing past the Kotri Barrage at Hyderabad, Sindh, it is time for not only Sindhis from all over the world, but for all human beings, to do whatever they can to prevent this imminent disaster before it is too late.

Like the rest of the great rivers of the world, including the Nile, Amazon, and Mississippi, the great River Indus should be allowed to flow freely, with its seasonal ebbs and tides that are most essential for the natural existence of flora, fauna, marine, land, and avian species dependent on the river.

The Sindhis have a glorious past as a part of a great civilization that dates back over 5,000 years. However, standing amidst the ruins of a great civilization and offering to the world its elegant artifacts could never be a penance to the Sindhi nation alone. Sindhis need to be a globalized society in a globalized world. Avenues for the progress, prosperity, and emancipation of Sindhis are increasing, provided they remain fully aware and conversant with what is going on around them and they are able to compete with the rapidly changing circumstances around the globe.

A promising future for Sindhis and their motherland, Sindh, the Sindhi language, culture, and Sindhiyat lay in store if we, the Sindhis, become one nation in Hind, Sindh, and elsewhere around the globe—if we become the global Sindhi citizens of the world. Sindhis will have to rise above the division that has developed among them on the basis of religion. They will have to break the glass wall that separates them. They will have to bury the past and bid farewell to bad blood among them. Time is a great healer. The following could be some indicators to lead us Sindhis into a bright future:

> *Leaving behind their land, homes, and businesses, the rich traders and Zamindars of Sindh boarded trains and ships empty-handed like migrant laborers, thankful to have escaped partition unscathed. Once in India, poverty and dependence actually dawned upon many Sindhis, but they had neither the time to contemplate their miseries nor the luxury of returning home. Distracted by, and caught up in, their immediate concerns, many didn't know whether to search for missing relatives, to earn a living, or to simply swallow their pride and live as refugees. When I asked my uncle, Udhavdas Makheja, whether he tried to look for his friends and family after he landed in Bombay, he said, "Silly, who had the time?"*[170]

Sindhis in India, as author and scholar Wadhyo Gajwani put it, "have a boat but not the river."

---

[170] Rita Kothari, Eds. Michel Boivin and Matthew A. Cook "Unwanted Identities in Gujarat," *Interpreting the Sindhi World: Essays on Society and History* (Karachi: Oxford University Press, 2010) 59.

However, Sindhi leaders and writers have been able to get the Sindhi language recognized in the schedule of other national languages in the Constitution of India. This was a historic contribution. The person most credited with getting the Sindhi language constitutionally recognized in India is Jairamdas Daulatram, who was then a member of Parliament. There are many Sindhi leaders who have attained national stature in Indian politics. They include leaders like L. K. Advani, Ram Jethmalani, and Pappu Kalani. Wadhyo Gajwani sums up the present state of Sindhis as follows:

> *There is spirit of sacrifice and management in all other nations but it's lacking among us Sindhis. Sindh was our homeland that we should not have abandoned at first place. Every human has their land a mother and we should not have left motherland out. It was better to bear the brunt of the death than to be separated from motherland. A nation that cannot take care of itself, how could it take care of others?*

In his book, *The Future of Sindhis in India*, Wadhyo Gajwani goes on to state:

> *We Sindhis say to each other that we are trading people. We do not know how to participate in protests and hunger strikes. In democracy you do not rely on wealth but unity. For the rights of our Sindhi people, we need to be united leaving other chores behind. To provide the proof of our being united, we must be united. This is the only way we can get our people their rights. There are many Sindhis who*

> *are millionaires. Can they get Sindhis their rights from the government? No. They will never get it. In democracy, the government always respects to the majority. Keeping this all in view, all Sindhis will have to be one voice and united in order to achieve their rights. Every Sindhi be united. Be they our traders, shopkeepers, lawyers, public servants, or private employees, engineers, or laborers, but government will never give them rights until they become one and united.[171]*

However, scholar Subhadra Anand, who has studied India's Sindhi society and culture on a scientific basis, offers her findings as follows:

> *Sindhis have become so individualist that they have not been able to form strong group ties. Since they settled down anywhere in India, it was not left to them to choose their associates. So a strong bond amongst them is missing.*

Shedding light on historic but ongoing relationships between Sindhis in Thar and Sindhis in Rajasthan, Subhadra Anand wrote:

> *The relationship between Sindh and Rajasthan is ancient. The invaders of the Indus Valley were ultimately checked in their march by the inaccessible*

---

[171] Wadhyo Gajwani, *The Future of Sindhis in India* (Ulhasnagar: Sagar Publications, 1999) 102-108.

> deserts. Those who were driven by the invaders also sought refuge in the adjoining desert spread over to Kutch, Kathiawar, and the border areas of Rajasthan mitigating the Sindhi character intact. From Rajasthan during the time of drought, the people migrated to Sindh. This was an annual event. Thus the people of Kutch border Rajasthan never went back and got assimilated into the Sindhi population. The ancient Indus cities extending from beyond the present-day limits of Sindh covered the land of the ancient Saraswati, which disappeared in the tectonic disturbances that destroyed the Indus Valley Civilization. The cultural affinity between the two regions can be seen from the similarity between Uderolal of Sindh and Ramdev Pir of Rajasthan.[172]

The Sindhi diaspora, especially those living in India, must reestablish and restore their bonds with their motherland. The Sindhis across both borders and elsewhere can make Sindh great again by investing in Sindh and transforming Sindh's economy based on modern models. Sindhis are naturally a democratic nation; they have practiced pluralism for thousands of years. Their future is closely tied to continued democratic rule in Pakistan. Years of undemocratic rule, subjugation, and militarization has resulted in increasing trends of extremism among Sindhis. This must be prevented at any cost.

---

[172] Anand, *National Integration of Sindhis*, 177-183.

The best way to conquer a people is to convince them that they are incapable of governing themselves. It is said that at the peak of the Quit India Movement, Mahatma Gandhi was asked, "How could the British leave India? India has so many problems; who will take care of these if we the British leave?"

To which the mahatma responded, "We know India has a lot of problems, but these are our problems, not theirs, so we will take care of these."

Unfortunately, over the last few decades, similar rhetoric has been used against Sindhis. They are repeatedly told that they are uneducated, lack merit, and are corrupt, thus are not capable of governing themselves. This convinces us that we need outsiders to govern us, to the point that most Sindhis, especially our educated elite, are now convinced of this. This is the saddest and scariest part of what has happened to Sindhis as a nation.

Sindhis must conquer the attempts to stereotype them; they must overcome the inferiority complexes that may have crept into their collective psyche. They must never lose faith in themselves; they must never forget their great history. They should be proud of their national identity and teach their future generations the same. The nationalities living in the Valley of Indus, extending from Karachi to Kashmir, since the beginning of times have always lived in harmony and peace, with utmost respect for each other's territories and cultural flavors. This balance must be regained, maintained, and encouraged to flourish. Just as each flower in a bouquet complements and enhances the beauty and fragrance of every other flower in it, so do each of the nationalities living in the valley of Sindhu.

Excellence in Education, Sciences, Arts, and Literature

Sindhi youths must excel in all sciences, especially advanced natural sciences, social information, and other engineering technologies. Technologies over land, beneath seas, and in space—Sindhis should excel in all of them. The classroom of the future will be transformed into a laptop.

The war on Sindhis' rights will not be fought on the battlefield but through libraries, universities of advanced learning, and international communities, including the United Nations, public and all diplomacies, sports, art, and literary venues. Sindhi literature is among the top literature in the world; it must be translated into the world's languages.

Introducing ecologically friendly, mechanized, organic agriculture; strengthening of rural middle classes; reconstructing modern villages and countrysides; and abolishing the caste system and tribal blood feuds can be the byproduct of bidding farewell to feudalism in Sindh. By organic and ecologically friendly methods of agriculture, Sindh could be turned into an agriculture-based industry proven to be the food basket of Asia.

As they say, "Charity starts at home." Sindhis are known for philanthropy all over the world. It is now high time for Sindhi philanthropists globally to also start taking care of the most disadvantaged among their own Sindhi in the land of their forefathers. At the same time, Sindhi philanthropists in Sindh should take responsibility and join this most worthy cause.

According to G. M. Syed, "Since the independence of Pakistan, Sindhi nation has seen very little development, and yet more than 50% of gross national product of the central government of Pakistan comes from Sindh."[173]

For example, Sindh has the following resources:

More than 40,000,000 acres of very fertile agricultural land

- *Large meadows for animal farming*
- *Variety of crops like rice, wheat, sugarcane, cotton, etc.*
- *Various minerals like coal, oil, gas, and precious stones*
- *Ver y prosperous fishing industry*
- *Easy and convenient access to the sea*
- *Great potential for industrialization*

"We the people of Sindh must feel quite confident because our nation is potentially prosperous, with a lot of resources to survive as an independent state."

In his last speech on the occasion of his ninety-second birthday on January 17, 1995, addressing the congregation and Urdu-speaking inhabitants of Sindh, Syed said:

---

[173] G. M. Syed, *Sindh Ja Soorma (Heroes of Sindh)*. Karachi: Naeen Sindh Publications, 1974.

> *The land [of Sindh] is a beautiful bouquet of different religions, civilization, outlooks, and creeds. The nature has been kind to you that having been thrown out from your own soil, it has provided you the lap of such land, which has remained a great center of love, tolerance, and brotherhood. Therefore, don't lose this golden opportunity, and get yourselves harmonized with the original people of this soil and be part of them.[174]*

A study of the postindustrial era around the globe will tell us that no nation in the world has made significant progress without shifting their traditional agriculture-based economy to one based on industry, as there is no method more effective to create a dynamic, educated middle class than being an economy based primarily on industry. Therefore, the need of the hour is for the Sindhi diaspora all over the world to conquer their religious prejudices, forget and forgive the mistakes of the past, and rebuild their bond with the land of their forefathers.

There is no better way to rebuild their roots than to invest in it and build industry in Sindh. This will not only go a long way in uniting Sindhis across their religious divides, but will also transform the society of Sindh by taking its economy from the medieval agricultural economics to a modern industry-based economy.

Sindhis of the world will have to come together to protect Sindh's geographic, demographic, linguistic, cultural, social, and ecological identities and interests if they want Sindh to survive

---

[174] G. M. Syed, *Sindh Ja Soorma (Heroes of Sindh)*.

the next century. Otherwise, there may be Sindhis left in the world, but—alas!—there will be no Sindh.

In the end, in the words of the great poet Shaikh Ayaz:

جي هانءُ نه هارين ڪوهيارل!

جي هانءُ نه هارين ڪوهيارل! هي ڍينهن بہ گهاري وينداسين،
چو پير پساري ويٺو آن، اٿا! ڍونگر ڍاري وينداسين.
ڪنهن لاءِ تڪين ٿو ڪندِيءَ تان، هي هيڙي ڪاہ نہ اڇٽي آ،
جي تون بہ اچين او وٽجارا! توکي بہ اڪاري وينداسين.
دريا اندر جا دهشت آ، ڪنهن وقت قيامت ٿي ويندي،
تون مان تہ رڳو هن سنڌوءَ تي، ڪا لهر اپاري وينداسين.
ڪا جهرمر جهرمر جگنوءَ جي، ڪا ٽم ٽم ٽم ٽم تاري جي،
گهنگهور گهٽا جو گهيرو آ، ڪنهن جي تہ سهاري وينداسين.
آ مرٽو هر ڪنهن ماٿهوءَ ڪي، پر هيئن نہ مرنداسين ساٿي،
ڪا آڳ لڳائي وينداسين، ڪو ٻارڻ ٻاري وينداسين.
تون آءُ تہ اوريون او راٽا، چو جيءُ سهي هي جهوراٽا؟
تون چا ڪان چرڪين ٿو راٽا! اڄ ڪاڪ ڪناري ويندسين.
چو گهہرائين ٿو ڪوٽ ڍسي، هي اوچي اوچي اوٽ ڍسي،
زندان اڈائي ويندسين، زنجير پگهاري ويندسين.
تنهن وقت بہ مون هي چاتو هو، هي ڪاريهر سان ناتو هو،
جي ساٿي ساٿ سجاتو تو، هي ماري ماري ويندسين.
تون ڪر، جيڪو توڪي ڪرٽو آ، هي دور بہ نيٺ گذرٽو آ،
ڪنهن وقت ڈهيسر مرٽو آ، بنواس گذاري ويندسين.

Do not lose hope my friend, these days will also pass
Why are you lying dejected, we will conquer the mountain
Standing on the banks, who are you looking for, no ship is coming for you
Join your hands with mine, together we will reach our destination
There is torrent in the river, apocalypse will happen any time
Lest You and I, create our wave on the Sindhu
The flickering of a firefly, and twinkling of a star, with their light
We will find out path, though surrounded by dark clouds
Every human has to die one day, but we will not die in vain, my comrade
We will light a flame, we will start a fire
Let us struggle together, why should we suffer these atrocities
Why are you afraid, my prince, soon we will reach our destination
Why are you worried by these garrisons, these tall towers
We will destroy these prisons, and melt these chains
I have always known that I am up against a serpent
With our friends, we will destroy this killer
Let them do what they want to do, this era will also pass
The tyrant will vanish soon, we will survive this exile

Selected Bibliography

Advani, Bherumal Meharchand. *Sindh Je Hindu Ji Tarekh (History of Hindus in Sindh)*. Bombay: Shardha Prakashan, 1991.

Ahloowalia, B. S. *Invasion of the Genes: Genetic Heritage of India*. New York: Eloquent Books, 2009.

Ahmed, Feroz. *Ethnicity and Politics in Pakistan*. (New York: Oxford University Press, 1998.

Ahmed, Makhdoom Amir, Trans. *Chachnamo (Sindhi)*. Jamshoro: Sindhi Adabi Board, 2004.

Aijaz, Nasir. *Hur: The Freedom Fighter*. Karachi: Culture and Tourism Department, Government of Sindh, 2015.

Ajwani, L. H. *History of Sindhi Literature*. Karachi: Sahitya Akademi, 1970.

Akbar, M. J. *Tinderbox: The Past and Future of Pakistan*. New York: Harper Perennial, 2012.

Albinia, Alice. *Empires of the Indus: The Story of a River.* New York: W. W. Norton & Company, Inc., 2010.

Ali, Tariq. Tariq Ali, *Can Pakistan Survive?* London: Penguin Books, 1983.

Allchin, Raymond and Bridget. *The Rise of Civilization in India and Pakistan.* New York: Cambridge University Press, 1982.

Allen, Brooke. Brooke Allen, *Benazir Bhutto: Favored Daughter.* ICONS Series. New York: New Harvest Houghton Mifflin Harcourt, 2016.

Anand, Subhadra. *National Integration of Sindhis.* New Delhi: Vikas Publishing House Limited, 1996.

Ansari, Sarah. *The Musselman Races Found in Sind, Baluchistan and Afghanistan.* Karachi: Indus Publications, 1996.

Asif, Manan Ahmed. *A Book of Conquest: The Chachnama and Muslim Origins in South Asia.* Cambridge: Harvard University Press, 2016.

Baloch, Inayatullah. *The Problem of "Greater Baluchistan": A Study of Baluch Nationalism.* Cambridge University Press, 1987.

Baloch, Nabi Bakhsh Khan and A. Q. Rafiqi, Eds. Clifford Edmund Bosworth and M. S. Asimov. *The Age of Achievement: AD 750 to the End of the Fifteenth Century: The Achievements (History of Civilizations of Central Asia.)* UNESCO Publishing, 1998.

Bhatia, Shyam. *Goodbye Shahzadi: A Political Biography of Benazir Bhutto.* New Delhi: Lotus Roli Books, 2008.

Bhavnani, Nandita. *The Making of Exile: Sindhi Hindus and the Partition of India.* New Delhi: Westland and Tranquebar Press, 2014.

Bhutto, Benazir. *Daughter of the East.* New United Kingdom: Hamish Hamilton, 1989.

Boivin, Michel. *Historical Dictionary of the Sufi Culture of Sindh in Pakistan and India.* Karachi: Oxford University Press, 2015.

Brohi, Ali Ahmad. *Jaam Jamote aen Jaamra.* Hyderabad: New Fields, 1984.

Burnes, James. *A Narrative of a Visit to the Court of Sinde: A Sketch of the History of Cutch, From Its First Connexion With the British Government in India Till the...Remarks on the Medical Topography of Bhooj.* Edinburgh, 1829.

Burton, Richard F. *Sindh and the Races That Inhabit the Valley of the Indus.* Oxford University Press, 1973.

Cavalli-Sforza, L. L., Paolo Menozzi, and Alberto Piazza. *The History and Geography of Human Genes.* Princeton: Princeton University Press, 1996.

Cavalli-Sforza, L. L. *Genes, Peoples, and Languages.* University of California Press, 2001.

Channa, Sahib Khan, Eds. Muhammad Qasim Soomro and Gh̲ulāmu Muḥammadu Lākho. "Charle Napier in Sindh: Challenges and Achievements." *Sindh, Glimpses into Modern History: Proceedings of PHIRC on the History of Sindh, 1843-1999*. Jamshoro: Department of General History, Faculty of Social Sciences, University of Sindh, 2008.

Chitkara, M. G. *Jiy-e-Sindh: G. M. Syed*. New Delhi: APH Publishing Corporation, 1996.

Cook, Matthew A. *Willoughby's Minute: The Treaty of Nownahar, Fraud, and British Sindh*. Oxford University Press, 2013.

Daily Dawn. "One Unit: A Dark Chapter of Our History," *The Daily Dawn*, October 16, 2011.

Doniger, Wendy. *The Hindus: An Alternative History*. Oxford University Press, 2010.

Duiker, William J. and J. Jackson Spielvogel. *World History, 9th Ed*. Cengage Learning, 2018.

Dutt, Nalinaksha. *Buddhist Sects in India*. Delhi: Motilal Banarsidass Publishing House, 1978. Dwivedi, Om Prakash, Ed. *Tracing the New Indian Diaspora*. Amsterdam: Brill | Rodopi, 2014.

Ebrahim, Zofeen T. "Economy vs Environment: Thar Coal and Tests of Pakistan's Priorities." *The Daily Dawn*, February 22, 2017.

Frawley, David and Vamadeva Shastri. *Myth of the Aryan Invasion of India*. New Delhi: Voice of India, 1994.

Frazier Jessica, Ed. *The Continuum Companion to Hindu Studies*, New York: Continuum, 2011.

Freedomforum.org; Pakistan, October 2006.

Gajwani, Wadhyo; *Bharat mein Sindhian jo Aindo (The Future of Sindhis in India)*. Ulhasnagar: Sagar Publications, 1999.

Gates, Jr., Henry Louis. *Finding Your Roots*. University of North Carolina Press, 2014.

Gibbons, Ann. *The First Human: The Race to Discover Our Earliest Ancestors*. Doubleday, 1981.

Green, Michael R. and Joseph Sambrook. *Molecular Cloning: A Laboratory Manual (Fourth Edition) Vol. 1, 2 & 3*. Cold Spring Harbor Laboratory Press, 2012.

Haig, Malcolm Robert. *The Indus Delta Country: A Memoir Chiefly on Its Ancient Geography, History, and Topography*. Walton Press, 2010.

Hiranandani, Popati. Hero Thakur, Ed. Sindhoo (essay); "Behtareen Sindhi Mazmoon." ("The Best Sindhi Essays"). Gandhinagar: Gujarat Sindhi Academy, 1990.

Hiranandani Popati. *Sindhis: The Scattered Treasure*. New Delhi: Malaah Publications, 1980.

Human Rights Watch. "Reforms or Repression: Post-Coup Abuses in Pakistan." *Human Rights Watch*. New York, October 2000.

Jatoi, Hyder Bux. Ed. Mohammed Ibrahim Joyo. "Bhali aeen je aeen Daryl Shah." *Quarterly Journal.* Mehran/1955/3, Hyderabad: Sindh, Pakistan.

Joshi V. T. *Pakistan: Zia to Benazir.* New Delhi: Konark Publishers, 1995.

Jotwani, Motilal. *The Sindhi Through the Centuries.* New Delhi: Aditya Books Pvt. Limited, 2006.

Jotwani Motilal. *Sufis of Sindh.* New Delhi, 1986.

Junejo, Abdul Qadir. *The Dead River.* Lahore: University of Management and Technology, 2015.

Junejo, Khursheed. *Yaadein Bhutto Ki (Memories of Bhutto).* Lahore, 2008.

Kenoyer, Jonathan Mark et al. *The Indus Civilization; Art of the First Cities the Third Millennium BCE from the Mediterranean to the Indus.* Oxford University Press, 1998.

Khan, Adeel. *Politics of Identity: Ethnic Nationalism and the State in Pakistan.* New Delhi: Sage Publications, 2005.

Khilnani, N. M. *Panorama of Modern Indus Valley.* Delhi: Westville Publishing House, 1994.

Khuhro, Hamida. *Sindh Through the Centuries.* Karachi: Oxford University Press, 1981.

Khuhro, Hamida. *Mohammed Ayub Khuhro: A Life of Courage in Politics.* Oxford University Press, 2000.

Khushalani, Gobind. *Chachnamah Retold: An Account of the Arab Conquest of Sindh.* New Delhi: Promila Books Publisher, Bibliophile South Asia, 2006.

Kothari, Rita. Eds. Michel Boivin and Matthew A. Cook. "Unwanted Identities in Gujarat," *Interpreting the Sindhi World: Essays on Society and History.* Karachi: Oxford University Press, 2010.

Lahiri, Nayanjot. *Finding Forgotten Cities: How the Indus Civilization was Discovered.* London New York Calcutta, 2013.

Lahiri, Nayanjot. *Decline and Fall of the Indus Civilization.* New Delhi, 2000.

Lakho, Ghulam Muhammad. *Samman ji Saltanat.* Jamshoro: Sindhi Adabi Board, 2005.

Lambrick, H. T. *Sindh before the Muslim Conquest. (History of Sind series, v. 2.)* Karachi: Oxford University Press, 1973.

Lari, Suhail Zaheer. *A History of Sindh.* Oxford University Press, 1994.

Malkani, K. R. *The Sindh Story.* Sindhi Academy, archives.org, 1984.

Markovits, Claude. *The Global World of Indian Merchants (1750-1947): Traders of Sind from Bukhara to Panama.* Cambridge University Press, 2000.

Marshall, Sir John. *Mohenjo-Daro and The Indus Civilization*. Varanasi: Indological Book House, 1983.

McIntosh, Jane R. *The Ancient Indus Valley: New Perspectives*. Santa Barbara: ABC- CILIO Inc., 2008.

McIntosh, Jane R. *A Peaceful Realm: The Rise and the Fall of the Indus Civilization*. Westview Press, 2002.

Mehdi, S. Q. et al. "Clinical and Evolutionary Genetics of Pakistani Populations," ICGEB 10th Anniversary Symposium. Trieste, Italy 1997.

Mehdi, S. Q. et al; "Where West Meets East: The Complex mtDNA Landscape of the Southwest and the Central Asian Corridor." *The American Journal of Human Genetics* Vol. 74, Issue 5. April 2004.

Mohammed, Qazi Faiz. *Muhinjo Safar (My Journey)*. Hyderabad: Sindhi Sahat Ghar, 1999.

Mujtaba, Hasan. "Bhutto: Man and Myth," *Newsline*, Karachi, January 1994.

Naipaul, V. S. *Among the Believers: An Islamic Journey*. New York: Vintage, 1981.

Naqvi, Saiyid Ali. *Indus Waters and Social Change: The Evolution and Transition of Agrarian Society in Pakistan*. Karachi: Oxford University Press, 2013.

The Nation Weekly, Volume 96, page 595. New York, January 1913.

New York Times. Opinion, "Dangerous Coup in Pakistan," *New York Times*, October 13, 1999.

Nizamani, Qadir Bux. *Jang-e-Miani*. Baloch Adabi Society, 1947.

Noori, Shakir. Interview with Ram Buxani. "In Dubai, Risks Come with Rewards." *Gulf News*, July 10, 2018.

Notovitch, Nicolas. Trans. Alexina Lorianger. *The Unknown Life of Jesus Christ, by the Discoverer of the Manuscript*. Chicago: Indo-American Book Company, 1916.

Omvedt, Gail. *Buddhism in India: Challenging Brahmanism and Caste*. New Delhi: Sage Publications, 2003.

Panhwar, M. H. *Chronological Dictionary of Sindh*. Jamshoro Sind-Pakistan: Institute of Sindhology University of Sind, 1983.

Papiha, S. Surinder, Ranjan Deka, and R. Chakraborty, Eds. *Genetic Diversity Application in Human Population Genetics*. Boston: Springer, 1999.

Parpola Asko. *The Roots of Hinduism: The Early Aryans and the Indus Civilization*. New York: Oxford University Press, 2015.

Possehl, Gregory. *The Indus Civilization: A Contemporary Perspective*. Boston: AltaMira Press, 2002.

Postans, Thomas. *Personal Observations on Sindh: Manner and Customs of Its Inhabitants*. Longman, Brown, Green and Longman, Paternoster-Row, 1843.

Rafiuddin, Colonel. *Bhutto Ke Akhri 323 Din (The Final 323 Days of Bhutto)*. Lahore: Jang Publishers, 2013.

Ramey, Steven W. *Hindu, Sufi, or Sikh: Contested Practices and Identifications of Sindhi Hindus in India and Beyond*. New York: Palgrave Macmillan, 2008.

Ranade, Rekha. *Sir Bartle Frere and His Times*. New Delhi: Mittal Publications, 1990.

Ratnagar, Shereen, Ed. *Trading Encounters: From the Euphrates to the Indus in the Bronze Age*. Delhi: Oxford University Press, 2004.

Reetz, Dietrich. *Hijrat: The Flight of the Faithful: A British File on the Exodus of Muslim Peasants from North India to Afghanistan in 1920*. Berlin: Klaus Schwarz Verlag, 1996.

Rind, Saeed Ahmed. "Rise of Sindhi Diaspora in USA: A Comparative Study of SANA, WSC and WSI." Islamabad: National Institute of Pakistani Studies, January 2017.

Ross, David. *The Land of the Five Rivers and Sindh: Sketches, Historical and Descriptive* London: Chapman and Hall, Ltd., 1883.

Samrat, Gangaram. *Sindhu-Sauvir: History Begins at Sindh*. Ahmedabad: G. Samrat, 1984.

Shah Nafisa and Hasan Mujtaba. "The Raider of the Past." *Newsline*, February 1995.

Shankarananda, Swami. *History of Mohenjo-Daro and Harappa.* Calcutta, 1965.

Siddiqui, Iqtidar Husain. *Indo-Persian Historiography Up to the Thirteenth Century.* Delhi: Primus Books, 2010.

Sindhi, Dada. *Daee Dunbh Dadan (Sindhi ڏٺٺ ڏٺٺ ڏٺٺٺ).* 2016.

Singer, Bilge. *Biodiversity: Biomolecular Aspects of Biodiversity and Innovative Utilization.* New York: Kluwer Academic/Plenum Publishers, 2002.

Stearns, Peter N. and Stephen S. Gosch. *Pre-Modern Travel in World History.* New York: Routledge, 2007.

Suresh, K. and Usha Sharma. *Cultural and Religious Heritage of India, Volume 7, Zoroastrianism.* New Delhi: Ancient India, Mittal Publications, 2006.

Syed, Anwar H. *The Discourse and Politics of Zulfikar Ali Bhutto.* New York: St. Martin Press, 1992.

Syed, G. M. *Sindhudesh: A Nation in Chains.* Karachi: 1974.

Syed, G. M. *Sindh Ja Soorma (Heroes of Sindh).* Karachi: Naeen Sindh Publications, 1974.

Tahir, Naeem. *Melluhas of the Indus Valley, 8000 BCE-500 BCE.* Pakistan National Council of the Arts, 2008.

Talbot, Ian. *Pakistan: A New History.* New York: Palgrave (Macmillan), 1998-2005.

Talpur, Parveen. G. A. Allana, Foreword. *Indus Seals (2600-1900 BCE) Beyond Geometry: A New Approach to Break an Old Code.* BookBaby, 2017

Talpur, Parveen. *Mohenjo-Daro: Metropolis of the Indus Civilization (2600-1900 BCE).* United States, 2014.

Van Buitenen, J. A. B. Ed. and Trans. *The Mahabharata. 1. The book of the Assembly Hall 2. The Book of the Forest i-ii.* 1973.

Vaswani, T. L. *India in Chains.* Madras, 1921.

Viyogi, Naval. *The Founders of Indus Valley Civilisation and Their Later History: v. 1 (The history of the indigenous people of India).* Samyak Prakashan, 2015.

Wade, Nicholas. "Tracing Ancestry: Researchers Produce a Genetic Atlas of Human Mixing Events." *New York Times*, February 13, 2014.

Weaver, Mary Anne. "Bhutto's Fateful Moment." *The New Yorker*, October 1993.

Weber, Steven A. and William R. Belcher. *Indus Ethnobiology: New Perspectives from the Field.* New York: Lexington Books, 2003.

Wilson, H. H. Rigveda *Sinhita: A Collection of Ancient Hindu Hymns of the Rig-Veda*. Hard Press Publishing, 2013.

Wolpert, Stanley A. *Zulfi Bhutto of Pakistan*: His Life and Times. Oxford University Press, 1993.

Wright, Rita P. *The Ancient Indus: Urbanism, Economy and Society— Case Studies in Early Societies.* New York: Cambridge University Press, 2009.

Zamindar, Vazira. *The Long Partition and the Making of Modern South Asia: Refugee, Boundaries, Histories.* New York: Columbia University Press, 2007.

Zardari, Mohammed Laiq. *Tehreek Pakistan mein Sindh jo Hiso: Hur Tehreek*. 1984.

Ziring, Lawrence. *Pakistan in the Twentieth Century: A Political History*. Delhi: Oxford University Press, 1997.

Acknowledgments

First and foremost, I would like to acknowledge my dear friend Sufi Munawar Laghari, without whose encouragement, prodding, perseverance, and brotherly love this would never have been possible. He introduced the idea of writing to me and then relentlessly pursued it. It was his patience and faith that kept this candle lit many a time when I was ready to throw in the towel.

The other dear friend of mine who made this possible is Ada Hasan Mujtaba. The long hours, days, and nights he put into research, discussions, revisions, and formatting with me is reflected in every page of the manuscript.

I sincerely appreciate all of Adi Fatima Gul's contributions, input, encouragement, and help.

A special thanks to Ms. Clarissa Myers for the first round of proofing and initial corrections of the manuscript.

The heart and soul of this whole effort could not have been depicted better by anyone other than Saeen Khuda Bux Abro, who created and formatted the graphics for this manuscript.

My most sincere gratitude to Ms. Jenny Watz for her outstanding editing and final touches. I would never have crossed the finish line without her expertise and help.

Of course, my heartfelt gratitude to my family, especially my beloved sons, Shahmeer and Mahmeer Halepota, without whose love, affection, and encouragement it would have been impossible for me to complete this endeavor. They are the inspiration behind all my perspiration for this labor of love.

My hope is that this book will always remind them and their future generations of their roots while they prosper in their new homeland, the great United States of America.

I would also very humbly express my gratitude in advance to each of the readers who will read this book. This by no means is intended to be a didactic work on the history of the Indus Valley; these are purely reflections of an individual.

My intention is not to disrespect or hurt the feelings or offend the sensibilities of any individual or group. I have tried my best to state the facts as objectively as possible. But I fully appreciate and accept the fact that, like all other human beings, I am also not free of biases and prejudices, out of love for my motherland. So please let me know if you find any historical inaccuracies in the book, and I will be more than happy to make the necessary corrections.

Although I have tried to stay within the confines of documented history, I have relied on some oral traditions also. As it is, I am of the firm belief that what is considered documented history is nothing but the perspective of events as documented by the victor. Seldom have the vanquished had the opportunity to relate their version of what actually transpired through the history of humankind.

I urge each reader to read this book with an open mind and heart. I know some of the facts discussed in this book are going be perceived as being too bitter to accept. But unless each one of us develops the courage to accept the bitter facts of our past, we will never learn from our past mistakes. So the only way to avoid repeating the mistakes of our past is to accept them so that we can improve ourselves and evolve into better humans, individually and collectively. That is the only way we will be able to deal with the harsh realities and challenges of the future.

Last, but not least, I would like to recognize:

- Manhattan Research Library Initiative (MaRLI) Program, New York Public Library
- Butler Library, Columbia University
- Elmer Homes Bobst Library, New York University (NYU)

None of this would have been possible without the extensive research material available at each of these institutions.

About Dr. Maqbool A. Halepota, MD, FACP, CPE

Dr. Maqbool A. Halepota, MD, FACP, CPE, is a medical oncologist in Scottsdale, Arizona. He is the current elected president of Sindhi Association of North America (SANA), is the founding president of Sindhi American Political Action Committee, and chairman of the board directors of Sindhi Foundation. He is also a founding member of the Fund for Educational Development in Sindh and has served as a member of the board of directors for the American Civil Liberties Union in Arizona. Before moving to Arizona, he worked in Kentucky, where he earned a commission in the Honorable Order of Kentucky Colonels for his outstanding service and care for the indigenous population in one of the poorest counties in the state.

He has organized, conducted, and chaired many international conferences and meetings, including annual conventions of SANA, international meetings of Sindhi intellectuals, politicians, and other thought leaders in Karachi, London, New York, and Washington, DC. His articles have been published in many journals, including *South Asia Tribune* and peer-reviewed medical journals. He is currently working on another book on the historical roots of Sufism in the Indus Valley.

He is highly respected and well-known among the Sindhi communities in US, Canada, and all over Sindh for his non-partisan advocacy and philanthropy on behalf of the most oppressed sections of the society.

www.ingramcontent.com/pod-product-compliance
Lightning Source LLC
Chambersburg PA
CBHW050924240426
43668CB00020B/2421